U0957444

谨以此书献给

历史的镜头　罕见的珍本

二次大战照片精华

Outstanding Photographs of World War II

群言出版社

前　　言

为纪念世界所有为反法西斯战争做出贡献的人们，群言出版社重编新版的《二次大战照片精华》在社会各方的大力支持协助下，以更加翔实丰富的内容、庄重精美的版式，与广大读者见面了。

1942年夏，复旦大学新闻专业出身的记者、摄影家舒宗侨和美国人温福立，在盟军设在重庆的新闻处的支持下，联合了当时美国、英国、苏联和中国的战时宣传机构，成立了旨在以摄影、幻灯等形式来宣传报导战争进程的“联合国幻灯电影图片社”，数月后即在此基础上改组成立了我国抗战时期最重要的新闻画报——《联合画报》社，温福立任社长，舒宗侨任主编。《联合画报》由重庆的盟军新闻处发行，其特殊的背景和地位，使其图片资料来源非常充足，有画报社同仁分赴各战地现场拍摄的，也有从各方面征集的，还有盟军各国的通讯部队、战地记者在世界各战区拍摄后，通过电传、甚至用军用飞机直接送至的。内容丰富、真实、及时，价值极高，倍受世人关注。在鼓舞中国及盟军的斗志，瓦解敌寇的士气方面起了很大的作用。

二战结束后，《联合画报》社以每月1美元的象征性租金转让给了舒宗侨私人经营，并将社址迁至上海。在上海，舒宗侨继续进行广泛蒐集二战题材照片的活动：在旧货摊上淘寻旧资料、旧照片；到敌伪、日军家属居住过的地方找寻被遗弃的画报、相册；向外国通讯社购买；通过友人征集；特别是还得到了上海中共代表团办事处的支持，从延安经南京辗转送来了二百多幅八路军、新四军及各地游击队英勇抗日的珍贵照片。1946年9月，舒宗侨用上述艰难征集来的图片，加上《联合画报》数年间积累的大量资料照片，编集出版了《第二次世界大战画史》，洋洋四五十万言，一千余幅照片，其史料、参考及收藏价值均极高。1947年5月，又与文化名流曹聚仁合作，编集出版了又一部鸿篇巨著《中国抗战画史》，朱自清先生当时曾评价说“书中取材翔实，图片更可珍贵”。1948年2月，又与另一位摄影家魏守忠一起，从大量的二战题材照片中精选出232帧，编成出版了《二次大战照片精华》，一个个真实的历史镜头，生动地再现了第二次世界大战的全过程。两本画史和一本画册，对社会产生了巨大的影响，其中的许多图片曾多次被翻拍、转载和引用。美国哈佛、斯坦福等大学在二战研究中均将上述画史作为重要参考资料；1984年新华通讯社摄影部编、新华出版社出版的《日本侵华图片史料集》中也有三十多幅照片采自舒宗侨的这两本画史。特别值得一提的是，1948年国民政府在上海审判日本战犯时，这两本画史曾被作为日寇战争罪行的有力证据，出现在庄严的法庭上。

岁月荏苒，世事沧桑，曾经如此辉煌、如此珍贵的这批画史画册，逐渐淡出了人们的记忆，原书存世数量也越见稀少，至今已成罕见的珍本。为了保存、再现这些珍贵的史料，我们在舒宗侨先生及其家属的全力支持和配合下，决定整理重编《二次大战照片精华》。

这次新版的《二次大战照片精华》，是以1948年2月出版的《二次大战照片精华》为底本，再把1947年3月第三版的《第二次世界大战画史》以及1947年5月出版的《中国抗战画史》中以八路军、新四军抗日活动为主的一部分照片补入，重编而成的。原版《二次大战照片精华》的序、第二次世界大战简史、每幅照片下的说明文字等，均以中、英两种文字书写，我们在重编过程中除保留了这中、英两种文字外，并增补了日文。另外，对从《第二次世界大战画史》、《中国抗战画史》中补入的照片，都用中、英、日三种语言增加了说明文字。为示区别，并能让读者窥见《二次大战照片精华》的原貌，凡补入的照片和新增的文字，均在目录上附注了*号。

60年来，对第二次世界大战中许多问题的研究已取得了巨大的成果，因此成书于近60年前的《二次大战照片精华》中的一些提法和观点就似乎略显陈旧或不妥了。我们是本着保存史料的目的出版这本《二次大战照片精华》的，所以除了对明显是笔误或排版印刷的错误径予改正外，其它地方一律保持原貌。这就需要读者在阅读、使用其内容资料时自己加以鉴别了。如本书第174页“史迪威公路”，这幅表现滇缅公路艰险路段的照片当年曾震撼了西方国家，直接影响了美国决策层，由此加强了对中国武器物资的支援。这段名为“二十四道拐”的盘山路一直被认为就在滇缅公路的云南省境内，可是二三年前却被证实不属滇缅公路，它在贵州省的晴隆县城约1公里处的莲城镇五一村半官坡。

重阅这本画册，可以让人们缅怀那段血与火的历史，牢记那场浩劫带给人类的灾难，重温万众一心、共赴沙场的烽火岁月。当年《联合画报》的社长温福立曾说：“在世界各战场流血作战的千千万万的军人的鲜血，为我们的图画增添了无限的光彩。一个小小的镜头，也许就是成千上万人血的结晶。”《二次大战照片精华》的原序中也有这样一段文字：“请求阅者不要以看普通图书或电影杂志的心情来看这些镜头。这里一幅照片的出现，也许已经付出成千成万人的生命来做代价，它代表着光明与黑暗，正义与暴力的决斗，呈现着历史所遗留下的必然的路径。”

让我们牢牢地记住这段沉痛的历史，为促进世界和平与发展的崇高事业而努力奋斗吧。

本画册能顺利出版，首先要感谢舒宗侨先生及其子女舒似槿、舒似茵、舒达明、舒达远，是他们无私地提供了画册的原件底本和一些重要的背景资料；还要感谢雅昌企业集团北京雅昌彩色印刷有限公司，是他们把许多已漫漶不清的照片修整得甚至比原件更清晰。另外，南京大学唐建清教授帮助审阅了画册的英文，天津市商务委员会的王建新女士参加了图片说明的日文翻译工作，我们谨在此一并表示衷心的感谢。

但愿这本画册的重新整理出版也能给各界喜爱珍藏历史镜头的朋友们提供宝贵的精神财富。

群言出版社编辑部

2005年8月15日

PREFACE

In honour of that contributed to Anti-Fascist, reedited *Outstanding Photographs of World War II* is finally republished with the help of all sections.

In the summer of 1947, Shu Zongqiao, a journalist and a photographer graduated from Fudan University, with American Winfred, combining the wartime propaganda agencies of U.S.A., U.K., U.S.S.R. and China, founded the "U.N. Magic Lantern Photographs Service" in order to report the process of war in the form of photographs and lanternslides. On the basis of which *United Pictorial*, the most important news pictorial press in China came into being several months later. Winfred assumed the office of president, and Shu Zongqiao was the editor in chief. Because of its special background and superior position, *United Pictorial* was rich in pictorial resources, some of which were taken by colleagues of the press, some were collected from the public, and some, taken by the Allied communication troops and war correspondents, were got through fax or by military airplanes. Having rich, reliable, timely and valuable contents, these photographs attracted the attention of the public and played an important part in inspiring the Allied and Chinese troops as well as undermining the enemy's morale.

After the Second World War, *United Pictorial* was transferred to Shu Zongqiao as a private press on a nominal rent of one dollar permonth, and moved from Chongqing to Shanghai. There, Shu zongqiao kept collecting photographs about World War II. He sought for old photos and materials on old stalls and in the houses where the traitors or Japanese once lived, purchased them from the foreign news agencies and amassed them from his friends. Furthermore, supported by the Chinese Communist Office in Shanghai, he collected over 200 precious photos about the heroic battles of Eighth Route Army and New Fourth Army, the guerillas against Japanese army. In September 1946, with the pictures mentioned above and the accumulated photos from years of *United Pictorial*, Shu Zongqiao compiled *A Pictorial History of the World War II*, which composed of more than 400,000 words and 1,000 photographs and was of great historical value for reference and collection. In may 1947, he cooperated with Cao Juren, a cultural elite, to compile another monumental work, *A Pictorial History of China's War of Resistance Against Japan*, on which Zhu Ziqing commented:"This pictorial book has a faithful account and the photographs are valuable." In February 1948, He, together with Wei Shouzhong, another photographer , chose 232 from lots of photos on the subject of World War II and published the *Outstanding Photographs of World War II*, which successfully gave the reader a vivid historical impression of the World War II. These pictorial books had a great effect in the society, in which most of the photographs were copied, reproduced and cited many times. Many American universities, such as Harvard, Stanford and etc, regarded them as important reference data for World War II study. In 1984, *Collection of Historical Photographs of Japanese Invasion to China*, published by Xinhua Press, cited over 30 photographs from these books. In particular, these books were esteemed as the powerful and solemn evidences of the Japanese invaders's guilty when the Kuomintang Government accused the Japanese war criminal in 1948.

Time flies and things change. The pictorials, which were once splendid and precious, have faded away from people's memory. Many of the original books were lost, and the remains are precious. In order to preserve and represent these valuable historic footnotes, under the generous support from the family of Mr. Shu Zongqiao, we decided to reedit the *Outstanding Photographs of World War II*.

The new edition is on the basis of the original one published in 1948, supplementing some photos about Eighth Route Army and New Fourth Army from the third edition of *A Pictorial History of the World War II* and those from *A Pictorial History of China's War of Resistance Against Japan* published respectively in March and May, 1947. The preface and the explanatory words in the original edition of *Outstanding*

Photographs of World War II were in Chinese and English. This time, we also provide Japanese translation. And so do, the new photos added. In order to distinguish from the original edition, all newly supplemented words and photos are asterisked.

We have achieved more on the research about World War II during the past 60 years. Some viewpoints in *Outstanding Photographs of World War II* maybe out of date and not that pertinent. For the purpose of conserving the historical sources, we published this book and in its original style with few corrections. It is necessary for the reader to distinguish and enjoy it with his or her own eyes. For example, Stiwell Road, which once shocked the western countries for its hardships and dangers and directly influenced the White House to aid China with more weapons and resource, has been believed a portion of Burma Road in Yunnan province for quite a long time. In fact, the zigzag road in this photo has been found at Banguanpo, Wuyi village, Liancheng town, which is one kilometer away from Qinglong county, Guizhou province.

These photos will help rekindle memories on that historic period, which brought so much misery to the human being. They will also bring back the days when the whole nation rallied together to fight against foreign invasion. Winfred, the president of the *United Pictorial* once said:"Hundreds of thousands of soldiers were fighting and bleeding in every battlefields. Their bloodshed adds infinite glory to our pictures. A small picture may be the result of hundreds of thousands of lives." In the original preface of *Outstanding Photographs of World War II*, we can also find the following words:"…… it is hoped that this book will not be taken for a mere picture book or a motion picture magazine for even one single scene in the photographs reproduced here may have cost millions of lives, representing a struggle between the forces of light and darkness, right and violence, which inevitable path left behind by history."

Let us firmly keep this heavy and dark episode of history in our mind, and work together for the lofty career of world peace and development.

In preparing this book the editor is greatly indebted to many institutions and friends, foreign and Chinese, and it is appropriate that this be mentioned with hearty thanks.

Thanks to Shu Zongqiao ,and Shu Sijin, Shu Siyin, Shu Daming , Shu Dayuan, offspring of Shu Zongqiao, without the original you offered, this book can not come into the world.

Thanks to Beijing Artron Color Printing co., LTD, for your masterful retouch technology.

Thanks to Professor Tang Jianqing in Nanjing University and Ms. Wang Jianxin in Tianjin Commerce Commission for your selfless help.

We wish this book would bring more pleasure to the friends who like to collect historical photographs.

August 15, 2005

前　書　き

世界反ファシズム戦争において戦った人々を記念するために、群言出版社は社会各方面の多大な支持と協力の下、『二次大戦照片精華』を再編出版しました。更に精確で豊富な内容、趣のある精巧で美しい新版になって、多くの読者に会わせることができました。

1942年夏、復旦大学新聞専門出身の記者、撮影家の舒宗僑とアメリカ人オンフレットは、同盟軍が重慶で設立した新聞社のサポートを得て、当時のアメリカ、イギリス、ソ連、中国の戦時宣伝機構と協力して、撮影、スライドなどの形式で戦争の過程を宣伝報道する「国連スライド写真社」を成立させました。また数ヶ月後それを基に中国抗日戦争時期におけるもっとも重要なニュース画報『聯合画報』社を創立させました。オンフレットが社長に、舒宗僑が編集長に就任しました。『聯合画報』社の特殊な背景と立場が功を奏して、写真資料の出所が非常に充実していました。同雑誌社のカメラマンが各戦地の現場に赴いて撮影したものから、各方面から集めたもの、各国同盟軍の通信部隊や戦地記者が世界各戦場で撮影したのをＦＡＸ或いは軍用飛行機で直接送付されたものまで取り揃えていました。その内容は豊富で、真実味があり、タイムリーで、価値が極めて高いため、世間で注目されていました。中国及び同盟軍の士気を高め、敵軍の士気を崩壊させるのに大きな役割を果たしました。

第二次世界大戦終結後、『聯合画報』社の経営権を月１ドルという象徴的な租金で舒宗僑先生個人に譲り、同時に上海に移りました。上海では、舒宗僑先生が引き続き第二次大戦を題材にした写真の蒐集活動に従事していました：蚤の市で古い資料や写真を、日本軍家族の生活居住区で捨てられた雑誌やアルバムを探したり；海外の通信社から購入したり、友人から集めたりしていました。特に上海中共代表団事務所の協力も得られ、南京経由で延安から二百数枚の八路軍、新四軍及び各地遊撃隊が勇敢に抗日する貴重な写真も転送されてきました。1946年９月、舒宗僑先生は一枚一枚集めた写真に加え、『聯合画報』社が数年間に亘り蓄積してきた大量な資料写真を用いて、『第二次世界大戦画史』を編集出版しました。それは四、五十万の文字数と、千枚余りの写真からなり、その史料としての参考及び収蔵価値は極めて高かったのです。1947年5月、名高い文化人の曹聚仁先生と共同で『中国抗戦画史』という大作を編集出版しました。朱自清先生は当時「本の取材は精確で、写真は更に貴重だ」と評価していました。1948年2月、更にもう一人の撮影家魏守忠先生と一緒に、大量の第二次大戦を題材にした写真の中から232枚を精選し、『二次大戦照片精華』を編集出版しました。一つ一つ真実の歴史的ショットが第二次世界大戦の全過程を生々しく再現しました。この二冊の画史と一冊の写真集は、社会に多大な影響を及ぼし、そのうち数多くの写真は数回複写され、転載、引用されました。アメリカのハーバードやスタンフォード等の大学が二次大戦を研究する際も、上記画史を重要参考資料にしてました。1984年新華通信社撮影部編集、新華出版社が出版した『日本侵華図片資料集』の中にも三十数枚の写真は舒宗僑先生のこの二冊の画史から採用されました。特に言及しなければならないのは、1948年国民政府が上海で日本戦犯を審判する際も、この二冊の画史は、日本侵略軍の戦争犯罪の有力な証拠として厳粛な法廷に登場しました。

歳月は速く過ぎ、世事は変転し、かつてこんなに輝いた貴重な写真集も次第に人々の記憶から薄れてしまいました。原本の保存数は少なく、今では極稀な珍書となりました。これらの貴重な史料を保存、再現するため、我々は舒宗僑先生及びその家族の全面的なサポートと協力の下、『二次大戦照片精華』を整理再編することに決めました。

この新版の『二次大戦照片精華』は、1948年2月に出版された同書に基づき、1947年3月『第二次世界大戦画史』の第三版及び1947年5月に出版された『中国抗戦画史』中の八路軍、新四軍の抗日活動をメインとした一部の写真を補充し、再編されました。元版の『二次大戦照片精華』の序、第二次世界大戦略史、全ての写真の下の説明文等は、中文、英文で書かれていました。我々は再編する際、この二ヶ国語以外に日本語を加えました。また『第二次世界大戦画史』、『中国抗戦画史』から補充した写真も全て中、英、日文の説明を加えました。従来の『二次大戦照片精華』と区別するためにも、読者により分っていただくためにも、全ての補充写真及び文書に関しては、目録に＊記号を附加しています。

60年来、第二次世界大戦に対する多くの研究成果は既に挙げられてきました。よってこのほぼ60年前に出版された『二次大戦照片精華』の中のいくつかの表現の仕方や観点は少し古い、或いは妥当でなくなっているかもしれません。我々は史料保存を目的にこの『二次大戦照片精華』を再出版しましたので、明らかな書き間違いや印刷ミスの改正以外は全て原状維持しています。読者が本書を読まれる際、或いはその資料を使用する際は、各自での鑑別をお願いします。例えば第174ページの「スティルウェル道路」について、この滇(雲南省）緬（ビルマ）道路の険しさを表現していた写真は、当時の西側諸国を震撼し、アメリカ上層部に直接影響を及ぼしたため、対日抗戦する中国軍へ軍用物資の支援も強化されました。この「二十四カーブ」と名付けられた曲がりくねった道は雲南省境内の滇緬道路の一部だと思われていましたが、二、三年前に、滇緬道路の一部ではなかったことが証明されました。それは貴州省の晴隆県から1キロ離れた蓮城鎮五一村半官坂という場所にあったことが分かりました。

この写真集を再び世に出すことは、人々にあの血と火の歴史を追想させ、人類に災難をもたらした戦争を心に刻ませ、心を一つにして共に戦場に赴く歳月を思い出させます。当時の『聯合画報』社長オンフレットはかつてこのように述べていました：「世界の各戦場で流れた数千数万の軍人の血は、我々の写真に無限な色彩を与えた。一つ一つのショットは数千数万人の血の結晶でしょう。」『二次大戦照片精華』元の序文の中にもこのように記されている：「普通の写真集や映画雑誌を見るような軽い気持ちでこれらのショットを見ないで欲しい。ここに掲載された一枚の写真が、もしかしたら何万人ものの命の代償だったかもしれない。それは、明光と暗黒、正義と暴力の決闘である。歴史が残した必然的な道筋を示している。」

この沈痛な歴史をしっかり憶え、世界の平和と発展を促進する崇高な事業のために努力奮闘しましょう。

この写真集の出版にあたり、まず舒宗僑先生及び家族舒似槿女史、舒似茵女史、舒達明先生、舒達遠先生に感謝の意を表したいと思い、彼らは写真集の元本と重要な背景資料を提供してくださいました。また雅昌企業集団北京雅昌カラー印刷有限公司にも感謝いたし、彼らは数多くのぼやけた写真を元よりも鮮明に修正してくださいました。また、南京大学唐建清教授はこの写真集の英文を校閲してくださいました。天津市商務委員会の王建新女史は写真の説明文書の日本語翻訳に携わってくださいました。ここで謹んで心より感謝致します。

この写真集が新たに整理出版されたことは、歴史資料や古い写真の収蔵愛好家達に貴重な精神的な財産をもたらすことを心より願います。

群言出版社編集部
2005年8月15日

目　录

日本战败

*法西斯罪魁和汉奸的下场

CONTENTS

The Collapse of Germany and Italy

China's Contribution to Allied Victory

Bloody Fighting in the Pacific

The Defeat of Japan

*The End of the Fascists and the Traitors

目　次

北アフリカの砂漠戦場

ドイツとイタリアの崩壊

中国は連合国勝利のために戦った

太平洋の血戦

日本の敗戦

＊ファシストの主犯者と売国奴の結末

原　　序

这是一部纯粹图画的战争史料，从九一八到日本投降，记录了这一世纪又一次世界战争的全貌。

公理终归战胜强权，尽管强权在某一时期称雄一时。法西斯主义者挑起了战争，而它本身也葬送在这一次战争中；民主力量的团结，争取到了胜利，也指出了人类今后合理的生活方式是什么。

本书之目的，在给予阅者对于这一次战争一个清楚明确的印象，请求阅者不要以看普通图书或电影杂志的心情来看这些镜头，这里一幅照片的出现，也许已经付出成千成万人的生命来做代价，它代表着光明与黑暗，正义与暴力的决斗，呈现着历史所遗留下的必然的路径。

这是战争到和平的结晶，在今天动荡和黯淡的世界中刊行，并不是多余，反之，也许我们由此得到警惕。我们已经更深切地知道战争所要付的代价有多大，鲜血汇成巨流，正是人类经验与智慧的源泉，在这源泉之前，我们树立过一块和平基石，这块基石不能再经我们的手将它破坏。维护和平，摒弃战争，是我们这一代不可逃避的责任。

本书之编印，曾得很多中外机关与友人帮忙，谨在此郑重致谢。

编者　　一九四八年二月一日

PREFACE

This is purely a pictorial war history from "September 18th, 1931" to the surrender of Japan to the Allies, recording the Second World War of the present century.

It is Right that always prevails over Might in the end, although the latter may appear triumphant over the former for a certain length of time. Fascism stirred up the war and war finally destroyed Fascism in the tremendous struggles. This war was won through the unity of the democratic forces, which well demonstrated the manner by which men should live together.

This pictorial book is intended to give the reader a vivid, and almost indescribable impression of the war. Thus it is hoped that this book will not be taken for a mere picture book or a motion picture magazine for even one single scene in the photographs reproduced here may have cost millions of lives, representing a struggle between the forces of light and darkness, right and violence —— the inevitable path left behind by history.

Embodying the resultant peace which followed this war we hope it is not superfluous to publish this book today when the world is shaken with fresh disturbances. Indeed, it may serve as a reminder of the terrific price we have paid in this last war, a vast stream swelling with myriads of tiny blood-pools, but a rich source of experience and wisdom. In front of this source we have erected a headstone to peace and this headstone of peace let us not destroy with our own hand. To maintain peace and denounce war is a duty from which none of us can shrink today.

In preparing this book the editor is greatly indebted to many institutions and friends, foreign and Chinese, and it is appropriate that this be mentioned with hearty thanks.

February 1, 1948

序　文

これは単なる絵による戦争の史料である。九一八の満州事変から日本の投降まで、今世紀の再び起こした世界大戦の全貌を記録している。

強権は一時的に脅威を見せても、最終的には正義がいかなる強権にも勝る。ファシズムが今回の戦争を起こしたが、それ自身も今回の戦争によって葬られてしまうこととなった。民主の力の団結が勝利を勝ち取ったと同時に人類の今後の合理的な生活も導いた。

本書の目的は、読者に今回の戦争への明確な印象を与えることである。普通の写真集や映画雑誌を見るような軽い気持ちでこれらのショットを見ないで欲しい、ここに掲載された一枚の写真が、もしかしたら何万人ものの命の代償だったかもしれない。それは、明光と暗黒、正義と暴力の決闘である。歴史が残した必然的な道筋を示している。

これは戦争から平和に至る結晶である。今日のような、揺れ動いている暗い世の中に刊行されたことは、余計なことではなく、我々に警鐘を鳴らしている。戦争の代償の大きさについて我々はすでに認識している。血が大きな流れを成し、これはまさに人類経験と知恵の源泉であろう。この源泉の前に、我々は平和の記念碑を建てた、この記念碑を自分たちの手で破壊してはいけない。平和を維持し、戦争を廃棄するのは、我々の逃れられない責任である。

本書の編纂出版にあたり、数多くの国内外の団体及び友人の協力を得られまして、ここで謹んで心より感謝申し上げます。

編修者　　一九四八年二月一日

第二次世界大战简史

第二次世界大战，是本世纪人类第二度的大流血，战争起于1931年九一八沈阳事变，到1945年8月大战结束，先后将近14年。

这次世界战争，以亚洲为起点，欧洲战争发生，德意日从政治与精神的结合，发展到军事结合，1941年德苏战争与太平洋战争的爆发，东西两半球的战火燃烧成一团，把世界划分为法西斯与反法西斯，轴心与反轴心，侵略与反侵略的两大壁垒，能够逃出战争漩涡的国家，已是很少。

战争开始，发动侵略的轴心国家把握住主动的优势。初期战争中只能听到敌人攻势的炮声。同盟国家的反攻准备，直到1943年才算逐渐完成，1944年才大规模展开。盟国攻势开始，轴心国家亦即走上下坡路，意大利墨索里尼首先支持不住下了台，希特勒跟着传出死讯。德军在夹攻之下投降，欧洲战争先收了场。日本没有德意，精神上更孤单，它的自杀攻击，抵不住盟军绝对优势的炮火，最后迫着这个称霸东方半世纪的“东方之强”屈了膝，在密苏里号上签下降书。

战争的起因　造成这次战争的是德意日三个轴心国家，日本在1918年第一次大战结束后，国力日渐强大，亟想向亚洲大陆侵略，日本军阀与财阀散布法西斯思想，鼓动着人民从事侵略行动。意大利上次大战得到利益不多，墨索里尼组织法西斯棒喝团，以恢复罗马帝国的光荣为号召，也能得到人民的喝彩。德国在上次大战以后，经济政治均陷于解体，德国人愤恨现状达于极点，它需要权力，需要德意志的精神重生。所以德意日这三个极权国家，在时间与地点方面，都是法西斯势力最好培植的摇篮。

首次大战产生的凡尔赛和约，德国人认为是一条枷锁，希特勒就利用推翻凡尔赛和约来完成政治的蠢动，达到军事征服的目的。

法西斯飞快地发展时，强国如英法，却在推行一种现实的妥协外交，即所谓绥靖政策。日本侵略中国东北，德军重整军备，入莱因，占萨尔，意大利侵犯阿比西尼亚，德意参与西班牙内战，英法均取冷眼旁观的态度，生怕引起战争；那知英法的退让，直接鼓励着法西斯的侵略行动，1938年德国兼并了奥地利，又开始向捷克开刀，捷克牺牲之后，又临到波兰。

中国是反法西斯的前锋　日本在1931年攻占中国宝库东北，没有受到阻碍，即大踏步的向亚洲大陆进犯，3个月时间占据全东北。1932年又在上海行动，是年底攻长城，试叩华北的门户，中国毫无准备，一再容忍。接着日军又来攻绥远，察哈尔，发动自治运动。其时全国民族意识异常强盛，民情沸腾，西安事变解决，全国对外敌忾同仇，万众一心，对日抗战形势已成，当1937年7月7日民族抗战的号角从卢沟桥头响起时，中华民族团结成一个巨人，从事神圣的挽救民族的战争。

战事先在平津一带展开，8月13日上海又发生战事，国军坚守3月，退向南京；南京失陷，中国首都移至四川重庆。华北方面，逐战逐退；1938年春发生徐州会战，日军大败于台儿庄。徐州失守后，日军转兵攻武汉，至是年10月，武汉及华南重镇广州被敌占据。15个月以来的中国抗战，虽重要城市相继失陷，而抗战意志，始终坚定，国人一致从事对日的长期战争。

欧战爆发　1939年9月1日德国继续用兵于波兰，开始了一个空前冒险的征服欧洲的计划。英法被迫对德宣战，但不及援助波兰，波兰已被德国闪电战所攫取。此后，德国进行了6个月的神经战，按兵不动，只是一味恫吓，直到1940年4月9日又以闪击姿态，12小时亡了丹麦，同时以第五纵队为内应，经2个月战争亡了挪威。

1940年夏天，希特勒的枪头指向荷兰，比利时，卢森堡，绕道西欧低洼国家攻法国。英法比荷为德国强烈攻势阻成数段，比王下令投降德军，英军被逼至敦刻尔克，作冒险的撤退。法国北部法军虽图振作，以组织涣散，士气消沉，6月14日巴黎失陷，法兰西的罪人贝当，遂宣布对德媾和。

德国进到英吉利海峡，希特勒瞻望英伦，准备跨海西征，先展开一个空中攻势——不列颠之战，一连着84天的恶斗，英人牺牲重大，到最后5分钟，德国却软化了。

征英不成，德国继续在巴尔干挑动战争，指使意大利攻希腊，罗马尼亚侵入保加利亚，迫匈牙利，罗马尼亚加入轴心，用兵南斯拉夫，英国虽竟以军事外交力量支持巴尔干各国，但结果还是轴心占着上风。

在大西洋上，英国与德国的海军在广大的海洋上，正从事封锁与反封锁的恶战。

美国也受着纳粹的直接威胁。在罗斯福总统英断之下，美国以人力物力，协助被侵略国家作战。

非洲战场　法国崩溃，1940年秋意大利乘机向埃及进攻，想与德国控制中东和地中海，意军占英属索马利，8月间自利比亚攻埃及，英军情势危急，于冬季增援反攻，重入利比亚。希特勒鉴于意军力量薄弱，调非洲师团由隆美尔指挥猛攻，后轴心军又入埃及。1941年德苏战争与太平洋战争爆发，德意军在非洲无法推进，兵力分散，1942年11月盟军在北非洲大规模登陆。至翌年5月，轴心军已在非洲被肃清。

德苏战争 德国在欧非作战年余，从波罗的海到地中海攫得土地资源，超过战前数十倍，与苏联在地理上发生冲突，同时它更想从苏联手中得到重要的作战物资如煤油粮食及各种矿藏，德国于是又来侵犯苏联。

1941年6月22日到12月底，德军集中200万精兵和五分之四的空军闪击苏联，企图一鼓而下莫斯科。在1,500哩漫长的战线上，苏军起初作战很为不利，德军在北路进至列宁格勒，中路进展迅速，占白俄罗斯首府明斯克，逼近莫斯科近郊，苏联首都迁到古比雪夫，南方占乌克兰首府。苏军积极保卫莫斯科，损失极重。到严冬来临，苏军利用季候展开反攻，始抵住了侵略者。

希特勒的攻势在1942年从春季延到夏季，变更战略，集中160个师准备在顿河与高加索歼灭苏军主力，攻占斯大林格勒，再沿伏尔加河经古比雪夫绕攻莫斯科，同时南下取巴库油田；德军获得进展。至8月间，斯大林格勒争夺战开始，双方以火力与血肉作孤注一掷，死伤遍野，德军疯狂进攻，苏军冒死抵御。这是二次大战一大高峰，德军最后的惨败，注定了在这次战争中的命运。

太平洋战争 日本占领了半个中国，为实行其征服亚洲，于1941年12月7日清晨偷袭美国在太平洋的基地珍珠港；美国一无准备，损失惨重。日本靠了优势兵力，同时进攻上海，香港，荷属印度，马来亚，菲律宾，关岛，泰国；中英美加澳自由法国等相继对日宣战。新加坡军港于1942年2月失陷。在菲律宾登陆之日军，取马尼拉，美军退至巴丹半岛及柯里几多，由麦克亚瑟领导作艰苦之抵抗，先后5月。东南亚方面，日军强在泰国登陆，压迫越南"联防"，藉以进攻缅甸；中国军队入缅协助英军作战，后以日军由泰国经缅甸東，侧击腊戍，瓦城失陷，中英军乃相率退入印度。

珍珠港奇袭成功，使日军得以一时称霸东方，彼时德军正在苏联发动进攻，大有在近东会师之势。

美国舰队于1942年在珊瑚海与中途岛，两次与日发生海战，阻止了日本继续进犯。

欧洲的解放 1943年盟国反攻准备已逐渐完成，开始向希特勒堡垒防线进攻。德国从闪击战的主动地位被迫而作防御战了。

盟军的战略是在南欧与西欧登陆，再与东线苏军三面夹攻德军，另以空军实行大规模的战略轰炸。盟军在西西里登陆，打了2个月的硬仗，9月2日盟军在意南登陆。就在这时，意大利内部发生分裂，墨索里尼被反对党逼迫下了台，意大利政府首先向盟国投降。但在德军控制下之意大利本土之意军，仍与盟军作战。罗马终在1944年6月4日，拱手让与盟军。

罗马失陷之日，养精蓄锐，训练经年，准备摧毁希特勒欧洲堡垒之数百万盟国大军，已登上4,000艘攻欧船舰。

6月6日，欧洲以及世界人士殷望之第二战场终于开辟，盟军由天空与海岸在法国北部诺曼底一带登陆。希特勒占领下的欧洲，曾先经年余轰炸，欧洲堡垒的屋顶业已震塌，德国空军作防御战都感到困难，秘密武器飞弹不能阻止盟军攻势，大西洋长城之梦已经幻灭。瑟堡半岛为登陆后之争夺中心，盟军飞机坦克的活跃，使德军穷于应付。仅仅克恩之战，德军便丧失了6个坦克师。

盟军于8月15日陆续在法国南部登陆，法国内地军与爱国者们加紧活动，25日解放巴黎。盟军过塞纳河，向比利时进扑，继而双方在莱因河对峙。

东线方面，1942年冬末苏联即已开始大反攻，高加索与顿河各大城市发生争夺战，中路苏军的进展，解除了莫斯科的威胁，夺回奥勒尔，冲过聂伯河，1943年底，苏联已收回失土四分之三。第二战场开辟后，苏军更开始总攻，向波兰作扇形展开，政治与军事双管齐下，屈服了罗马尼亚，保加利亚，进入南斯拉夫，解放了匈牙利。中路方面，12月攻占华沙。1945年1月苏军进入德国本土。

希特勒在东南西三面围攻中，东西线主攻，均以柏林为目标，德军以全力保卫柏林。12月间曾在西线作反攻，图重行回到巴黎，而艾森豪威尔部下数百万大军却在350哩前线开始全面总攻，再打回莱因河。苏军与西线盟军作争夺柏林之赛跑，苏军九路围攻柏林，柏林市区发生激烈巷战，4月26日美苏会师于莱比锡以东之突尔高。德国南部城市，亦相继被攻克，柏林经多日巷战，大势已去，杜尼兹海军上将宣布希特勒死亡，德国决定投降。至此，称霸欧洲十余年之纳粹德国，终为英美法苏盟军占领。

日本投降 德意败亡，三个轴心国家已去其二，盟国乃得转移兵力，集中打击日本。1944年盟军在太平洋反攻已收复了瓜加林岛，塞班，关岛，帛硫岛，菲律宾之雷伊泰，这些攻势均以海空军为先导，继之以敌前登陆。1945年盟军再登陆于吕宋，硫璜岛，大硫球，切断其南洋交通线，进入日本内卫圈，空中堡垒自塞班和大硫球及航空母舰上之轰炸机经常轰炸东京，横滨，名古屋各大日本城市，一次出动常在千架以上，投弹数千吨，使日本军事防御与工业陷于解体。在亚洲大陆上，中国军队已打通中印公路，取得国外的接济，空军轰炸台湾，东北，越南各地，收复桂林，正准备配合联合国作总反攻。日本在德国失败后，精神上已崩溃，再后虽然还想以武士道的作战方式——自杀攻击，来挽回帝国的厄运，但是盟国的联合力量，压倒一切，当波茨坦的决议付诸实施——苏联对日宣战，再加上两颗小小的原子弹，日本只好由天皇出面宣布投降结束了二次大战。

一九四八年二月

A Brief History of World War II

In World War II we witnessed the second colossal tragedy of human bloodshed of the current century. From the very first scene of this world-wide conflict (which consisted of the Mukden Incident of September 18, 1931), to the final conclusion of the whole war in August 1945, a period of nearly fourteen years was spanned.

The War had its beginnings in Asia. But when hostilities broke out on the European Continent, the political and spiritual alliance between Germany, Italy and Japan was extended to embrace a military alliance of the Unholy Three. When in due course war broke out between Germany and the Soviet Union, and later in the Pacific in 1941, the flames of war which surged over both the Eastern and Western Hemispheres were joined into a single and inseparable conflagration. The whole world was divided into two principal camps —— the Fascists and the anti-Fascists; the Axis powers and the anti-Axis powers; the aggressors and the resisters of aggression. Few indeed were the nations which could escape from being embroiled in the world's most gigantic combat of strength.

In the early stages of the War, the Axis powers who launched their aggressive schemes held in their hands the superiority of the initiative. The thundering assaults of the enemy's offensives predominated the early scenes of the conflict. The preparations on the part of the Allied Nations for their counter-offensive were only gradually being brought to perfection in 1943, and it was not until a year later that their large-scale counter-attack could be launched.

But once the Allies began their counter- offensive, the Axis powers found themselves on the downgrade. Mussolini of Italy first collapsed. This was soon followed by news of Hitler's death. The German Army, hemmed in by strong forces on all sides, surrendered. The war in Europe was thus ended. Deprived of her war-mates of Germany and Italy, the spiritual isolation of Japan was accentuated. Her "suicidal" offensives could not check the absolutely superior firepower of the Allies, and this "Strong-man of the East", who for half a century held hegemony over East Asia, was finally forced to bend her knees and to sign her surrender on board the U.S.S. Missouri.

Causes of the War

The war was brought into being by the Axis powers of Germany, Italy and Japan. With her growing prowess achieved, since the end of World War I in 1918, Japan began to nurse designs on the Asiatic Continent. Her militarists and financial overlords freely disseminated Fascist ideas among the people who were encouraged to undertake acts of aggression. In Italy, which did not obtain much gain from the first war, Mussolini organised his Black Shirts, and his cry for the restoration of the glories of the ancient Roman Empire found enthusiastic response from the people. In Germany, whose political and economic structure disintegrated following defeat in the first World War, the people's dissatisfaction with conditions at that time was worked up to the highest pitch and a popular demand for power, for the rebirth of the spirit of Germany, was easily created. For these reasons, time and the geographical situation all helped to make these three totalitarian states of Japan, Italy, and Germany the ideal cradle for the growth of Fascism.

The Versailles Treaty, given birth by the first World War, was considered by the Germans to be shackles over them. The unsuccessful political maneuvres launched by the Germans for the abrogation of Versailles was quickly exploited by Hitler who sought to achieve his results through military conquest.

While the forces of Fascism were thus seeking rapid expansion, the strong powers like Britain and France were pursuing a realistic diplomacy of compromise, the so-called policy of appeasement. Japan was invading China's Northeastern provinces; the German Army, rearmed, entered the Rhine and occupied Saarland; Italy. invaded Abyssinia; and both Germany and Italy participated in Spain's civil war. To all these atrocities Britain and France merely looked on askance-fearing lest any positive stand might lead to war. But the compromises and concessions made by the Anglo-French powers only served to encourage directly more aggressive acts on the part of the Fascists. In 1938, Germany absorbed Austria, and Czechoslovakia suffered the same fate. When the latter country was also sacrificed, Poland became the next victim.

China as the Advance Guard of Anti-Fascism

In 1931, the Japanese met with no obstacles when they began their invasion of the Northeastern provinces, China's treasurehouse. They immediately began to embark on a large-scale invasion of the Continent, and. in three months occupied the whole of China's northeastern provinces. Early in 1932, they staged an incident in Shanghai. Towards the end of the same year, the Japanese attacked the Great Wall, experimenting, no doubt, on the possibility of breaking through this back-door of North China. Unprepared at that time, China tolerated all these criminal assaults without hitting back effectively. The Japanese soon extended their aggression to Suiyuan and Chahar. and launched the socalled "self-government" movements in the areas.

The national consciousness of the Chinese people became highly aroused and public agitation against the alien invader was heightened. Meanwhile, the Si-an Incident was being settled: and the whole country became united as one in their determination to deal with the aggressors in the proper manner. The situation calling for the war of resistance against Japan had been strongly built up. And so when on July 7, 1937, the fighting at Marco Polo Bridge (Lukouchiao) sounded the bugle call of the war for racial existence, the Chinese people built themselves into a giant to fight their holy war for the preservation of their race.

Fighting first broke out in the Peiping-Tientsin area. It was extended to Shanghai on August 13, 1937. After holding this part of the country for three months, the Chinese forces withdrew to Nanking. Later when the latter city was also lost, the Chinese Government moved to Chungking, which became the war time capital. On the North China Front, the Chinese forces gradually withdrew but always after engaging the enemy in a good fight. Thus in the spring 1938 was staged the Battle of Hsuchow, when the Japanese forces met with their first major defeat at Taierhchuang. The Japanese eventually captured Hsuchow and turned their forces against the Wuchang-Hankow area. In October, 1938, both Hankow and Canton, bastion of South China, fell into enemy hands. The first fifteen months of China's war of resistance thus resulted in the loss to the enemy most of the major cities of the country but nevertheless the war consciousness of the nation remained more unshakable than ever, and the people became fully resigned to their determination to prosecute a prolonged war with Japan to the bitter end.

War Breaks Out in Europe

On September 1, 1939, Germany sent her armies into Poland, to initiate an unprecedented adventurous scheme for the conquest of all Europe. Britain and France were forced to declare war on Germany; but they were too late to render effective assistance to Poland which was soon grabbed by Germany with blitzkreig tactics. For the next six months Germany called a temporary halt to her military operations, in the meantime engaging in a war of nerves, putting up all forms of threats to all and sundry.

On April 9, 1940, however, the Germans moved again, and their blitzkreig strategy resulted in the conquest of Denmark in twelve hours. At the same time, with the aid of her fifth columnists in Norway Germany also overrun that country after a campaign, which lasted only two months.

In the summer of 1940, Hitler's guns were turned towards the Netherlands, Belgium, and Luxemburg, with the objective of launching an attack on France via these low basin areas of Western Europe. The British, French, Belgian, and Netherland forces were cut up into several sections in face of the fierce attack of the Germans. The King of the Belgians ordered his army to surrender to the Germans. The British expeditionary forces were forced to undertake the most risky withdrawal at Dunkirk. The French army in Northern France made a last stand but faulty organization and sinking morale made themselves felt and Paris was captured by the Germans on June 14. Marshal Petain, who proved himself an unworthy son of his country in this war, declared that France would conclude peace with Germany.

The Germans had now reached the English Channel. Looking across it towards the west Hitler conjectured up pictures of an even greater conquest on the other side. He launched, as a prelude to his contemplated invasion across the Channel, an air offensive. Thus was fought the Battle of Britain, a war of the most devastating consequences taking place principally in the skies, and for 84 days the British people were subjected to the most harrowing experiences and offered the greatest sacrifices. Finally the Germans weakened and called off the campaign.

The invasion of Britain having failed, the Germans turned their attention to the Balkans where the forces of destruction were soon easily let loose. Italy was made to attack Greece, Hungary and Roumania were forced into the orbit of the Axis powers and the invasion of Bulgaria and Yugo-Slavia was also launched. Britain exerted all the military and diplomatic resources at her disposal to maintain the status quo in the Balkans but for the moment the Axis powers gained the upper hand in the situation.

On the high seas in the Atlantic Ocean, over the seemingly unending expanse of water, the contending navies of Britain and Germany were engaged in their own battle of blockade and counter-blockade.

Meanwhile, the United States of America was beginning to feel the threat, directly and indirectly, of Nazi-ism. Under the resolute leadership of the late President Roosevelt the United States pledged her enormous manpower and resources to the aid of the victim nations.

The African Front

Following the collapse of France in the autumn of 1940, Italy took the opportunity to undertake the invasion of Egypt in an attempt to control, jointly with Germany, the Middle East and the Mediterranean. The Italians soon occupied British Somaliland. Using Libya as their base, the Italians in September 1940 attacked Egypt. The British garrison there for a time was in danger but with reinforcements in the winter, a counter attack was launched and the British re-entered Libya. Sensing the weakness of the Italians Hitler ordered the German African Divisions under the command of General Rommel, to that theater and the Axis once more invaded Egyptian territory.

The outbreak of war between Germany and Soviet Russia, and that of the war in the Pacific, produced a stalemate in the progress of the Germano-Italian campaign in Africa and the situation for the Axis powers there worsened as large contingents of the United Forces landed on the North African coast in November 1942. By May 1943, the Axis strength in Africa was completely annihilated.

The German-Russian War

After more than a year of intensive operations in both Europe and Africa, Germany had seized large tracts of land and material resources stretching from the Baltic to the Mediterranean, the acquisition being estimated to have enriched Germany to the extent of many times of her pre-war wealth. She now came into direct contact with Russia geographically, while at the same time she was anxious to obtain from the Russians some of the much coveted war resources, including coal, oil, food, and other minerals. She decided to include Soviet Russia in her scheme of conquest.

Between June and December, 1941, Germany mobilized 2,000,000 of her picked forces and 80 per cent of her Air Force for a blitzkrieg attack on Russia with the objective of taking Moscow by surprise. On a front extending over 1,500 kilometers the Soviet Army at first suffered reverses. On the northern front the Germans reached Leningrad. On the central front, where German progress was even more marked, the invaders, captured the White Russian capital of Minsk and threatened the approach to Moscow. The Russians moved their capital to Kuibyshev but continued to undertake the defence of Moscow in spite of huge losses. On the southern front the Germans took the Ukrainian capital in their stride. It was not until the arrival of the severe winter that the Russians were able to make full use of the weather and opened a counter-offensive which kept the aggressors in check.

In the early part of 1942 Hitler adopted a new strategy in the war with Russia. One hundred and sixty divisions were mobilised for a concerted attack on the main strength of the Soviet Army, concentrated in the Don basin and the Caucasus, the capture of Stalingrad, and thence the taking of Moscow by marching along the Volga and going through Kuibyshev. At the same time an attack was to be launched for the capture of the Baku oilfields. The Battle for Stalingrad began and both parties put in all they had into the struggle. Corpses covered the battlefields, the Germans attacked with unbelievable fierceness and the Russians defended with equally incredible bravery. The battle was one of the epics of World War II and the Germans ultimately suffered defeat, a development which practically sealed their fate in the whole war.

The Pacific War

After occupying about half of China, Japan, in carrying through her plan for the conquest of all Asia, in the early morning of December 7, 1941, launched a surprise attack on Pearl Harbor, a United States base in the Pacific. The Americans, taken unawares, suffered greatly in the episode.

The Japanese with their military superiority staged simultaneous attacks on Shanghai, Hongkong, Netherlands Indies, Malaya, the Philippines, Guam and Siam. China, Britain, the United States, Canada, Australia, and the Free French, one after another, declared war on this Asiatic aggressor.

The naval base at Singapore fell into Japanese hands in February 1942. Japanese forces landed on the Philippines, captured Manila, and the United States forces withdrew to Bataan and Corregidor where under the command of General Macarthur, they offered stiff resistance to the enemy for five months. In Southeastern Asia, the Japanese landed in Siam, forced French Indo-China into a joint defence undertaking, and planned to attack Burma. The Chinese Army entered Burma to assist the British forces in that area. The Japanese, coming from Siam and capturing Lashio and Mandalay through a rear frontal attack, forced the Sino-British units to withdraw into India.

The success of the cowardly attack on Pearl Harbour for a time placed Japan in the position of overlord of the East. At about this time the Germans were engaged in their offensive against Soviet Russia. There was then a dream among the Axis powers that they would effect a junction of their forces somewhere in the Near East.

In the course of 1942 the United States Navy engaged the Japanese Navy in battle in the Coral Sea and near Midway Islands, and these encounters succeeded in checking the further expansion of the Japanese advance.

The Liberation of Europe

By 1943 the Allies had completed their preparations for the counter-offensive and attacks against Hitler's bastions were begun. The Germans were forced to change from their blitzkreig initiative to assume a position of defence.

Allied strategy consisted of landings in both southern and western Europe and thence to join with the Russians in a three-front attack of German forces, at the same time releasing a colossal air force for large-scale strategic bombings. First landing in Sicily where they were engaged in two months of fierce fighting, the Allies on September 2, 1943 found themselves on the southern mainland of Italy. Just then, Mussolini was overthrown by political rivals following an extended period of internal dissension. The new Italian Government was the first among enemy nations to surrender to the Allies. But Italian forces, in Italy and elsewhere, under the control of the Germans, continued to engage Allied units in battle. Finally, on June 4,1944, Rome was officially taken over by the Allies, and the conquest of Italy was complete.

About the time of the fall of Rome, millions of Allied forces, carefully trained for the final onslaught on Hitler's European bastions, were embarking on their historic mission in 4,000 landing craft.

On June 6, 1944, the second front in Europe to which the people of that continent and all over the world had been looking forward for some time, was finally opened. Allied troops landed from boats and aircraft on the Normandy coast in Northern

France. For more than a year before this time, of course, Europe under Hitler had been subject to severe air attacks. The roofs of Hitler's bastions, so to speak, had been removed, and the German Air Force found it beyond their power to carry out an effective defence. The secret weapons, rocket missiles, employed by the Germans were futile in checking the Allied advance. The dream that the Atlantic would serve as a natural and insurmountable barrier was shattered. The first object of contention after the Allied landing was the Cherbourg Peninsula. Allied operations, greatly strengthened by the activity of planes and tanks, proved beyond the match of the Germans. In the battle of Caen alone, the Germans lost six tank divisions.

On August 15, 1944, the Allies began to land on southern France also. The French Forces of the Interior (F.F.I.) and partisan units immediately sprang to vigorous activity, and Paris was liberated on August 25. The Allies crossed the Seine, and marched towards Belgium. The Germans and the Allies were confronting each other on opposite banks of the Rhine.

Towards the end of 1942, Soviet Russia had already commenced her counter-offensive against Germany. Battles royal were fought for the control of various cities in the Caucasus and along the Don. The progress of Russia's central front soon removed the threat to Moscow. Orel was recaptured and the Dnieper was crossed. By the end 1943, the Russians recovered 75 per cent of their lost ground.

After the opening of the second European front, the Russians also opened a general counter-offensive and launched a two-pronged attack on Poland. Political forces were marshaled to augment military success, Roumania and Bulgaria were subdued, Yugo-slavia was entered, and Hungary liberated. In December 1944, the Russians took Warsaw and one month later they entered German territory.

Surrounded on the three sides, the east, the south and the west, two of the three forces having for their common objective the capture of Berlin, Hitler mustered all his resources for that city's defence. In December 1944, a counter-offensive was attempted in the western front with the objective of recapturing Paris. But General Eisenhower, with his large Army was already beginning an all-out attack on a 350 mile front and the Germans were easily pushed back. The Soviet forces and the Allied troops on the Western front began a race for Berlin. The Russians approached the German capital from nine routes and there was fierce street fighting in the city. On April 26, the Russians and Americans effected a junction of forces at Torgau, east of Leipzig. Cities in southern Germany were falling into Allied hands in quick succession. Berlin, after days of street fighting, was finally doomed. Hitler's death was announced by Admiral Doenitz, and Germany decided to surrender. Thus Nazi-Germany, which reigned supreme in Europe for more than a decade, was finally subdued by the allied forces of Britain, the United States, Soviet Russia, and France.

Japan's Surrender

The defeat of both Italy and Germany left Japan the lone survivor among the Axis trio, and the Allied powers were now in a position to concentrate their attention to dealing with her. In the counter-offensives in 1944, the Allies had recaptured the Carolines, Saipan, Guam, Palan Island, and Leyte Island (in the Philippines). In each case, air and naval units led the attack prior to the landing of troops.

Early in 1945, the Allies succeeded in landing in the Luzon, Iwo Jima, Ryukyu Islands, cutting off the southern communication lines of Japan and entering the inner defences of' the latter. Flying fortresses, based at Saipan and Ryukyus, and from aircraft carriers, staged regular raids on the Japanese cities of Tokyo, Yokohama and others. Attacks were launched by fleets of 1,000 planes and thousands of tons of dynamite were released. Japanese military industry was by then already rendered ineffective.

On the Asiatic mainland the Chinese Army reopened the overland route between China and India and foreign supplies were then available. The Chinese Air Forces also attacked Taiwan, the Northeastern Provinces and French Indo-China. Kweilin was recaptured. Preparations were being rushed for a coordinated general counter-offensive.

With Germany's defeat, Japan had, of course, already undergone a spiritual collapse. In the very last days a desperate attempt was made to exploit her Bushido concepts in war through the launching of suicide attacks to save the fate of the Japanese Empire. But the united resources of the Allies held sway over all. The implementation of the Potsdam decisions ——the entry of Soviet Russia into the war with Japans——and the unleashing of two small atomic bombs finally led to Japan's surrender in the name of her Emperor.

World War II was thus brought to an official termination.

February 1948

第二次世界大戦略史

第二次世界大戦は、本世紀人類史上二度目の大流血であった。戦争は1931年九一八の満州事変から、1945年八月の大戦終結まで、14年近く続いていた。

この戦争は、アジアから始まり、ヨーロッパでの戦争の勃発、ドイツ、イタリア、日本の三か国は政治と精神の結合から軍事の結合まで発展していた。1941年ドイツ・ソ連戦争及び太平洋戦争の勃発は、東西半球の戦火が一つになって、世界はファシズムと反ファシズム、枢軸と反枢軸、侵略と反侵略の二つの陣営に分割して、戦争の渦から逃れられる国家はもはや少なかった。

戦争の初めは、侵略を起こした枢軸国家が主導的な優勢を握っていた。戦争の初期では、敵の進攻の砲声ばかり聞こえた。同盟国家の反撃準備は、1943年までようやく完成し、1944年からやっと大規模展開し始めた。同盟国の攻撃開始により、軸心国家は下り坂を始めた。イタリアのムッソリーニの失脚を始め、ヒトラーの死に関する噂が続いた。四方の強い力によって取り巻かれたドイツ軍は降伏された。ヨーロッパ戦争はこのようにして終焉を告げた。日本は、ドイツ、イタリアの戦争仲間を失い、精神上は孤立し、その自殺的な攻撃はもはや同盟軍の絶対優勢な砲火に耐え切れず、この東アジアで半世紀に亘り制覇していた「東方強国」は、米戦艦ミズリーにおいて降伏文章の調印を余儀なくさせられた。

戦争の起因　戦争はドイツ、イタリア、日本の枢軸強国によって生み出された。日本は、1918年第一次世界大戦終結後、国力は日に日に強大化し、アジア大陸への侵略を企てた。日本の軍閥と財閥は、ファシズムを拡め、民衆に侵略行為に従事するよう扇動した。イタリアは、前回の戦争で余り利益を得られなかったから、ムッソリーニは、ファシズム黒シャツ隊を組んで、ローマ帝国の栄光の回復を唱え、同じく民衆の喝采を得られた。ドイツは、前回の大戦以降、経済政治は解体に状態に陥り、ドイツ国民の現状への不満がピークに達していた。ドイツは再生するのに、権力や、ドイツ精神が必要だった。これらの理由で、時間及び地理条件上、ドイツ、イタリア、日本、この３カ国は、ファシズム育成のための理想的な揺りかごとなった。

ドイツ人は、第一次大戦によって生み出されたベルサイユ条約を足枷と感じた。ヒトラーはこのベルサイユ講和条約を覆すことで、政治的蠢動、軍事征服の目的を達成しようと企らんでいた。

ファシズムは急速に拡大した時、イギリスやフランスのような強国は、一種の現実的な妥協外交、いわゆる宥和政策を推進しようとした。日本は中国東北地方への侵略、ドイツは軍備を建て直し、ラインラントやザールランドへの占領、イタリアのエチオピアへの侵犯、ドイツ、イタリアのスペイン内戦への介入に対し、イギリス、フランスは戦争が再び起きることを恐れたため、それらの行動を全て容認してきた。しかし、イギリス、フランスのこの譲歩は、直接ファシズムの侵略行為を激励する結果となった。1938年、ドイツはオーストリアを併合し、続いてチェコスロバキアにメスを入れた。その次は、ポーランドが犠牲になった。

中国は反ファシズムの前衛　1931年、日本は妨げられることなく、中国の宝庫である東北地方に侵攻できたため、更に大股でアジア大陸を侵犯し始め、わずか三ヶ月で全東北地方を占拠した。1932年上海で行動を起こし、年末には華北の門戸をこじ開けようと万里の長城に侵攻した。中国は全く抵抗の準備できず、再三の侵略行為に容認した。日本軍は続いて綏遠，察哈爾を攻撃し、自治運動を発動させた。その時、全国の民族意識は非常に強く沸き立った。西安事変の解決が全国の外敵に対する敵対心を燃やし、心を一つにした。対日本の抗戦態勢はすでに形成された。1937年7月7日の盧溝橋事件をきっかけに、抗日戦争のラッパが鳴り響き、中華民族は一人の巨人と化し、この神聖なる民族救済戦争に従事した。

最初の戦いは、北平、天津地方で展開された。8月13日、再び上海で事件が起きた。中国軍隊は3ヶ月間死守した後、南京へ退けたが南京も陥落したため、首都を四川の重慶に移した。華北方面は、戦いのたびに陥落していった。1938年春には　徐州会戦が勃発し、日本軍が台児荘で敗戦した。徐州を失った日本軍は、武漢を目標に変えた。同年10月、武漢及び華南の重要都市広州も占拠された。重要都市が相次いで陥落したにもかかわらず、国民が終始強い抗戦意識を持ち、十五ヶ月間にも及ぶ中国の初期な抗日戦争に粘り強く従事した。

ヨーロッパ戦争の勃発　1939年9月1日ドイツはポーランドへ武力侵攻し、空前のヨーロッパ征服の計画を開始した。イギリ、スフランスはドイツに対して、宣戦せざるを得なかったが、ポーランドは既にドイツの電撃戦によって奪取された。その後、ドイツは六ヶ月の間に兵隊を動かさず、ただひたすら脅しをかける「精神戦」を続けた。。1940年4月9日に再び電撃戦を発動し、12時間でデンマークを落とした。それと同時に内部からは第五縦隊の応援を受け、二ヶ月間でノルウェーを落とした。

1940年夏、ヒトラーは矛先をオランダに向けた。ベルギー，ルクセンブルクを回ってフランスを攻撃した。イギリス、フランス、ベルギー、オランダはドイツの強烈な攻撃の下で、数段に分かれた。ベルギー国王はドイツ軍に投降するよう発令した。イギリス軍はダンケルクに追い込まれ、冒険とも言える撤退を余儀なくされた。フランス北部のフランス軍は奮起しようとしたが、組織が緩み、士気が消沈したため、6月14日にはパリが陥落してしまった。フランスの罪人ペタンは、ドイツとの講和を宣告した。

ヒトラーはロンドンが狙いで、イギリス海峡まで侵攻し、西部戦線征服を企てた。まず前哨戦対英航空戦（バトル・オブ・ブリテン）を展開したが、84日にも及ぶ悪戦苦闘の結果、イギリス側は重大の損失を負ったけれど、最後の5分でドイツ軍が後続力の不足でイギリス上陸の作戦を中止した。

イギリス征服が失敗に終ったドイツが今度はバルカン諸国に戦争を手がけた。イタリアにギリシャ、ルーマニア、ブルガリアへの侵攻を指図した。ハンガリー、ルーマニアを枢軸国に強制的加盟させ；続いてユーゴスラヴィアに侵攻した。イギリスは軍事外交の力でバルカン諸国を支持したものの、結局枢軸国側が優位に立っていた。

大西洋において、イギリスとドイツの海軍は広い海洋で、封鎖と反封鎖の悪戦に広めていた。

アメリカもナチスの直接な脅威を受けた。ルーズベルト大統領の英断の下、人力及び物資を援助することで、侵略された諸国の作戦に手を貸した。

アフリカ戦場　1940年秋のフランスの崩壊を機に、イタリアはドイツと共に中東及び地中海をコントロールしようとして、エジプトに侵攻した。イタリア軍はイギリス領ソマリランドを占領した。9月にリビアからエジプトを攻め、英軍情勢が危ぶまれたが、冬季に援軍を増員し、再びリビアに入り反抗を始めた。ヒトラーはイタリアの軍力の衰弱を鑑み、「ドイツアフリカ軍団」を与え、ロンメルの指揮の下で猛攻を始め、再びエジプトに入った。1941年ドイツ・ソ連戦争と太平洋戦争が勃発したため、ドイツ、イタリア軍の兵力が分散され、もはやアフリカでの侵攻が不可能となった。1942年11月、連合軍は北アフリカに大規模上陸した。翌年5月には、アフリカにいた枢軸国軍を追放した。

独ソ戦争　ドイツがヨーロッパ、アフリカでの数年間の戦いの結果、バルト海から地中海まで、戦前の数十倍を超える土地資源を獲得した。これはソ連と地理的に衝突を生じさせた。同時に、石油、食糧及び各種鉱物のような重要な戦争物資をソ連から得るため、ドイツはソ連を侵犯し始めた。

1941年6月22日から12月末まで、モスクワを一気に落とすため、ドイツ軍は200万の精鋭兵と五分の四の空軍を集め、電撃戦でソ連を攻撃した。千五百キロに及ぶ戦線上、最初はソ連軍が極めて不利であった。北戦線では、ドイツ軍がレニングラードに到達した。中部戦線では最も進展が速く、 ベロルシアの首府であるミンスクを占領した。モスクワの近郊まで攻められたため、ソ連は首都をクイビシェフに遷した。南部戦線ではウクライナが独軍に占拠された。ソ連軍は積極的にモスクワを死守し、損失が極めて大きかった。やがて厳しい冬季が到来し、ソ連軍は気候を利用し侵略者を抑えて攻撃を始めた。

ヒトラーは、攻撃が1942年の春から夏に延びたため、戦略を変えた。百六十師団を集め、ドン川及びカフカス地域でソ連軍の主力を殲滅することで、スターリングラードを占領、ヴォルガ川に沿ってクイビシェフを通ってモスクワを攻める予定であった。8月までは、ドイツ軍の進展は順調だったが、スターリングラード攻防戦が始まり、双方は全ての火力と血肉をこの戦いに注いだ。ドイツ軍は気が狂ったように進撃し、ソ連軍は必死にそれに抵抗した。これは第二次世界大戦のピークとされ、このドイツ軍の最後の惨敗が今回の大戦の運命を決定付けた。

太平洋戦争　日本は中国の半分を占領した後、アジア征服のため、1941年12月7日早朝、アメリカ太平洋艦隊の基地である真珠湾に奇襲攻撃を仕掛けた。アメリカは全く無防備だったため、損失が大きかった。日本は優位な兵力を用いて、上海、香港、オランダ領のインド、マレーシア、フィリピン、グアム、タイを同時攻撃した。中国、イギリス、アメリカ、カナダ、オーストラリア、自由フランスが相次いで日本に宣戦した。シンガポールの海軍基地は、1942年2月に日本に陥落した。日本軍はマニラを狙い、フィリピンに上陸した。アメリカ軍はバターン半島とコレヒドールまで撤退し、マッカーサーの指導の下五ヶ月間抵抗を続けた。東南アジア方面で、日本軍はタイに上陸し、ベトナムに「共同防衛」を強制し、ビルマ侵攻した。中国軍はイギリス軍に協力するためビルマに入った。後、日本軍がタイからビルマの西を経て、横から攻撃し、ヤンゴンが陥落したため、中国とイギリス軍は止むを得ずインドまで退いた。

真珠湾奇襲の成功は、日本軍に一時的に東アジアでの制覇を成功させた。時を同じくして、ドイツ軍はソ連で侵攻を発動し、近東で合流する勢いだった。

米国艦隊は、1942年に珊瑚海とミッドウェーで、二回日本軍と海戦を展開し、日本の更なる侵犯を食い止めた。

ヨーロッパの解放　1943年連合国の反抗準備はほぼ完成し、ヒトラーの堡塁防衛線に進攻しようとした。ドイツ軍は電撃戦のような主導的な優勢から一変して防御戦に転じた。

連合軍はドイツ軍に対し、陸上ではそれぞれ南欧と西欧に上陸し、東戦線のソ連軍との三面から攻撃する上、空からは大規模な爆撃をする戦略だった。連合軍はシチリアから上陸し、二ヶ月の激しい戦いの後、9月2日にはイタリアの南に上陸成功した。この時、イタリア内部では分裂が発生し、ムッソリーニは政治上のライバルによって失脚した。新しいイタリア政府はまず連合軍に降伏を宣告したが、ドイツ軍にコントロールされていたイタリア本土のイタリア軍はまだ連合軍と戦っていた。ローマは結局1944年6月4日に連合軍の手に渡った。

ローマが陥落した日、長年訓練を重ね、英気を養ってきた数百万の連合国大軍は既に四千艘ヨーロッパを攻めるための戦艦に乗り込んだ。

6月6日、ヨーロッパ及び世界中の人々が望む第二の戦場も切り開かれた。連合軍は空と海からフランス北部のノルマンディーに上陸した。ヒトラーの占領下のヨーロッパ根拠地は長年の爆撃で既に崩れていた。ドイツの空軍は防御戦にすら困難を感じた。「飛弾」という秘密兵器も連合軍の攻勢に耐え切れず、「大西洋長城」の夢が幻滅してしまった。シェルブール半島は争奪の中心となり、連合軍の戦闘機及び戦車の（空と陸での）活躍は、ドイツ軍を窮地に追い込ませた。カーンの戦いだけでも、ドイツ軍の六つの戦車師団を殲滅した。

連合軍は8月15日に続々とフランスの南部に上陸した。フランスの内地軍と愛国主義者は活発に活動し、25日にはパリを解放した。更に連合軍は、セーヌ川を渡り、ベルギーに入った。双方はライン川を挟んで対峙した。

東戦線方面は、1942年末ソ連はすでに大々的に反撃を始めていた。フカス地域及びドン川の各大都市での争奪戦では、ソ連中央軍の進展がモスクワへの脅威を取り除いた。オーレルを奪回し、トニエプル川を突破し、1943年末には、ソ連は失った国土の四分の三を奪回できた。第二の戦場が切り開かれた後ソ連軍は更なる攻撃を始めた。ポーランドで扇型のごとく作戦を開始、政治と軍事の両方から攻めたため、ルーマニア、ブルガリアを屈服させ、ユーゴスラビアに入り、ハンガリーを解放した。中部方面では、12月ワルシャワを攻め落とした。1945年1月ソ連軍はドイツ本土に進入した。

ヒトラーは東南西の三面から囲まれた。東西は主にベルリンを目標にしていたため、ドイツ軍は全力でベルリンを守ろうとした。12月には、パリに戻ろうとして西戦線で反撃をしたが、アイゼンハワー司令官の数百万の大軍が350マイル手前で攻撃を始まっていたため、再びライン川へ追い戻されてしまった。ソ連軍と西連合軍戦線はベルリン争奪競争をしていた。ソ連軍は九つのルートからベルリンを包囲し、激しい市街戦が勃発した。4月26日、アメリカとソ連はライプチヒ東のトルガウで合流した。ドイツ南部の都市は相次いで陥落し、ベルリンも数日の市街戦で勢いを失くし、デーニッツ海軍上将は、ヒトラーの死を宣告し、ドイツは降伏を決定した。これでヨーロッパを十数年余り制覇したナチスドイツは最終的にイギリス、アメリカ、フランス、ソ連連合軍に占領された。

日本の降伏　ドイツイタリアの敗北により、枢軸国が三分の二を失った。連合国は兵力を移転し、日本を集中打撃した。1944年、連合軍は太平洋での反撃で、既にカロリン諸島、サイパン、グアム、フィリピンのレイテ島を奪回した。これらの攻勢は皆海軍空軍を先導にして、次は陸軍が上陸する。1945年、連合軍は更にルソン島、硫黄島、硫球諸島を上陸し、日本の南方での交通路線を断ち切った。日本の外囲に入り、航空母艦やサイパン、硫球からの空爆戦闘機は東京、横浜、名古屋各大都市を爆撃した。攻撃は、一回の出動は常に千機以上、そして毎回数千個ものダイナマイトを放出した。日本の軍事防御及び工業を解体するほどに陥った。その時、アジア大陸では、中国軍隊は既に中国インド間の道を開通でき、国外からの応援もあって、台湾、東北、ベトナム各地を爆撃し、桂林の奪回も成功し、ちょうど連合国に協力して反撃を準備していたところだった。日本は、ドイツの敗北の知らせを受け、事実上精神的に既に崩壊したにもかかわらず、武士道の作戦方式自殺攻撃で帝国の悪運を挽回しようとした。しかし、連合国の結合した力は全てを圧倒した。やがてポツダム宣言が実施されソ連の日本に対する宣戦布告に加え、二発の原爆弾が、天皇に日本を代表してに降伏を宣告させた。ついに二次大戦が終結を迎えた。

一九四八年二月

战争前奏曲

战争！战争！二次大战的号角响了！

日本，近百年来都在做着征服亚洲的美梦；在西方一次大战后产生两个大独裁者——墨索里尼和希特勒，他们宣传着极端国家主义，号召打破现状，扩张领土；德意日缔结反共协议，形成轴心——一个大规模的侵略集团，预定由德国统治欧洲，意大利统治地中海，日本统治远东；因为英法的妥协政策，轴心侵略气焰愈加猖狂，中国被日本蚕食，德国并吞了奥地利，接着捷克被牺牲。

Prelude to the War

War! War! The clarion call to the second world-wide conflagration was being sounded.

For nearly a hundred years Japan had been nursing a beautiful dream of the conquest of Asia. In the west, the end of World War Ⅰ produced two dictators, Mussolini and Hitler. They advocated the ideals of totali-arianism, with the objective of breaking up the status quo and the expansion of their respective territorial possession. Germany and Italy soon joined hands with Japan in concluding the anti-Comintern Pact and created the Axis —— an imposing group of aggressors who among them drew up plans for the division of the world with Germany controlling Europe, Italy holding sway over the Mediterranean, and Japan exercising hegemony in the East.

The appeasement policy adopted by Britain and Franc fanned the flames of aggression on the part of the Axis aggressors, Japan was worming her way into China. Germany absorbed Austria. Czechoslovakia was next sacrificed.

戦争前奏曲

戦争！戦争！第二次世界大戦のラッパが鳴り響く。

日本は、ここ百年以来アジア征服を夢見ていた。西側では第一次世界大戦後２大独裁者が誕生したムッソリーニとヒトラー、彼らは極端な国家主義を唱え、現状の打破及び領土の拡大を呼びかけた。ドイツ、イタリア、日本は反共協定を締結し、枢軸、即ち大規模な侵略集団を形成した。ドイツがヨーロッパを制覇し、イタリアが地中海を制覇し、日本が遠東を制覇することと企てた。イギリス、フランスの妥協政策で、枢軸侵略者側の攻撃の炎を扇いだ。中国は日本に蚕食され、オーストリアはドイツに飲み込まれ、続いてチェコスロバキアも犠牲となった。

战争前奏曲

Prelude to the War

日本准备侵略战争

日本自1894年中日战争以来，即抱定大陆政策以侵略中国，征服东亚，称霸世界为其国策，先后从中国劫去台湾，旅顺，大连等要地，复图进一步向大陆发展。日本法西斯数十年来致全力于扩张军备，处心积虑，以谋侵略行动的实现。图为日人献机典礼之热烈欢呼情况。

Japanese Craziness

Ever since the Sino–Japanese war of 1894, the Japanese were intoxicated by their dreams of expansion and empire–building. Successes on the Chinese mainland further swelled their heads to reach out for world dominance. Above shows Japanese shouting during a ceremony to present air–planes to the government.

日本の侵略戦争の準備

日本は1894年の日清戦争以来、大陸政策を以って中国侵略を企て、東アジアを征服し、世界制覇を国策とした。大陸への更なる侵入のため、前後して台湾、旅順、大連などの要塞を略奪した。日本ファシズムは数十年来全力で軍備を拡張し、侵略の実現に苦心してきた。写真は、日本人が飛行機を政府に贈る儀式の時の熱狂振りである。

希特勒当权

德国第一届备战纪念，总理希特勒在旗帜招展，万众欢呼下进入柏林市街，前往检阅30万大军。德国久已准备侵略战争，1935年宣布废除凡尔赛条约军事条款，恢复征兵，1936年3月7日进兵莱因东岸，1938年煽动奥地利政变，宣布德奥合并，1939年吞并捷克。

Hitler's Rise to Power

Adolf Hitler, Chanceller of Germany, rides through the banner-draped streets of Berlin amid cheering crowds en-route to review 300,000 soldiers on the occasion of Germany's first "preparedness day" observance. Actually Germany had prepared for its war aggression long before.

ヒトラー政権

ドイツ第一回備戦記念に、ヒトラーが30万大軍を検閲するため、旗幟が揺らぎ、群衆が喝采する中、ベルリン市街に入る様子。ドイツはずっと前から侵略戦争の準備をしていた。1935年にベルサイユ条約の軍事条項を廃止すると(ドイツ再軍備宣言)宣告し、徴兵制を回復した。1936年3月7日にライン川東に進軍して、1938年にオーストリア政変を扇動し、ドイツ・オーストリア併合を宣告した。1939年チェコスロバキアを併呑した。

德国秘密建军

德国秘密建军，到1936年已相当强大，像机械一般之德军行列于国社党行经纽伦堡希特勒旅邸，希特勒私自训练冲锋队与铁卫队作为侵略的资本。德国更和东方侵略者日本缔结反共同盟(1936年11月25日)，1937年11月6日意大利亦参加。

Reich's Secret Army

Germany started to rebuild her army long before 1936, despite Verssaille Treaty limitations. The Nazi again organized and trained their own SA and SS to prepare for future aggression. The above parade was held in Nuremburg before the inn where Hitler stayed.

ドイツの秘密軍備

ドイツの秘密軍隊は1936年には相当強力になった。機械の如く行列を成してニュルンベルクのヒトラーの宿屋までパレードした時の情景。ヒトラーは侵略の資本として突撃隊(SA)と親衛隊(SS)を無断で訓練した。1936年11月25日、ドイツは更に、東の侵略者日本と反共同盟を締結した。1937年11月6日にはイタリアもそれに参加した。

法西斯鼻祖

墨索里尼是法西斯主义的鼻祖，他在1919年组织一小党，提倡极端国家主义，反对共产主义，企图恢复罗马帝国的光荣，1922年领着40,000法西斯党员进军罗马，诱骗国王，任为首相，意大利人的自由被他剥夺尽了。1935年开始侵略埃塞俄比亚，1937年联合德国干涉西班牙内战。

Benito Musollini

A fascist extremist of 1919,Benito Musollini marched to ower at the head of his 40,000 followers in 1922. From then on he sat squarely on his people's freedom and very life. He invaded Ethiopia, took part in the Spanish civil strife, and then joined Hitler in the conquest of the world.

ファシズムの元祖

ムッソリーニは、ファシズムの元祖である。彼は、1919年に党を組織した。極端国家主義を提唱し、共産主義を反対し、ローマ帝国の栄光を回復することを企てていた。1922年に4万のファシスト党員を引き連れローマに進軍し、国王を騙し、首相に就任した。イタリア人の自由は彼に剥奪された。1935年にエチオピアに侵略し始め、1937年にドイツと一緒にスペイン内戦に介入した。

慕尼黑惨剧

希特勒吞并了奥地利（1938年），又预备对捷克开刀，英法想以牺牲弱小来满足希特勒的领土欲望，英首相张伯伦到了慕尼黑，希特勒假意地热烈欢迎他，签订了耻辱的慕尼黑协议（1938年9月29日），承认苏台区属德。可是到翌年3月15日，德国却进占了捷克全境。

Disaster at Munich

The treaty of Munich directly contributed to the aggrandizement of the nazi powers. Britain' Chamberlain and France's Daladier tried to pacify Hitler in securing the peace in our time, but Hitler answered them with the conquering of Czechoslovakia and the aggression of Poland in the next year.

ミュンヘンの陰謀

1938年ヒトラーがオーストリアを併合後、チェコスロバキアにメスを入れようとした。イギリス・フランスはヒトラーの領土への欲望を満たすためには、弱小を犠牲にすることに決めた。英首相チェンバレンが1938年月29日にミュンヘンへやってきて、ヒトラーは熱烈歓迎を装い、恥辱的なミュンヘン協定を締結させた。ズデーテン地方をドイツ領として承認した。しかし翌3月15日には、ドイツはチェコスロバキアの全領土を占領した。

轴心交欢

二次世界大战爆发前，日德意三国分别侵略他国领土，战争爆发以后，很快地结成轴心阵线，东西呼应，冀图征服世界。上为希特勒之青年团拜访东京，向欢迎之日人行纳粹礼，表示两国团结一致，1940年9月27日，日德意三国成立军事同盟。

Birds of a Feather Flock Together

The Hitlerite youth corps paying a visit to Japanese at Tokyo. The Military Alliance of the three axis powers was formed on Sept. 27, 1940.

枢軸国が喜び交わす

第二次世界大戦勃発前、日独伊の三国はそれぞれ他国の領土を侵略し、戦争勃発後には、枢軸戦線を結んだ。東西呼応して、世界の征服を企てた。上の写真は、ヒトラーの青年団(ヒトラーユーゲント)が東京に訪問した際、両国の団結を示すため、歓迎する日本人にナチス式敬礼をしている情景。1940年9月27日、日本、ドイツ、イタリア三国の軍事同盟が成立した。

日本侵略中国

战争首先开始于东方，日本军阀首先于1931年9月18日侵犯沈阳，很快的夺去了中国的宝库东北。翌年扰乱上海，挑动一二八战争，进而蚕食华北，中国一再容忍，至1937年，由于日军在卢沟桥的挑衅，逼使中国走上长期抗战的大道。平津与京沪经战斗后相继失陷，战争中心移至徐州，日军在台儿庄遭受重大损失。其后发生武昌大会战，中国迁都于重庆，继续长期战争。

Japan Invades China

The dogs of war were first let loose in the East. On September 18, 1931, the Japanese attacked Mukden, and very speedily grabbed the whole of the Northeastern Provinces —— China's treasures house.

The next year, 1932, saw the Japanese militarists showing their hands in Shanghai with the January 28 fighting in that city. North China was next invaded.

China tolerated all these crimes inflicted on her until 1937. The Japanese challenge at Lukouchiao (Marco Polo Bridge) on July 7, forced the Chinese nation to rise in defenses of their country in a prolonged war of resistance.

Peiping, Tientsin, country in a prolonged war of resistance, another fell into enemy hands after fierce engagements. Invaders were dealt a disastrous blow in the Battle of Taierchuang.

The Battle of Wuchang-Hankow followed. China's capital was moved to Chungking where the continuation of the war was directed.

日本の中国侵略

日本の中国侵略戦争は東洋から始まった。日本軍閥はまず1931年9月18日に瀋陽の侵犯から始まり、すぐさま中国の宝庫である東北地方を奪取した。翌年には、上海に手を伸ばし、一・二八戦争(第一次上海事変)を引き起こした、さらに華北地区を蚕食する、中国は何度も容認してきたが、一九三七年、日本軍の盧溝橋での挑発により、長い抗戦の道に余儀なく立たされた。北平、天津、上海では抵抗したが、結局相次いで陥落した。戦争の中心が徐州に移った後、日本軍は台児荘で重大な損失を負った。その後の武昌大会戦が起き、中国国民政府は都を重慶に移し、長期戦争を続けた。

日本侵略中国

Japan Invades China

沈阳事变

日本对华大侵略的开始是制造沈阳事变，于1931年9月18日借口中国军队炸毁南满铁路，向沈阳中国军队进行攻击，同时占领沈阳及东北各主要城市。日本对华侵略战争就此揭开。图为日军及南满铁路人员图以破碎枕木，军帽，枪支证明破坏铁路为中国军队所为之留影。

Mukden Incident

Here an excuse was fabricated by the Japanese military officers for their invasion of China's Northeast, on Sept. 18, 1931. The date was important because it turned the tide of the world situation. From then on, the world moved steadily toward war.

満州事変

日本の中国侵略は満州事変の捏造から始まった。1931年9月18日に中国軍隊が南満鉄道を爆破したことを理由にして、瀋陽の中国軍隊に攻撃を始めた。同時に瀋陽及び東北の各主要都市を占領した。日本の中国への侵略戦争はこれにて幕開けとなった。写真は、日本軍及び南満鉄道員が、鉄道の爆破は中国軍隊の行為であることを証明しようと、枕木、軍帽、銃を破損しているところ。

东北抗日义勇军

九一八事变后，中国东北各地的爱国官兵、工人、农民、商人、开明绅士等，纷纷拿起武器组织抗日队伍，英勇抵抗入侵的日本军队。最多的时候队伍发展到30多万人。东北抗日义勇军中涌现了一批像杨靖宇、赵尚志、赵一曼、王德泰那样的抗日民族英雄，他们用自己的鲜血谱写了东北抗战的凯歌。图为活跃中的东北义勇军。

Anti-Japanese Volunteers of the Northeast

After "September 18th, 1931", All kinds of patriotic powers in northeast China, commanders, warriors, workers, farmers, merchants, open-minded landlords and etc, took up arms against the Japanese enemy, standing up manfully against the Japanese invaders. Anti-Japanese Volunteers of the Northeast added up to 300,000 in its heyday. Anti-Japanese national heroes came forward in great numbers, such as Yang Jingyu, Zhao Shangzhi, Zhao Yiman, and Wang Detai, composing the song of victory with their own blood.

東北抗日義勇軍

九・一八事変後、中国東北各地の愛国将兵、労働者、農民、商人、見識、勢力のある人は、武器を携え抗日部隊を組織し、勇敢に日本軍に立ち向かった。一番多い時期には30万人を超える部隊まで発展した。東北抗日義勇軍の中からは、楊靖宇、趙尚志、趙一曼、王徳泰のような抗日民族英雄が現れ、彼らは自分達の血で東北抗戦の凱歌を作った。

东北抗日义勇军组图
Three Pictures of Anti-Japanese Volunteers of the Northeast
東北抗日義勇軍に関する図

东北义勇军战斗在白山黑水间
Fighting in the wild
東北義勇軍の東北地区での戦い

义勇军在白旗堡破坏日军的铁轨
Smashing Japanese railway at Baiqibao
義勇軍は白旗堡で日本軍の鉄道を破壊する

上海民众集会援助义勇军
Shanghai people assemble to aid the Volunteers of the Northeast
義勇軍を応援する上海民衆の集会

日军占领东三省

九一八事变发生，中国军队虽有抵抗，因事起仓卒，各地防卫不够，义勇军孤立作战，仅仅三月时间，东北辽，吉，黑三省已尽陷敌手。敌踪散布于东北原野。

Japanese Invasion of Manchuria

When the Japanese Kwangtung Army opened the attack at Mukden, the Chinese Government adopted a non-resistance policy in the hope that the League of Nations would do something. Within three months all three provinces of Liaoning, Kirin, and Heilungkiang had fallen into Japanese hands.

日本軍は東三省を占領した

九・一八事変後、あまりにも事件が突然に起きたため、中国軍隊は抵抗を示したものの、各地の防衛不足が原因で、義勇軍は単独で作戦せざるを得なかった。わずか三ヶ月の間、東北の遼寧、吉林、黒龍江の三省はすでに敵の手に渡ってしまった。敵の足跡は東北平野に散布された。

一二八淞沪战役

日本为威胁英美及国联，逐步达到侵略目的，1932年1月28日又在上海攻击中国军队，中国军队源源开赴前线应战，日军图以4小时占领上海，经十九路军及第五军阻击，抵抗两月以后中英美法意各国代表调解，签订停战协议。

Battle of Shanghai

To menace the American and British economic interests along the Yangtze Valley and to weaken the stand of the League, the Japanese created another war in January 1932. The Shanghai, Woosung area was greatly devastated. Above shows Chinese troops marching to the front.

一・二八上海事変

日本はイギリス、アメリカ及び国連を脅かす、侵略の目的を順次達成するため、1932年1月28日上海で中国軍隊を攻撃した。中国軍隊は続々と前線に出発して応戦する。日本軍は4時間で上海を占領しようとしたが、十九路軍及び第五軍の狙撃により、二ヶ月間の抵抗が続いた。その後、イギリス、アメリカ、フランス、イタリアの各国代表の調停で停戦協議に調印した。

七七卢沟桥事变

中国全面抗战，于1937年7月7日开始于卢沟桥。在这一天，中华民族展开了有史以来所未有的对于异族侵略的英勇战争。日军在卢沟桥演习，借口士兵一名失踪，坚欲入城搜索，卒为二十九军拒绝，战事遂于平津一带展开。上为有历史意义之卢沟桥一瞥。

Marco Polo Bridge Incident

The Sino-Japanese war flared up the Marco Polo Bridge outside the city of Peking. On July 7, 1937, the Japanese army, under false accusations, attacked the Chinese 29th Army. This bridge took on more historical importance.

七・七盧溝橋事変

中国の全面抗戦は、1937年7月7日の盧溝橋事変から始まった。その日、中華民族は有史以来かつてなかった異民族の侵略に対する勇敢な抵抗を展開した。日本軍は盧溝橋で演習した際、兵士が失踪したを理由に強引に入城捜索しようとしたが、二十九軍に拒絶された。戦火はすぐさま北平や天津あたりで展開した。上は歴史意義をもつ盧溝橋の写真である。

八路军

1937年，共产党领导下的红军改编成国民革命军第八路军，迈出了国共合作，联手抗日的重要一步。八路军在朱德总司令、彭德怀副总司令的率领下，与日寇英勇作战，组织了一系列的大小战役，取得了平型关大捷、百团大战等许多重大胜利，沉重打击了日军的嚣张气焰，在抗日战争、特别是华北地区的对日作战中起到了中流砥柱的作用。

Eighth Route Army

In 1937, the Red Army under the leadership of Chinese Communist Party was re-formed into the eighth route of the National Revolutionary Army as the first and most important step of the cooperation between Kuomintang and CCP for Resistance. Under the leadership of Zhu De and Peng Dehuai, Eighth Route Army fought bravely against Japanese Invaders. They organized a series of battles and obtained lots of victories, such as Great Victory in Pingxingguan and Great Campaign with One Hundred Regiments, greatly undermining the enemy's morale hard. They played an important part throughout the War of Resistance Against Japan.

八路軍

1937年、日本の侵略に抵抗するために、国民党と共産党は手を組んだ。共産党が創設した紅軍を国民革命軍に改編し、そのうち、華北主力を第八路軍とした。八路軍は朱徳総司令、彭徳懐副総司令に率いられ、日本軍と勇敢に戦った。一連の戦役を計画して、平型関の戦いや百団大戦など大きな勝利を収めた。猛威を振るっていた日本軍に強い打撃を与え、抗日戦争の中、特に華北地区で大黒柱のような役割を果たすことができた。

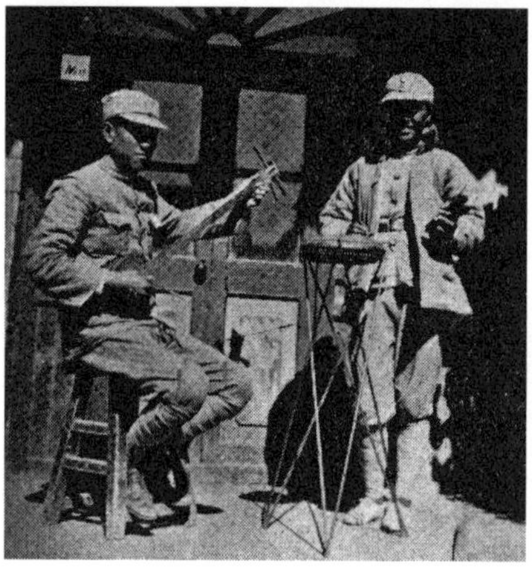

八路军组图
Six Pictures of Eighth Route Army
八路軍に関する図

八路军和百姓一起开荒
Our fighters and people are subduing the rough land
八路軍と百姓が一緒に開墾する

八路军与民众聚餐
The Army and the civilian enjoy meals together
八路軍は庶民と会食する

自敌堡移出战利品
To remove the capture from the enemy's fort
トーチカから戦利品を搬出する

向日军接收武器
Accept Japanese army's weapon
降参した日本軍から武器を収める

军队娱乐活动
Military entertainment
軍隊の娯楽活動

八路军占领正太路大铁桥
To occupy the Zhengtai Road Iron Bridge
八路軍が正太鉄道を占領する

八一三上海战争爆发

8月13日（1937年）日军在所谓虹桥事件的借口下侵犯上海，中国军队30万人与民众勇猛抵抗，战斗空前激烈，中国军队固守3月，终为日军占领。上为闸北夜晚激战时火烧情况。

Shanghai War Outbroke

The Hungchiao incident brought to Shanghai another aggressive war by Japanese on August 13, 1937. Chinese troops and civilians fight bravely. Defending for there months, the great Shanghai then was occupied by Japanese. Picture shows in Chapei, Shanghai, during a bloody fighting at night.

八・一三上海戦争勃発

1937年8月13日、日本軍はいわゆる虹橋事件を口実に上海を侵犯した。中国軍隊と民衆30万人は立ち向かって抵抗したが、三ヶ月後にはついに日本軍に占領された。図は閘北の夜激戦中の火事である。

日军侵入华北

平津沦陷，淞沪激战之际，敌军积极进攻华北，西侵绥远山西南沿平汉线攻入豫北，8个月期间国民党军队屡战屡退，山河变色，局势日非，为抗战最黯淡时间。图为山西战场中国军队在雪中行军。

Imperialistic Penetration

Peking and Tientsin were lost to the Japanese when war was raging to its climax in the Shanghai area. The Japanese soon carried out their plan to take the entirety of North China from which the Chinese had to retreat.

日本軍が華北に侵入する

北平、天津陥落、上海事変の際、敵軍は積極的に華北を侵攻した。西は綏遠省(現在は内モンゴル自治区の一部) 山西南部平漢線に沿って豫(河南)北に侵入した。八ヶ月の間国民党軍は何度戦っても退かされ、山河が色を変え、情勢は日に日に悪化し、抗戦の最も暗い時期であった。

新四军

1937年10月起，散布于南方8省14个地区的红军游击队陆续改编，成立了新四军。军长叶挺，副军长项英。皖南事变后由陈毅任代军长、军长，张云逸任副军长。在长江中下游的广大地区新四军抗击入侵日寇，沉重打击并牵制了数十万敌伪军，为抗日战争的胜利作出了巨大贡献。图为新四军江南游击队出击敌寇。

New Fourth Army

In October 1937, the Red Army guerillas, fighting throughout the 8 southern provinces, 14 regions, were re-formed into New Fourth Army. Ye Ting was the army commander, and Xiang Ying was the vice. After Southern Anhui Incident, Chen Yi took the place of commander, and Zhang Yunyi took the place of vice-commander. Over a wide area throughout the Yangtze valley, New Fourth Army fought bravely and struck heavy blows at the Japanese enemy, tied down hundreds of thousands of Japanese and puppet troops, contributing greatly to the success of the War of Resistance Against Japan.

新四軍

1937年10月から、華南の8省14地区に分布していた紅軍、遊撃隊が続々改編され、新四軍が成立された。当初葉挺を軍長とし、項英を副軍長とした。皖南事変後、陳毅が軍長代理から軍長に、張雲逸が副軍長に就任した。長江中下流域の広い地域で侵略してきた日本軍に反撃し、数十万の日本軍と傀儡軍を牽制し、大きな打撃を与えた。抗日戦争の勝利に大いに貢献した。図は新四軍の遊撃隊の活躍ぶりである。

台儿庄大战

台儿庄我军之机枪阵地。徐州之战的最高峰为台儿庄之决战，双方调集主力兵团，自3月中旬起，在台儿庄一带冲杀，最后被我军包围于台儿庄内，加以歼灭，此役日军伤亡万余人，俘轻重机枪数百挺，俘虏数千人，为抗战中最大的胜利之一。

Battle of Taierchuan

Chinese troops are fighting hardly at Taierhchuan which is the climax of the first stage of Sino-Japanese war. Japanese troops were surrounded by Chinese and ten thousand more men either killed or wounded. Taierhchuan marked one of the important victories in Chinese resistance war.

台児荘大戦

台児荘は我が軍の機関銃の陣地である。徐州における戦いの頂点は台児荘の決戦であった。双方は主要な兵力を集め、3月中旬から台児荘あたり突撃するものの、最終的に日本軍は我が軍に台児荘に包囲され、殲滅された。この戦いでは、日本軍は1万人以上が死傷し、我が軍は軽重機関銃数百丁を没収し、数千人を捕虜にした。抗日戦争の中の最大の勝利の一つである。

武汉会战

徐州失守，武汉保卫战展开，日军从长江窜扰河南，安徽，江西诸省，目标为武汉。图为在江西前线之炮兵。日军自6月开始攻武汉，其主力于9月中旬仍被阻于赣北与鄂东。

The Battle of Hankow

The loss of Hsuchow bared the defense of the Wuchong and Hankow area, whither the Chinese government had moved its headquarters a few back Chinese artillery units guarded the mountain pass in Kiangsi for several months.

武漢会戦

徐州陥落後、武漢会戦が展開された。日本軍は目標を武漢に定め、長江から河南、安徽、江西諸省に侵入した。写真は、江西前線の砲兵である。日本軍は六月から武漢を攻め始めたが、9月中旬になってもその主力は贛北(江西の北)と鄂東（湖北の東）に阻まれていた。

侵略者之墓

赣北万家岭一役，日军第一〇六师团损失惨重，伤亡逾万，其后肃清战场发现死尸死马及战利品极多。日军坟墓比比皆是。

All Invaders Lie in Alien Lands

More than ten thousand Japanese were lost in the battle of Wanchialing in northern Kiangsi. These graves were the relies of the ambitions dreams of an ambitious race.

侵略者の墓

贛北万家嶺の戦いでは、日本軍の第一〇六師団が受けたダメージがひどく、死傷者は１万人を越した。その後戦場を確認したところ、戦死者や馬の屍骸及び戦利品が数多く発見された。日本軍の墓は至る所にあった。

平型关大捷

1937年9月下旬，八路军一一五师在山西省灵丘县的平型关附近对日寇进行了一次伏击，歼敌一千余名。这是八路军首战便告捷的一次重大胜利。打破了日军不可战胜的神话，增强了全国军民的抗日信心。图为八路军由平型关出击。

Great Victory in Pingxingguan

In late September, 1937, 115 Division of Eighth Route Army ambushed the Japanese invaders in the vicinity of Pingxingguan, Lingqiu county of Shanxi province of annihilating more than one thousand enemies. It is a signal victory for Eighth Route Army to win the first battle, blowing the myth of Japanese troops' invulnerability as well as inspiring the countrywide armies and people. Picture above shows Eighth Route Army engaged from Pingxingguan.

平型関の快挙

1937年9月下旬、八路軍第115師団は山西省霊丘県の平型関附近で日本軍を待ち伏せ攻撃した。この戦闘により、日本軍兵士千人余りを殲滅した。これは八路軍が前線に出征して最初に勝利した戦いで、日本軍に勝利することは不可能という神話を打ち破り、全国軍民の抗日への自信を強めた。

日军伤亡重大

武汉会战，先后4个半月，大小战斗数百次，日军使用之12个师团，伤亡20万人，曾补充五六次之多。上为此役我军所获战利品之一部。

Japanese Losses

The Battle of Wuchong-Hankow area lasted more than four months. The Japanese high-command employed twelve divisions which suffered casualties that ran to tens of thousand. These were captured during the battles.

日本軍の損失

武漢会戦中の前後四ヵ月半、大小の戦いは数百回に上る。日本軍は12の師団を使い、20万人を死傷させ、五、六回以上補充を行った。上の写真は、我が軍の戦利品の一部である。

汪精卫叛国

国民党副总裁汪逆精卫，受失败主义影响，公然叛国，1938年11月潜行离渝飞河内，投向日人怀抱，以“反共和平”为号召，担任伪国民政府主席。

Traitor Wang Chingwei

Kuomingtang’s Vice-Chairman Wang Chingwei turned traitor in November 1938 and fled to Nanking via Hanoi to head a puppet government under the dominance of the Japanese army. He evaded punishment by dying before V-J Day.

汪精衛の反逆

国民党副総裁の汪精衛は、失敗主義の影響で、公然と祖国を裏切った。1938年11月重慶を離れハノイに潜行し、日本側に飛び込んだ。「反共平和」をキャッチフレーズにして、南京国民政府主席に就任した。

八路军发动百团大战

1940年8月，在八路军总部的直接指挥下，为粉碎日军的“囚笼政策”，八路军调集了105个团，在华北地区与日寇展开了震惊中外的百团大战，取得了重大的胜利。搅乱了日军的军事部署和后方交通系统，狠煞了侵略者的狂妄气焰。图为参加百团大战的八路军拂晓出击。

Great Campaign with One Hundred Regiments

In august 1940, under the order of the headquarters, for the sake of breaking down the Japanese enemy's "cage policy", Eighth Route Army summoned 105 regiments, and scored important victories in Great Campaign with One Hundred Regiments against the Japanese enemy in north China, upsetting the Japanese enemy's troop disposition and rear transport as well as undermining the enemy's morale. Picture above shows Eighth Route Army engaged at dawn.

八路軍発動した百団大戦

1940年8月、八路軍総本部の直接の指導の下、日本軍の「とうまる籠政策」を砕くため、八路軍は105個の師団を召集し華北地方で日本軍と、国内外を驚かせた所謂「百団大戦」を展開し、大きな勝利を収めた。日本軍の軍事部署と後方の交通系統を乱し、侵略者の狂暴な気勢を抑えた。

百团大战组图

Four Pictures of Great Campaign with One Hundred Regiments

百団大戦に関する図

百团大战攻击敌人井陉煤矿
Attacking the enemy's coal mine
百団大戦で敵の井陘石炭鉱山を進攻する

爆破井陉煤矿大烟囱
Exploding the chimney of Jingjing Mine
井陘石炭鉱山の大煙突を爆発する

被破坏的正大路东段
The damaged part of Zhengtai rail
破壊された正太鉄道の東部

百团大战战利品之一部分
Some of the capture of the War of Hundred Regiments
百団大戦の戦利品に一部

南京大屠杀

1937年12月13日，日寇攻陷南京，置人类基本道德和国际公法于不顾，兽性大发，见男人就虐杀；见妇女就奸杀；见财物就抢夺，连婴儿小孩也不放过。这场惨绝人寰的大屠杀，残忍地了杀害了30多万中国人民。犯下了人类历史上罕见的滔天罪行。图为日本兵围观杀人，以此取乐。

Victims in Nanjing

In December 13, 1937, Japanese invaders occupied Nanjing. In flagrant disregard of the cardinal virtues and the international law, they robbed the property madly, and killed more than 300,000 common people brutally including men, women, and even infants and children. Japanese invaders committed such monstrous crimes, which can hardly matched in human history.

南京大虐殺

1937年12月13日、日本軍は南京を攻め落とした。人類基本の道徳と国際公法を無視し、獣のように、男を虐殺し、婦女を強姦し、財産を略奪し、赤ん坊や子供さえ見逃さなかった。この悲惨な大虐殺では、30万余の中国人民が無残に殺戮された。日本侵略軍は中国で極悪非道の罪を犯した。

南京大屠杀组图
Four Pictures of Victims in Nanjing
南京大虐殺に関する図

日寇活埋中国军民
The Japanese soldiers buried the Chinese soldiers and civilians lively
日本侵略者が中国の軍人や庶民を生き埋める

中国人被日军反缚刺杀
The Chinese were stabbed by Japanese repeatedly
縛られている中国人が日本軍に刺し殺される

日本刽子手在残杀中国人
The Japanese killers were killing Chinese cruelly
残虐の日本人が中国人を殺している

日本禽兽砍下中国人的头提在手上
The Japanese beasts carrying the beheaded head of Chinese
野獣のような日本人が中国人の頭を斬って手にぶら提げている

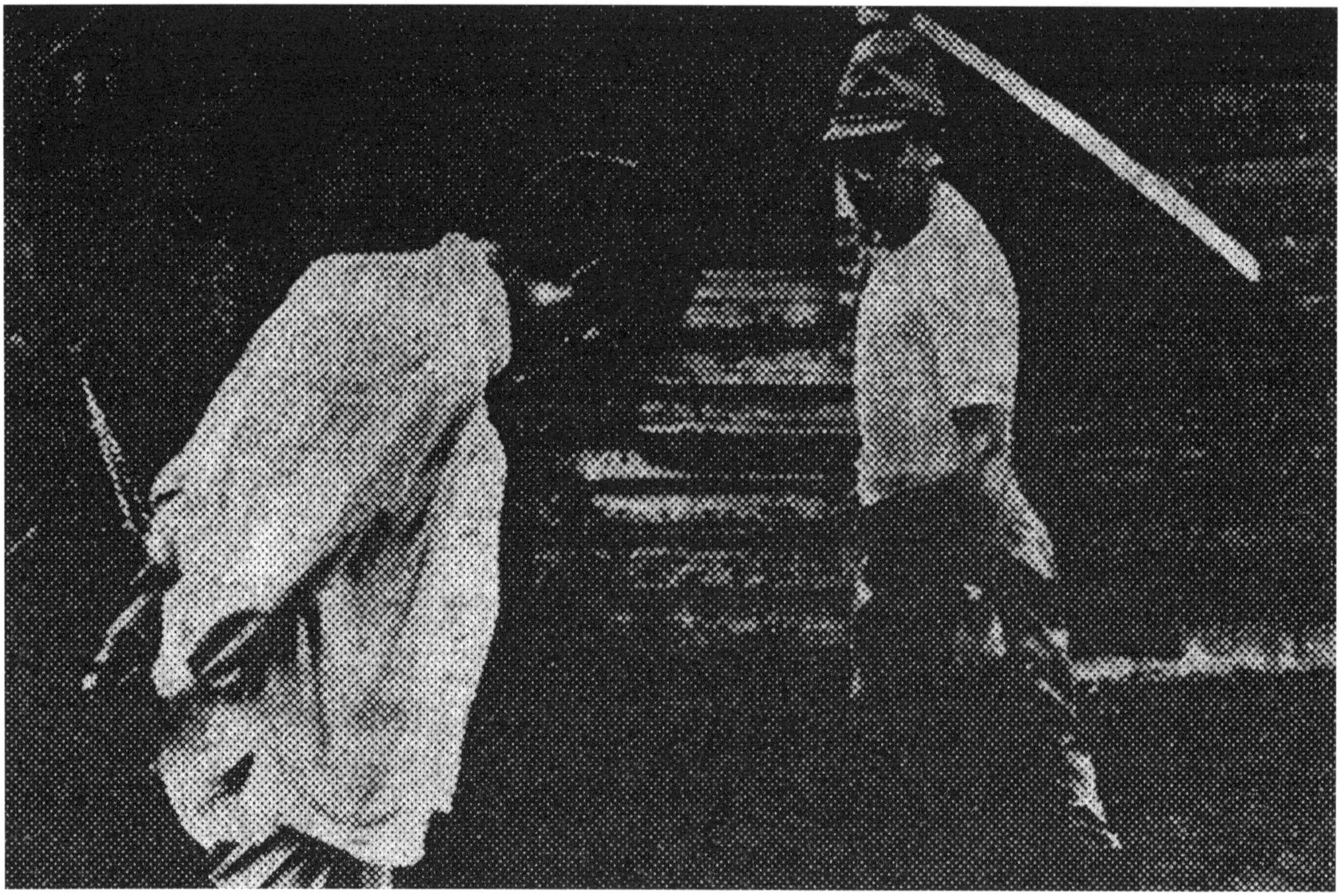

铁证如山，岂容抵赖

战后日本对南京大屠杀的罪行一直闪烁其辞，文过饰非，拒不认罪。自诩具有最勇敢最男子汉气慨的武士道精神的日本，显得是多么的卑怯和无耻。然而大屠杀的消息及屠杀现场的照片却白纸黑字地被披露在当时的东京《日日新闻》上，还有其他的地方都大量记录下了日军的罪行，铁证如山，岂容抵赖！图为凶恶的日本兵在虐杀中国人。

Irrefutable Evidence , Inescapable Guilty

After the war, Japan, who boasted himself to be the bravest and manliest nation, seemed so cowardly and shameless for his persistence in denying his guilty. The truth of Victims in Nanjing finally came out in the Daily News and other places in news and photograghys. Irrefutable evidence, inescapable guilty!

動かぬ証拠が否認は許されない!

戦後、日本は南京大虐殺の犯罪についてずっと言葉を濁し、過失をごまかし、決して罪を認めようとしなかった。自ら最も勇敢で最も男気のある武士道精神を誇りに思っている日本が、どんなに卑劣で臆病で恥知らずだろうか。しかし大虐殺のニュース及び殺戮現場の写真は当時の東京『日日新聞』にも掲載されていた。他にも日本軍の犯罪を記録した資料が大量に残されている。この動かぬ証拠を目の当たりして、どうして言い逃れることができるだろうか！

铁证如山组图

Six Pictures of Irrefutable Evidence

動かぬ証拠に関する図

大量南京军民被枪杀和活埋
Huge amount of soldiers and civilians were killed and buried lively
大量の南京軍人庶民は銃殺され、生き埋めされた

300多中国人被屠杀后推入池中染红了池水
The pool water was dyed red because of the blood of more than 300 Chinese
300人以上の中国人は虐殺されたら池に投げられ池水も赤く染められた

日本兵杀人后得意洋洋地擦拭刀上的血迹
The Japanese soldiers bloatingly wiped the blood on their sabers after killing
日本の兵士が殺人した後、得意満面しながら軍刀に付いている生き血を拭く

日军刺杀中国人
The Japanese killed Chinese
日本軍が中国人を刺し殺す

日寇虐杀中国人后，还在践踏尸体
The Japanese soldiers trampled on the bodies of the Chinese after killing them
日本侵略者が中国人を虐殺した後更に死体を踏みつけている

被强奸后剖腹的中国妇女
The women whose stomachs were opened after being raped
強姦された後更に腹も切り開けられた中国の婦女

鄂北反攻

日军为巩固武汉情势，1940年以来数度进攻鄂北鄂西，枣阳为战事一大中心。图为国军反攻枣阳城。

Counter-attack in Northern Hupei

To strengthen the position of Hankow, Japanese for several times launched stacks to northern and western Hupei since 1940. Tsaoyang, north-west Hankow was the center of the war. Chinese troops, in above picture, is counter-attacking Tsaoyang city occupied by the enemy.

鄂北（湖北北部）の反攻

日本軍は武漢情勢を固めるため、1940年以来数回鄂北鄂西に侵攻した。棗陽は戦争の一大中心であった。写真は、国軍が棗陽城を反攻しているところ。

欧洲闪击战

希特勒征欧准备完成的1939年9月首先闪击波兰，一个月时间占领全波兰。1940年用闪击战占据丹麦与挪威，通过荷比卢屈服了法国，他还预备乘胜越过英吉利海峡，征服英伦，然而不列颠之战失败，不得不转兵来肃清巴尔干。南斯拉夫，希腊，匈牙利，罗马尼亚均被迫加入轴心。从北欧到南欧，全是纳粹的天下，这真是希特勒最辉煌的时代。

美国遭受到战争的威胁，已在积极准备打击轴心。

The Blitz-kreig in Europe

Having completed his preparation for the conquest of Europe, Hitler in September 1939 chose Poland as the first victim of his blitz-kreig attack strategy. Within one month Poland was fully occupied.

In 1940, the blitz-kreig tactics again proved successful as the Germans occupied Denmark and Norway. Passing through the Netherlands, Belgium and Luxemburg, Germany also subdued France.

Plane for the subjugation of the British in the wake of these victories were however frustrated as the Germans lost the Battle of Britain. Hitler turned his attention to the Balkans, Yugo-slavia, Greece, Hungary and Roumania were forced to join the Axis.

From northern Europe to southern Europe, Nazi-ism held away. The height of Hitler's achievements had indeed been reached.

The United States of American, now felt the threat of war against herself, began active preparation to hit the Axis.

ヨーロッパの電撃戦

ヒトラーのヨーロッパ征服準備が完成して、1939年9月にはまず電撃戦で、僅か一ヶ月間でポーランド全土を占領した。1940年には、同じく電撃戦でデンマークとノルウェーを占拠し、オランダ、ベルギー、ルクセンブルクを通してフランスを征服した。彼は更に勝利の勢いに乗って、イギリス海峡を越え、イギリスを征服しようとしたが対英戦の失敗によって、やむを得ず、バルカン半島へ戦争を引き起こして。まもなくユーゴスラビア、ギリシア、ハンガリー、ルーマニアを強制的に枢軸国に加入させた。北欧から南欧まで、全てナチスの天下となり、これはまさにヒトラーの最盛期であった。アメリカは、戦争の脅威を感じ、積極的に枢軸国への打撃を準備し始めていた。

欧洲闪击战

The Blitz-kreig in Europe

德苏缔结互不侵犯协议

德国为求东线安定，准备必要时再进攻苏联，于1939年8月23日在莫斯科与苏联签订10年互不侵犯条约，苏外长莫洛托夫在条约上签字，斯大林元帅（莫氏之右）与德外长李宾特洛甫（莫氏之左）注视签字式。苏联签约目的在避免与德国发生冲突，然1941年6月22日，德国仍实行侵苏。

U.S.S.R. Signed Non-aggression Pact with Germany

The signing of this Pact On Aug. 23, 1939 was the biggest surprise of the year. Russian Commissar V.M. Molotov was putting his name on the paper while Marshal Josef Stalin and Germany's Foreign Minister Joachim von Ribbentrop watched.

独ソの不可侵条約

ドイツは東戦線の安定を追求するため、必要な時にソ連に侵攻すると考えた。1939年8月23日モスクワにてソ連と10年間不可侵条約を結んだ。図はソ連外相のモロトフが条約にサインし、スターリン元帥（モロトフの右側）とドイツ外相リッベントロップ（モロトフの左側）はサインに注目しているところである。ソ連がこの条約に同意したのは、ドイツとの衝突を避けるためであった。しかし、1941年には結局ドイツはソ連への侵入を実行した。

德国闪击波兰

德国吞并奥捷后，次一举动为闪击波兰，德军于1939年9月1日清晨微雨中发动99个师团兵力100万人，飞机6,500架，约占德国实力的三分之二，以饿虎搏兔之势，向波军进逼，英法遂对德宣战。波兰因实力相差过巨，撑持1月之后，除东部于9月17日为苏军进驻外，全被德军占领。上为希特勒赴波兰前线视察。

German Blitzkrieg over Poland

On September 1939, ninety-nine divisions of the Germany army with 6,500 planes crossed the polish border. Poland surrendered after 35 days of heroic resistance. Der Fuerer is evidently pleased with the Blitzkrieg.

ドイツのポーランド電撃戦

ドイツがチェコスロバキアを併呑後、次の行動はポーランドへの電撃戦だった。ドイツ軍は1939年9月1日朝小雨の中、その三分の二の兵力の99個の師団、100万人の兵力、6,500台の飛行機を発動し、まるで飢えた虎が兎に飛び掛かるの如き、ポーランド軍に迫っていた。イギリス、フランスはこれをきっかけにドイツに宣戦した。ポーランドは（ドイツとの）実力の差があまりにも大きく、一ヶ月間しか持たなかった。9月17日に、東部はソ連軍が進駐していた以外、他は全てドイツ軍に占領された。上の写真は、ヒトラーがポーランド前線を視察しに行くところ。

德军占领丹挪

德军于1940年4月9日仅以12小时时间，控制了丹麦，同日又在“保护”的名义下，由挪威奸细吉斯林为内应，登陆于挪威（上图）。挪军以寡敌众，其后并有英法军支持，抵抗至6月，伺英法撤退，挪威乃失陷。

Fall of Denmark and Norway

Hitler only needs twelve hours to conquer Denmark; that of Norway takes him longer, but still it is like a stride. Norway was betrayed from inside by her traitor, Quisling.

ドイツ軍のデンマーク、ノルウェー占領

ドイツ軍は1940年4月9日にわずか12時間でデンマークを占領した。同日、ノルウェーの売国奴のクヴィスリングの内部からの呼応によって、「保護」という名目で、ノルウェーにも上陸した（上の写真）。ノルウェー軍は少数対多数だったため、イギリス、フランス軍の支援にもかかわらず、6月まで抵抗したが、イギリス、フランス軍の撤退後に陥落した。

德军侵犯荷比卢

德军占领挪威后，于1940年5月10日开始侵犯荷兰、比利时、卢森堡及法国，先1日实行大规模轰炸，荷京阿姆斯特丹受重创，继以降落伞降落荷境，与开入比境之英法军队作战。5日后，德机又狂炸荷京，闹市夷为平地（上图），死30,000人，荷兰旋即投降。

Amsterdam Devastated

After conquering Norway in stride, the Germans converged their superior forces on Holland, Belgium, Lnxemberg and France. On May 9, 1940, Amsterdam was subjected to extensive bombing which killed thirty thousand persons and levelled many beautiful quarters.

ドイツ軍のオランダ、ベルギー、ルクセンブルクへの侵犯

ドイツ軍がノルウェーを占領した後、1940年5月10日にオランダ、ベルギー、ルクセンブルク及びフランスを侵犯し始めた。一日目は大規模な爆撃を実行し、オランダの首都アムステルダムは大きなダメージを受けた。続いて、パラシュートでオランダ境に入り、ベルギー境内に入ったイギリス、フランス軍と戦った。五日後、ドイツ機が再びオランダの首都を激しく爆撃し、繁華街は廃墟と化した（上の写真）。3万人が死亡し、オランダは直ちに降伏した。

敦刻尔克撤退

盟军对德作战失败，比国宣布投降，英国约40万人被迫退至敦克尔克海边，英军在陆地及天空攻击下，调集各种船只，以一星期时间，救出33万人，为二次大战撤退之光荣记录。

Retreat from Dunkirk

The retreat from Dunkirk in the summer of 1940 was one of the few historical examples that turned disaster into glory. The British people had accomplished the impossible. In a week they rescued 330,000 men under fierce attack from land and air.

ダンケルクの撤退

同盟軍の対ドイツ作戦が失敗し、ベルギーは降伏を宣告した。イギリス約40万人がやむを得ずダンケルク海岸まで退いた。英軍は陸と空の両方の攻撃される中、各種船舶を集め、わずか一週間で33万人の救出に成功した。第二次大戦における栄光な撤退であった。

德军在法北作战

德军由荷比向法北推进，势如破竹，盟军节节退至赛纳河，巴黎遂陷入德军围攻中，法兰西全境为失败主义所笼罩，虽仍保留相当武备，但已失去作战力量。图为德军进袭部队准备突击。

Attacking Paris

Extraordinary success marked the early days of Hitler's expansion. The Allied forces in northern France collapsed like fallen leaves before the advancing Germans. The Maginot Line failed to live up to previous expectations.

ドイツ軍のフランス北部での作戦

ドイツ軍はオランダ、ベルギーからフランス北部に侵入した。同盟軍はセーヌ川まで退かれ、パリはドイツ軍に包囲されてしまった。フランス全域が失敗主義に覆われ、相当な軍備を保持していたにも拘らず、作戦する気力を失っていた。写真は突撃を準備しているドイツ軍である。

意大利参战

当德国进侵法国时，大战中两大法西斯领袖希特勒与意相墨索里尼会晤于贝尼诺山隘，德军将意大利亦拖下水，1940年6月10日意向英法宣战，准备从背后夹攻法国。意大利对英法作战并无大表现，仅于德法停战后于6月24日与法签定停战协议，得了些小便宜。

Italy Enters War

Fascist leaders, Adolf Hitler (left) and Benito Mussolini, met at Brenner Pass station preceding Italy's entrance into war. It was announced a few days before France collapsed.

イタリアの参戦

ドイツがフランスに侵攻している時に、大戦中の二大ファシズムリーダーヒトラー（左）とイタリア首相ムッソリーニはブレンナー峠で会談した。ドイツはイタリアを巻き込んだ。1940年6月10日イタリアはイギリス、フランスに宣戦し、後ろからフランスを挟み撃ちしようとした。このイタリアの対イギリス、フランス作戦はあまり大きな動きを見せなかったが、ドイツとフランスが停戦後の6月24日にフランスと停戦協定を結び、少しだけ得した。

法国第三共和沦亡

1940年6月10日德军进巴黎，法国贝当政府求和，宣布第三共和告终，实行极权独裁制。法军150万人放下武器。德法停战协议21日在上次大战媾和之康边森林及所用的花车上由参谋总长李德尔向法代表宣读，希特勒坐在当年福熙元帅的椅子上，面对着被征服者。

End of the Third Republic

On June 10, 1940, the French army surrendered. Here, in Compiegne Forest, Hitler sits on the chair Marshal Foch used in 1918, and dictates terms to the French envoy through Keital.

フランス第三共和国滅亡

1940年6月10日ドイツ軍はパリに進軍した。フランスのペタン政府は投降し、第三共和国の終焉を宣告し、独裁制を始めた。フランス軍150万人が武器を置いた。ドイツ、フランスの停戦協定は21日に、前回大戦時の講和場所であるコンピエーニュの森で、花で飾られた車の上参謀総長からフランス代表に読み上げられ、ヒトラーは当年フォシュ元帥の椅子に座り、征服された人々を眺めている。

不列颠之战

法国投降以后，希特勒准备进攻英伦三岛，从1940年8月8日起以400架飞机袭轰英吉利海峡，机场，码头，铁路，后来增加到800架，英国受灾极重，幸有飓风式与喷火式战斗机予德国米塞史米德机以重创，不列颠之战，德国终至失败，德国丧失飞机2,375架，上为9月2日（1940年）飞机飞过圣保罗教堂上留下之白烟。

Battle of Britain

Standing up gloriously out of the flames and smoke of surrounding buildings, St. Paul's cathedral is pictured during the great fire raid of Sunday Sept. 2, 1940. The striking background of the vapour trails in the air depicts the heroic struggle of RAF planes warding off their enemies.

バトル・オブ・ブリテン

フランスの降伏後、ヒトラーはイギリスの三つの島を侵攻しようとした。1940年8月8日から400機の飛行機でイギリス海峡、飛行場、港、鉄道を爆撃した。後に飛行機の数を800機に追加した。イギリスが受けた損害はひどく、幸いハリケーン式と噴火式戦闘機がドイツのメッサーシュミット機にダメージを与えた。バトル・オブ・ブリテンにおいて、ドイツが最終的に失敗で終わった。2,375機飛行機を失った。上の写真は、9月2日（1940年）飛行機がセントポール大聖堂の上を通った時に残した白い煙。

伦敦在火烧中

德机攻英的最高峰为1940年11月29日，天黑之后伦敦落燃烧弹爆炸弹数千枚，500年以上之历史建筑摧毁无余，上为著名之圣保罗教堂在火舌吞吐中。不列颠之战，英死伤飞行员733人，平民14,000人，重伤20,000人，房屋炸毁百万所。

Old Gallant London

The Battle of Britain reached its climax On Nov. 29, 1940, when thousands of bombs were dropped on one day. Picture shows St. Paul's Cathedral standing gloriously amid the flames.

ロンドンが燃え上がる

ドイツのイギリスへの攻撃は1940年11月29日にピークを達した。空が暗くなってから、ロンドンに数千個もの爆弾が落とされた。500年以上の歴史を持つ建築物は余す所なく粉砕された。上の写真はかの有名なセントポール大聖堂が炎に包まれている光景。バトル・オブ・ブリテンでは、死傷したイギリス人パイロット733人、一般民衆14,000人、重傷20,000人、崩壊された家屋が百万箇所に及んだ。

快乐的天使

战争的恐怖，不能消灭孩子们的天真，这批在轰炸下的伦敦儿童，在被疏散时期暂时与爸爸妈妈隔离，但是他们还是那么纯真，愉快，顽皮。不列颠之战时，每天有数千儿童疏散下乡。

Happy Children

Thousands of youngsters were dispatched to safety everyday during the great raids on London. Though they had to leave their homes and parents, yet they were joyous over the prospect of living in the open country.

快楽の天使

戦争の恐怖は子供達の天真爛漫さを揉み消せなかった。これらの爆撃下のロンドンの子供達は、一時的に両親と離れ離れになっても、純真で愉快で活発に過していた。バトル・オブ・ブリテンでは、毎日数千人の児童が田舎に避難させられていた。

大西洋之战

盟国一方面要保持海上优势，一方面要确保美国的租借法案援助物资的安全到达英国，与德国在大西洋苦斗了数年。德海军以潜艇战争威胁盟国护航队，盟国以反潜艇战争突破封锁。图为随英海军在大西洋作战之美驱逐艇，发现德潜艇放出之深水炸弹爆炸。

The Atlantic Battle

The sea-route of the north Atlantic had to be kept open in order to keep Britain alive. When the British Navy was hard pressed, these American destroyers came to its rescue. Picture shows depth charges hurled by one U.S. destroyer.

大西洋の戦い

連合軍は、一方では海上の優位を維持し、一方ではアメリカからの援助物資が安全にイギリスに到着するのを確保しなければならないため、数年に亘って大西洋上でドイツ軍と戦っていた。ドイツ海軍はその潜水艦で連合軍の駆逐艦を脅かしていた。連合軍はその潜水艇を反撃することで封鎖を突破した。写真は英海軍と一緒に大西洋上で作戦するアメリカの駆逐艦がドイツの潜水艦から発射した爆雷を見詰めているところ。

英主力舰巴汉号被炸

1941年9月25日下午4时25分，英主力舰巴汉号与其它军舰在地中海距离亚历山大港200哩处作战时，为德国潜艇U.331袭击，集中之鱼雷于近距离向巴汉号烟囱与后炮座间左船舷放射，舰乃向左倾斜，中雷4分钟后倾倒时，火药库忽然爆炸，损失官兵859人。

H.M.S Barham Blew Up

At 4.25 in the afternoon of Nov. 25, 1941, H.M.S. Barham was attacked by the German submarine U.331. while operating with other ships 200 miles W.N.W.of Alexandria. Her magazine blew up and she sank with the loss of 859 officers and men.

英主力艦バーラム号爆撃される

1941年9月25日午後4時25分、英国主力艦バーラム号が他の軍艦とアレキサンドリア港から200マイル離れた地中海上で戦闘中、ドイツの潜水艇U331に襲撃され、魚雷は至近距離から集中的にバーラム号に向けて発射した。戦艦は左へ傾き、4分後火薬庫が突然爆発して、将兵859人が遭難してしまった。

轰炸德国潜艇

由于护航制度的推行，减轻了日益增长的德国潜艇威胁。图为德国潜艇人员在被炸时，另一炸弹又落下，蜷伏于潜望台旁之紧张情状。

Ash Can for German Submarine

The promoting of convoy system by the Allied ended the growing German submarine menace. German submarine crews, in above picture, crouch near conning tower as another ash can heads toward them.

ドイツ潜水艦爆撃

写真は、ドイツ潜水艦の乗組員が爆撃を受けてる最中に、もう一つの爆弾の落された際の緊張した面持ち。

德船被袭

英国空军战斗机于大西洋搜索德国船只，阻击武装敌船两艘，一艘沉没，一艘中雷后自行炸毁。上为第二艘武装敌船被攻击之近影。

German Trawlers Attacked

RAF Beaufighters intercepted two armed German trawlers on the Atlantic. One was sunk and the other was abandoned by its crew. This is the close–up of the attack on the second trawler.

ドイツ船襲撃される

英国空軍戦闘機が大西洋上ドイツの船舶を探している。武装した敵船二隻を狙撃し、一隻は沈没、一隻は爆弾を受け自爆した。上は二隻目の武装船が攻撃された時の写真である。

德潜艇俘虏

1943年8月至10月3个月中，德潜艇被盟军击毁者达60余艘，一次大规模的海上潜艇战中被俘虏之德国潜艇俘虏在解往俘虏营途中。

German U-boats Survivors

More than sixty U-boats were destroyed by the Allies in August, September and October 1943. Above shows German U-boats prisoners brought in after a big Atlantic Battles on their way to a P.O.W. camp.

ドイツ潜水艇捕虜

1943年8月から10月の三ヶ月間、連合軍に撃ち壊されたドイツ潜水艇は60隻余りに上った。ある大規模な海上潜水艇戦の際、囚われたドイツ潜水艇の捕虜を捕虜キャンプへ移送する途中の光景。

大西洋宪章

英首相丘吉尔与美罗斯福总统于1941年8月9日，首次会晤于大西洋纽芬兰海军舰上，罗邱会议后发表宣言，申述美英作战目的，此即所谓大西洋宪章。该宣言保证所有民族可自行选定其政府，恢复因德国侵略而损失之主权，公海航行自由，实行国际经济合作，以建立公正而永久之和平。

The Atlantic Charter

American President Roosevelt met British Prime Minister Churchill for the first time on board of a battleship in Newfoundland Bay in August, 1941, from which was enacted the famous Atlantic Charter, upholding the principles of basic human rights and a just and permanent peace.

大西洋憲章

英国首相チャーチルとアメリカ合衆国大統領ルーズベルトが1941年8月9日に、初めて大西洋のニューファンドランド軍艦上で会談した。両者は会談後イギリス、アメリカの作戦目的について述べた。これが所謂大西洋憲章である。この宣言は、全ての民族は自分でその政府の選定、ドイツの侵略で損失した主権の回復、公正で永久な平和を作り上げるため、公海航行の自由、国際経済協力の実行を保証した。

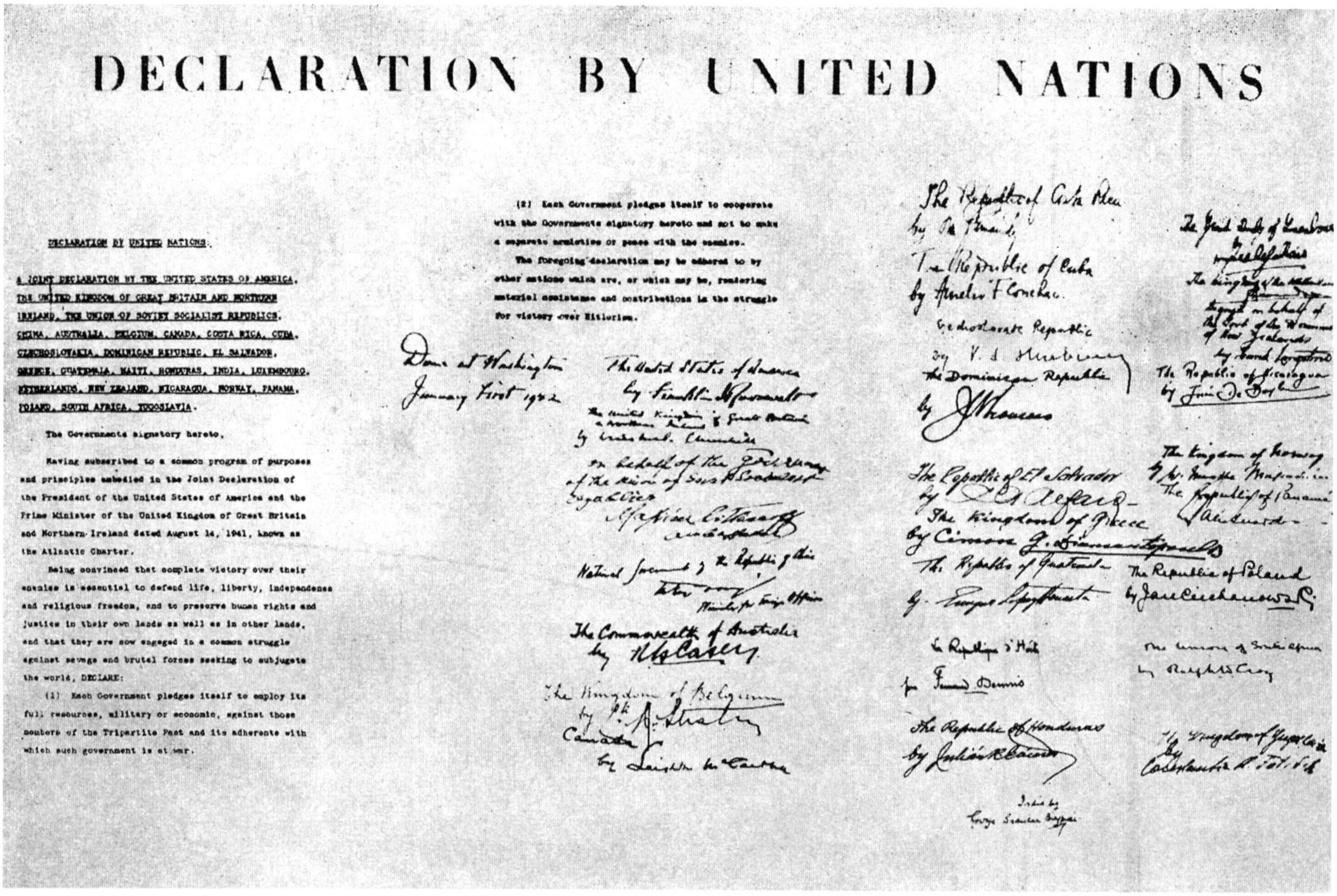

DECLARATION BY UNITED NATIONS

DECLARATION BY UNITED NATIONS.

A JOINT DECLARATION BY THE UNITED STATES OF AMERICA, THE UNITED KINGDOM OF GREAT BRITAIN AND NORTHERN IRELAND, THE UNION OF SOVIET SOCIALIST REPUBLICS, CHINA, AUSTRALIA, BELGIUM, CANADA, COSTA RICA, CUBA, CZECHOSLOVAKIA, DOMINICAN REPUBLIC, EL SALVADOR, GREECE, GUATEMALA, HAITI, HONDURAS, INDIA, LUXEMBOURG, NETHERLANDS, NEW ZEALAND, NICARAGUA, NORWAY, PANAMA, POLAND, SOUTH AFRICA, YUGOSLAVIA.

The Governments signatory hereto,

Having subscribed to a common program of purposes and principles embodied in the Joint Declaration of the President of the United States of America and the Prime Minister of the United Kingdom of Great Britain and Northern Ireland dated August 14, 1941, known as the Atlantic Charter,

Being convinced that complete victory over their enemies is essential to defend life, liberty, independence and religious freedom, and to preserve human rights and justice in their own lands as well as in other lands, and that they are now engaged in a common struggle against savage and brutal forces seeking to subjugate the world, DECLARE:

(1) Each Government pledges itself to employ its full resources, military or economic, against those members of the Tripartite Pact and its adherents with which such government is at war.

(2) Each Government pledges itself to cooperate with the Governments signatory hereto and not to make a separate armistice or peace with the enemies.

The foregoing declaration may be adhered to by other nations which are, or which may be, rendering material assistance and contributions in the struggle for victory over Hitlerism.

Done at Washington January First 1942

The United States of America

联合国宣言

英美苏中澳等26国代表，为确定联合国作战目的，于1942年1月1日，签定联合国宣言于华盛顿，声明共同承认大西洋宪章之原则，郑重实行两点：1.使用全部军事与经济资源对德意日作战，2.不单独与帝国停战或言和。此宣言为大战中一重大之历史文献。

Declaration by United Nations

To set up the aim of the war and relation among the United Nations, a Declaration by United Nations signed by representatives of 26 countries was published. Each country pledges itself to employ its full resources against the enemy and not to make a separate armistice or peace with the enemies.

連合国宣言

イギリス、アメリカ、ソ連、中国、オーストラリア等26カ国代表は、連合国の作戦目的を確定するため、1942年1月1日にワシントンにて連合国共同宣言（ワシントン宣言）に調印した。大西洋憲章の原則を承認し、以下2点を誓約した。1,各政府は、三国条約の締約国及びその条約の加入国でその政府が戦争を行つているものに対し、その政府の軍事的又は経済的な全部の資源を使用すること；2,各政府は、この宣言の署名国政府と協力すること及び敵国と単独の休戦又は講和を行わないこと。この宣言は第二次世界大戦において重要な歴史文献の一つである。

德苏战争

轴心势力在欧洲，特别是巴尔干的发展，与苏联利益发生冲突，德国更垂涎于苏联的资源，所以希特勒在十字军东征布尔什维克的口号下，先下手为强，于1941年6月22日进攻苏联。

德苏战争不是闪电战，而是惨烈的长期消耗战，先后达3年之久。

初期战争，德军占优势，以排山倒海之势直捣苏联心脏，莫斯科几至不守，幸德军攻势卒被阻止。1942年夏，德军再攻高加索及顿河流域，斯达林格勒为争夺中心，血战66天之后，德军全部覆没。1942年到1943年，苏军连续反攻，逐渐收复失土。

The Russo-German War

The expansion of Axis influence in Europe, and particularly in the Balkans, brought them into conflict with the Soviet Union. Germany, moreover, had aspirations to Russia's rich resources. Using the pretext of a crusade against Bolshevism, Hitler attempted to surprise the Russians when he ordered an attack on the Soviet Union on June 22, 1941.

The Russo-German war was no blitz-kreig eńcounter, but turned out to a most terrible and long-drown out conflict which lasted three full years.

In the early stages of this war, the Germans gained superiority. Striking with imposing strength at the very heart of the Soviet Union the Germans nearly took Moscow. Their advance was however successfully checked.

In the summer of 1942 the Germans launched another fierce offensive, in the Caucasus and Don basin areas. Stalingrad was the bone of contention in this battle. After the most bloody engagements in this battle. After the most bloody engagements in military history lasting 66 days, the German forces were annihilated.

During 1942 and 1943, the Soviet Army launched several successful counter-offensives and lost territory was gradually recovered from the German.

ドイツ・ソ連戦争

枢軸国のヨーロッパ、特にバルカン諸国における勢力の発展は、ソビエト連邦の利益と衝突になった。更にドイツがの資源に涎を垂らしていたため、ヒトラーは「十字軍がボルシェビキを征服する」を高唱しながら、先手を打とうとして1941年6月23日にソ連に侵攻した。独ソ戦は、電撃戦ではなく三年間にも及ぶ悲惨な長期戦であった。この戦争の初期段階にドイツは優位に立ち、勢いに乗ってソ連の心臓部に達した。モスクワはもう少しで占領されるところだったが、幸いドイツ軍の猛烈な進攻はソ連に食い止められた。1942年夏、ドイツ軍が再度コーカサスとドン川流域における激しい攻勢を始め、スターリングラードの激しい争奪戦は、66日間も続いた。接戦の結果はドイツ軍が撲滅された。1942年から1943年にかけて、ソ連軍の連続的反撃により次第に失った国土を取り戻した。

德苏战争

The Russo–German War

德国进攻苏联

1941年6月22日黎明，德军突从波罗的海岸到喀尔巴阡山麓，1,500哩的前线，集中200万人，用德国最新式的武器，分北，南，中三路进攻苏联，撕毁互不侵犯条约。图为德军喷火器正向苏军防御工事攻击。

Hitler's Attack on the U.S.S.R.

At dawn on June 22, 1941, the Germans crossed the Soviet border from the Baltic to the Carpathians. Two million men were used by Hitler in this adventure which brought him eventual defeat.

ドイツはソ連に侵攻

1941年6月22日未明、ドイツ軍はバルト海岸からカルパチア山脈までの1,500マイルの前線を突破し、200万人を集めドイツの最新式の武器を使い、北、南、中三つに分かれてソ連を侵攻し始めた。一方的に不可侵条約を破った。写真はドイツ軍の火炎放射器がソ連軍の防御工事を攻撃している光景である。

苏军阻敌前进

苏德初期战事，苏联仓卒应战，损失甚大，德军于开战3个月后已近至莫斯科防卫线，失地50万方哩，莫斯科之战展开。苏军于炮火下埋藏地雷阻止德军坦克车前进。

"Stop the Nazis, Comrades!"

The Russians suffered defeat in the first phase of the German–Soviet war. More than half a million sq. miles were lost in the first few months. The Germans were turned back only before the gates of Moscow.

ソ連軍は敵の前進を阻止する

独ソ戦争初期では、ソ連軍はドイツの攻撃を予期せず、防御の準備がないまま応戦したため、損失が非常に大きかった。開戦わずか三ヵ月後、50万平方マイルの土地を失い、モスクワの防衛線への近づきをも許してしまった。図はソ連軍がドイツの戦車の前進阻止するため、弾雨の中地雷を埋蔵しているところである。

保卫敖德萨

南路轴心军包括德罗匈意四国军队，入侵苏联，以占领克里米亚半岛夺取乌克兰富源为目的，敖德萨位于最前线，人民起来组织游击队，参加保卫祖国的战争。

Defending Odessa

The southern prong of the attacking Nazis consists of German, Rumanian and Italian forces. Odessa was the first Soviet city of importance on their way to Crimea and the fertile Ukraine basin.

オデッサを守る

南戦線では、ドイツ、ルーマニア、ハンガリー、イタリアの四カ国の枢軸軍がソ連に侵入した。ウクライナの豊富な資源を奪取するのが目的でクリミア半島を占領しようした。民衆は遊撃隊を組織し、この祖国防衛戦争（独ソ戦争）に参加した。

列宁格勒之战

德军攻到列宁格勒近郊（1941年8月），手指着近在眼前的城市，争夺两月，无法制胜，反而被打死了20万人，从此放弃在此路大规模进攻的计划。

The Siege of Leningrad

The battle of Leningrad began in August 1941 when the Germans succeeded in their penetration of the outer defense of the great seaport built by Peter the Great. But still the end of the war the Russian held them there.

レニングラードの戦い

ドイツ軍はレニングラード近郊まで侵攻し（1941年8月)、目の前の都市を指で指し、二ヶ月間の争奪にも拘らず勝利できず、20万人が戦死した。ドイツは余儀なくこのルートから大規模な侵攻計画を放棄した。

苏军转守为攻

莫斯科争夺战苏军表现了它的强大与坚韧性，德军两次总攻，莫斯科30哩外战况惨烈，1941年12月希特勒不得不暂时放弃夺取莫斯科的想念。苏联工兵正剪除敌人铁丝网，为反攻部队开路。

The Turning Point

In the battle of Moscow, Hitler learned for the first time the power and the tenacity of the Red Army. In wave after wave, the Germans attacked, but their hope of ever conquering Russia faded with the year 1941.

ソ連軍は守りから攻撃へ

モスクワの争奪戦では、ソ連軍のパワーと強韌性が表れた。ドイツ軍は二回総攻撃したが、全てモスクワから30マイルの所で撃退された。1941年12月ヒトラーは一時的にモスクワ奪取を諦めせざるを得なかった。ソ連工兵が反撃部隊に道を開けるために敵の金網を取り除いてるところ。

苏军冬季攻势

苏军于德军无力开展中，发动第一次的冬季攻势，冰天雪地中，苏军异常活跃，德军第十六军被围，列宁格勒以东地区被苏军收复。

Offensive in Winter

When the Germans were bogged down by the severe winter snow on the steppe, the Russians began to be active. The Reich's 16th Army was mercilessly defeated to the east of Leningrad.

ソ連軍の冬季攻勢

ドイツ軍の無力な会戦中、ソ連軍は初めての冬季攻勢を発動した。厳しい冬の最中、ソ連軍が非常に活躍した。ドイツ軍の第十六軍が包囲され、レニングラードより東の地区はソ連軍に回収された。

斯大林格勒之战

苏德战争的第二年（1942年）德军开始了夏季攻势，集中160个师，来歼灭顿河与高加索的苏军主力，然后占领莫斯科的前哨斯大林格勒。斯城血战，相持4月，猛烈程度超过上次凡尔登大战，上为斯城郊外德军与苏军之坦克战，德军坦克向苏联阵地进扑。

Battle of Stalingrad

The battle of Stalingrad that lasted fully four months from the end of 1942 to the spring of 1943 marked the beginning of German decline. Hitler used more than a million and one-half men to capture this river port on the Don but ended in complete failure and surrender.

スターリングラードの戦い

独ソ戦争の二年目の1942年、ドイツ軍は夏季攻勢を始めた。160師団を集め、ドン川及びコーカサス地方のソ連軍の主力を殲滅し、そしてモスクワの前哨基地にあたるスターリングラードを占領しようとした。スターリングラードの戦いは四ヶ月続き、その激しさは前回のヴェルダンの戦いよりも上回る。上は、スターリングラード郊外のドイツ軍とソ連軍の戦車戦で、ドイツ軍の戦車がソ連軍陣地に飛びかかろうとしているところ。

光荣的斯城

在不满百哩的斯城战线上，德军运用了75万兵力，飞机千架，斯城每一条街道，每一座房屋，均为德苏两军争夺的目标，苏方军民每日死伤7,000人，德方损失约占三分之一，战况猛烈可知。然到1943年2月初，德军终于失败，德军90,000人投降，造成二次大战一大转折点。上为斯城战后城中残留之巨厦脊柱，昂然立于夕阳下，显示苏军抗德战绩之无限光辉。

Pillar of Stalingrad

Hitler hurled more than 750,000 men and 1,000 planes into that short stretch of land along the Don, but the Stalingrad defenders engaged their enemies with unprecedented valour. The German surrender dashed the Reich's last hope of victory.

栄光なスターリングラード

百マイル足らずのスターリングラード戦線上、ドイツ軍は750,000もの兵力、千機以上の飛行機を動員した。スターリングラードの全ての道路、家屋が独ソ両軍の争奪の目標だった。ソ連側は毎日7,000人の死傷が、ドイツ側はその約三分の二の損失を負った。戦況の激しさが伺える。1943年2月初めになり、結局ドイツ軍が失敗し、90,000人が投降し、二次大戦の一大ターニングポイントとなった。上はスターリングラード戦後、残された巨大なビルの柱が昂然として夕日の下に立ち、ソ連軍のファシズムと戦う戦果の無限な輝きを示している。

珍珠港事变

日本为扫除征服亚洲的障碍，1941年12月8日凌晨，在美人迷梦未醒时偷袭珍珠港，把美国太平洋舰队几乎来了个一扫光。日本乘英美荷防务空虚，抢占太平洋各岛，日军还想向澳洲进犯，珊瑚海与中途岛的海战，阻止了它再进的企图。

珍珠港事变之后，美国已变为民主国家的兵工场，以大量的物资军火协助盟友对轴心作战。

Pearl Harbor Incident

In order to remove all possible obstacles to her conquest of all Asia, Japan in the early hours of the morning of December 8, 1941 (U.S. time Dec. 7,1941), when the Americans were still snugly occupied with their dreams, staged a surprise attack on Peal Harbour, and the American Pacific Fleet was almost wiped out.

Taking advantage of Anglo-Americans-Dutch unpreparedness at the time Japan occupied various Pacific Islands. The Japanese even contemplated pushing toward Australia but the sea battles of the Coral Sea and at Midway Islands checked their further expansion southwards.

With the Peal Harbour Incident the United States was officially converted into the Arsenal of Democracy and huge applies of material resources and military equipment were placed at the disposal of the Allied nations in their common on the Axis.

真珠湾攻撃

日本は、アジア征服するのに障害の排除するため、1941年12月8日未明、アメリカ人がまだ夢を見ていた頃に真珠湾を奇襲した。アメリカの太平洋艦隊をほぼ全滅させた。また、イギリス、アメリカ、オランダにおける国防の隙を見て、太平洋諸島の略奪に成功した。日本軍は更にオーストラリアにも侵攻しようとしたが、珊瑚海海戦及びミッドウェイ諸島での大失敗で断念せざるを得なかった。真珠湾攻撃後、アメリカは、民主国家の兵器工場となり、枢軸国家との戦いのため、同盟国の諸国に大量の物資と軍事装備品を提供した。

珍珠港事变

Pearl Harbor Incident

珍珠港被袭
Pearl Harbour Attacked
真珠湾奇襲

太平洋战争揭幕

1941年12月8日午前10时（美国时间为7日清晨8时）日本偷袭了珍珠港。珍珠港是美国太平洋的基地，日本原想这次奇袭，可以使美国在太平洋的海军全军覆没。美国事前毫无准备，珍珠港内的人还以为是在举行礼拜天早晨的演习。上为被袭时阿利桑那战舰。

Opening of the Pacific War

At ten in the morning of Dec.8,(U.S. time, 8 a.m. Dec.7,) 1941, the Japanese surprised-attacked Pearl Harbour, the American Naval base of her Pacific fleet. The Americans were caught completely unprepared. This is the Arizona, an American man-of-war, sinking in flames at Pearl Harbour after the vicious attack.

太平洋戦争の幕開け

1941年12月8日午前10時（アメリカ時間7日早朝8時）日本は真珠湾を奇襲した。真珠湾はアメリカの太平洋基地であった。日本はこの奇襲でアメリカの太平洋における海軍の全滅を狙った。真珠湾内の人々は日曜日早朝の演習だと思っていた。上は炎上する戦艦アリゾナの写真である。

火地狱

机场被炸燃烧，把珍珠港变成火地狱。珍珠港之奇袭惊醒了美国人，事变第二天国会通过对日宣战，中国也在这天公布对日宣战，英国则先一日对日本宣战，德意同时于12月12日对美宣战，从此二次世界大战转入一新的阶段，轴心与联合国间对垒形势划分清明。

The Inferno that was Pearl Harbour

Pearl Harbour marks another milestone in World War Ⅱ. The American people were rudely awakened to the grim fact of how far the aggressors would go, and were compelled to relinquish their foolhardy dreams. In next day of Japanese attack, both American and China declared war with their common enemy.

火の地獄

飛行場が爆撃され燃え上がり、真珠湾を火の地獄と化した。真珠湾奇襲はアメリカ人を目覚めさせた。その二日後、アメリカ議会は日本に対して宣戦布告を行い、中国も同じ日に日本に宣戦した、イギリスは更に一日早く日本に宣戦した。ドイツ、イタリアは12月12日にアメリカに対して宣戦した。二次大戦は新たな局面を迎えた。枢軸国と連合国の間の対峙情勢は明らかになった。

惊天动地

日本出动飞机100余架，以美国军舰机场船坞为轰炸目标，事前之充分准备，使袭击非常成功，港上炸弹如雨点一般，山崩海裂，惊天动地。此次美国计损失主力舰5艘，驱逐舰3艘，布雷舰1艘，其它小型舰多艘。陆军机273架之大部及海军机202架中之150架均被毁。官兵阵亡者2,117人，受伤1,272人，失踪者960人。这是美国立国以来最可耻的失败。

Peaceful Japanese?

The Japanese attack at Pearl Harbour was a complete success. American losses: 5 battleships, 3 destroyers, 423 planes, 4,349 casualties plus American Harbour.

驚天動地

日本が出動した飛行機は百余りで、アメリカ軍艦船や飛行場などを爆撃の目標とした。事前の周到な準備で臨んだ真珠湾での日本の攻撃は完全な成功でした。港では爆弾は雨のように降り注いでいた。今回のアメリカの損失: 5隻の主力戦艦、3隻の駆逐艦、1隻の水雷艦、その他多数の小型戦艦、陸軍機273機の殆ど及び海軍機202機のうちの150機は皆壊された。官兵死亡者2,117人、負傷者1,272人、失踪者960人に上った。これはアメリカ建国以来最も屈辱的な敗戦であった。

美国人，记住珍珠港！

初被偷袭时，珍珠港之鸟瞰。正中美舰正遭轰炸，日机在俯冲轰炸后正翱翔于其上空。美国在太平洋实力素逊于日本，被袭后，就仅有日海军实力的四分之一。

Americans, Remember Pearl Harbour

A general view of the Pearl Harbour when Japanese surprised–attack took place in the morning of Dec. 8, 1941. In the middle, American war ships still under bombing and Japanese plane flying over it after a dive operation.

アメリカ人、真珠湾を忘れないで！

図は奇襲された時の真珠湾の光景。日本機が急降下し、真ん中のアメリカ戦艦を爆撃して、上空に向かって飛び上がっているところ。アメリカの太平洋に於ける軍事力はもともと日本に劣っていた、奇襲後更に日本海軍の実力の四分の一にしか及ばなくなかった。

日军进入上海租界

太平洋事变爆发，日军进入上海租界。仅仅数小时的战斗，租界即为日军占领。上海遂全变为敌人与汉奸的世界，英美人士备受污辱与虐待。

Japanese Occupied Shanghai International Settlement

When the Pacific war outbreak, Japanese troops in Shanghai march into the International Settlement. Only several hours fighting with American and British forces, Shanghai occupied entirely by Japanese.

日本軍は上海租界に進入

太平洋戦争勃発後、日本軍は僅か数時間の戦闘で、上海租界に進入した。租界は日本軍に占領され、全上海は敵と漢奸の天下になった。欧米人も侮辱や虐待されていた。

日军登陆岷达拉峨

抵御日军在南太平洋的进攻中，菲律宾防御战是比较持久的。日军在珍珠港事变后的第三天在吕宋北岸登陆，继攻岷达拉峨，麦克亚瑟将军队集中在多山的巴丹半岛，一直苦守了3个多月，给予美国士气以重大的鼓励，造成有名的巴丹死亡战斗。1942年4月9日，美军弹尽粮绝而投降，巴丹失守，柯里几多之战又继续一月。

Mindanao Burning under Japanese Fire

The only accountable resistance in the Pacific was that of the Philippines. General Douglas Macarthur,s soldiers held the Japanese at Bataan and Corregidor for more than four months.

日本軍はミンダナオに上陸

日本軍は真珠湾を奇襲した三日間後、ルソン島の北岸に上陸し、続いてミンダナオに攻撃し始めた。マッカーサーは軍隊を山の多いバターン半島に集中して、三ヶ月あまり粘り強く防衛した、米軍の闘志が励まされた。しかし、結局は1942年4月9日米軍の弾薬がなくなったため、日本軍に投降した。バターン半島はついに陥落した。コレヒドールの戦いはそれからまた１カ月ほど続いた。

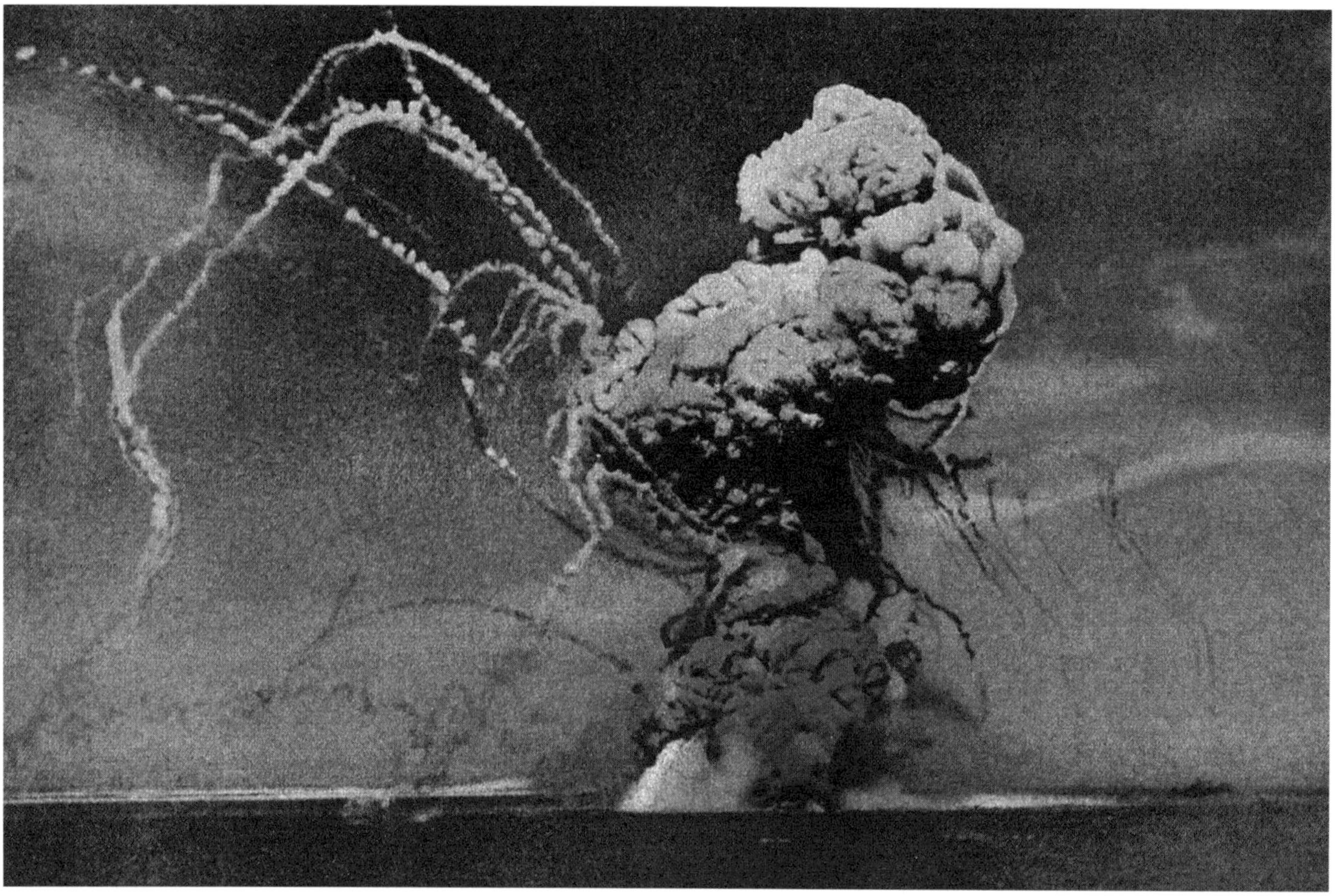

美军火船在地中海爆炸
U.S. Munition Ship Explode in Mediterranean Sea.
米軍の船は地中海で爆発

美机被击落

太平洋战争初期，美国在陆海空军各方面均处于劣势地位，若干地区均无法进行大规模的抵抗。在天空中美机被日机打成两半截。

An American Plane Downed

In the early days of the Pacific war, the allies fought against tremendous odds. This American plane had offered what its crew could in the battle of the sky.

米軍戦闘機の撃落

太平洋戦争の初期は、アメリカが陸、海、空に於いていずれも力が日本に劣っていたため、大規模な作戦はできない状態であった。図はアメリカの戦闘機が日本軍の戦闘機に撃たれ、二つになって落下する場面である。

荷属东印度群岛

日军在袭击马来亚，缅甸和菲律宾时，同时以陆海空军自三面夺取荷属东印度群岛，准备向南疾取澳洲，东取夏威夷。上为日军自马来亚进攻苏门答腊。荷人纵火焚烧油池，1942 年 3 月 9 日爪哇失陷，荷属东印度群岛完全沦入日军之手。

The Dutch East Indies

While the attacks on Malaya, Burma and Philippines were in progress, the Japanese did not forget the Dutch East Indies. Fire was burning in Sumatra. Java fell in March 1942 completing the Japanese occupation of the Dutch East Indies.

オランダ領東インド（現在のインドネシア）

日本軍はマレーシア、ビルマ、フィリビンを進攻すると同時に、陸、海、空軍を出動してオランダ領東インドを占領しようとした。図は日本軍がマレーシアからスマトラに攻撃している光景である。

新加坡英军投降

在进袭珍珠港之时，日军同时攻香港，上海租界，马尼拉，新加坡，中途岛威克岛和关岛，香港在圣诞节失陷了，马来亚方面日军利用在泰国和越南的基地，向南疾进，英军因为全力摆在欧非，马来亚之战，经过70天的样子，英军70,000人于1942年2月15日向日军投降了。上为英军向日军投降，正中凭刀而坐者为“马来之虎”日将山下奉文。

Singapore Surrender to Japanase Army

Seated in the extreme left, facing the camera is Japan,s Gen. Tomoyuki Yamashita, Tiger of Malaya. He is accepting the surrender of Singgapore from the British commanders.

シンガポールの英軍降参

真珠湾を襲撃と同時に日本軍は香港、上海の租界、マレーシア、シンガポール、ミッドウェイ諸島、グアムにも進攻していた。香港はクリスマスの日に陥落した。英軍の主力はヨーロッパに分布していたため、マレーシアで日本軍との70日間の戦いだけで、7万人の英軍は日本軍に投降してしまった。図は1942年2月15日英軍が日本軍に投降する儀式の場面で、正面真ん中のは「マレーの虎」と呼ばれる日本の山下奉文将軍である。

珊瑚海之战

1942年5月初美澳军舰在掩护新几内亚与所罗门群岛作战时，于5月7日在珊瑚海上与日本舰队相遇，美舰击沉日航舰翔鹤号，次日日舰反攻，水雷击中当时美国四大航舰之一的立克辛敦号（33，000吨），内部发生爆炸，上为船主下令弃船，船员纷纷系绳跳入海中，由他船救起。日本损失船舰10余艘，使其不敢再向澳洲冒险。

Battle of the Coral Sea

The decisive battle of the Coral Sea in May 1942 turned back to the Japanese forces for the first time in their victorious march on the Pacific. After that, they never advanced further south. Picture shows American carrier Lexington being abandoned.

珊瑚海の海戦

1942年5月7日、米軍と日本軍は珊瑚海で激しい海戦を繰り広げた。米軍は日本軍の航空母艦「翔鶴丸」を撃沈した。翌日日本軍は米軍の航空母艦「レキシントン」に水雷を発射し命中した。図は米軍の航空母艦「レキシントン」号の艦体が爆破され、船員達は海に跳び降りる場面である。

中途岛海战

1942年6月3日，日本庞大舰队两队赴美军基地中途岛，拟实行海空进击，发生太平洋战争以来第一次大规模海战，日本丧失航舰4，主力舰2，重巡洋舰2，美损失航舰约克敦号，及驱逐舰哈蒙号。中途岛之战，使美国在太平洋战争中转入一个新阶段。上为美舰炮战中。

The Battle of Midway

In June 1942, the Japanese Navy attempted to attack Midway, but it was frustrated with heavy losses. It marked the resurgence of American power in Pacific. This U.S. battleship is shooing hard.

ミッドウェー諸島海戦

1942年6月3日、日本は膨大な艦隊を二列に分けミッドウェー諸島の米軍基地に行き、海空から攻撃を企てた。これは太平洋戦争以来、第一回目の大規模な海戦である。この海戦で日本は戦艦4隻、主力艦2隻、大型巡洋艦2隻等を失ってしまった。米国は戦艦と駆逐艦各1隻を損失した。ミッドウェー諸島海戦は太平洋戦争のターニングポイントとなった。図は米国戦艦の戦いぶりである。

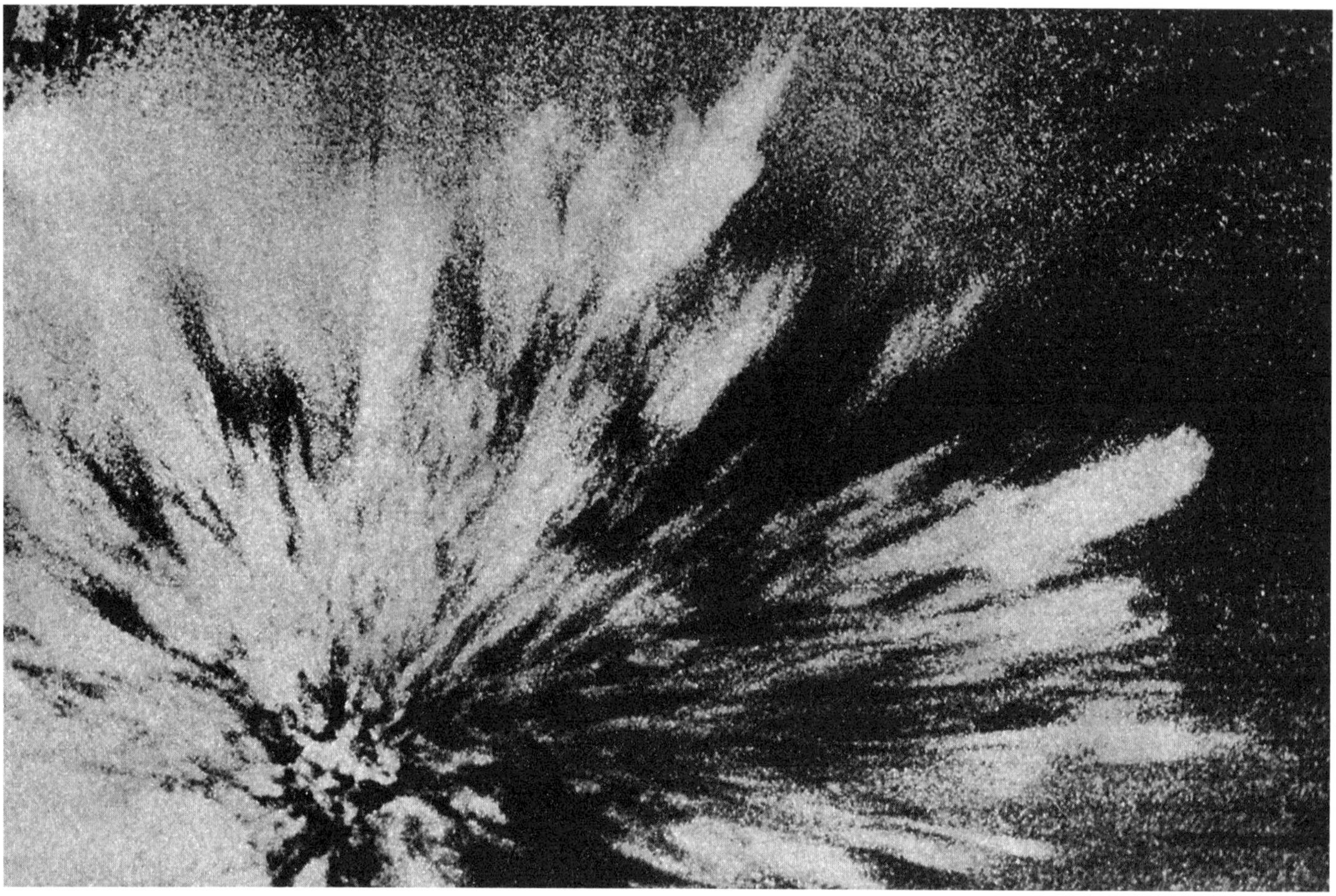

企业号中弹

美国航空母舰企业号在太平洋上的光荣战绩，1942年8月24日在西南太平洋作战时为日本飞机炸中，炸弹落于飞行甲板上。此难得与著名之照片，为美海军摄影员李德所摄，为摄此影之照相机虽幸获保存，而李德亦为此照片牺牲其生命。

A Hit on the Flight Deck of U.S.S. Enterprise

On Aug. 24, 1942, the Carrier was hit by a Japanese bomb in the south-western Pacific. This unique and famous picture was taken by Pho M3/c Robert Frederick Read, USNR, and cost him his life.

「エンタープライズ」が爆撃され

米空母の「エンタープライズ」は太平洋戦争に於いてかなりの戦功がある。1942年8月24日西太平洋の海戦中、日本の戦闘機から爆撃された。この写真は米国海軍のカメラマンリードさんが爆弾が艦体に命中して爆発の瞬間を撮った貴重な場面である。しかし、この写真を撮る為に彼は命を失ってしまった。

桑达克鲁士海战

1942年10月，桑达克鲁士海面发生海战，满天均为炮火所笼罩。著名之美国航空母舰企业号后由日机俯冲轰炸，投下炸弹适在爆炸，右部一主力舰后之驱逐舰正在发炮。海上白浪，为摄此影之巡洋舰驶过留下之余波。

Sea Battle of Santa Cruz

In October 1942, battle occurred near Santa Cruz. Fire and smoke spread over the sky. A Japanese bomb splashes astern U.S.S. Carrier Enterprise as the enemy plane pulled out of its dive. A battery was fired by the battleship on extreme right.

サンタクルーズ海戦

1942年10月にサンタクルーズ海戦が勃発した。有名な米国の航空母艦のエンタープライズの後で日本の戦闘機が急降下し、投下した爆弾が爆発した。右は主力艦の後ろについている駆逐艦が発砲している。海上の白波は、この写真を撮影するための巡洋艦が通過後に残されたものである。

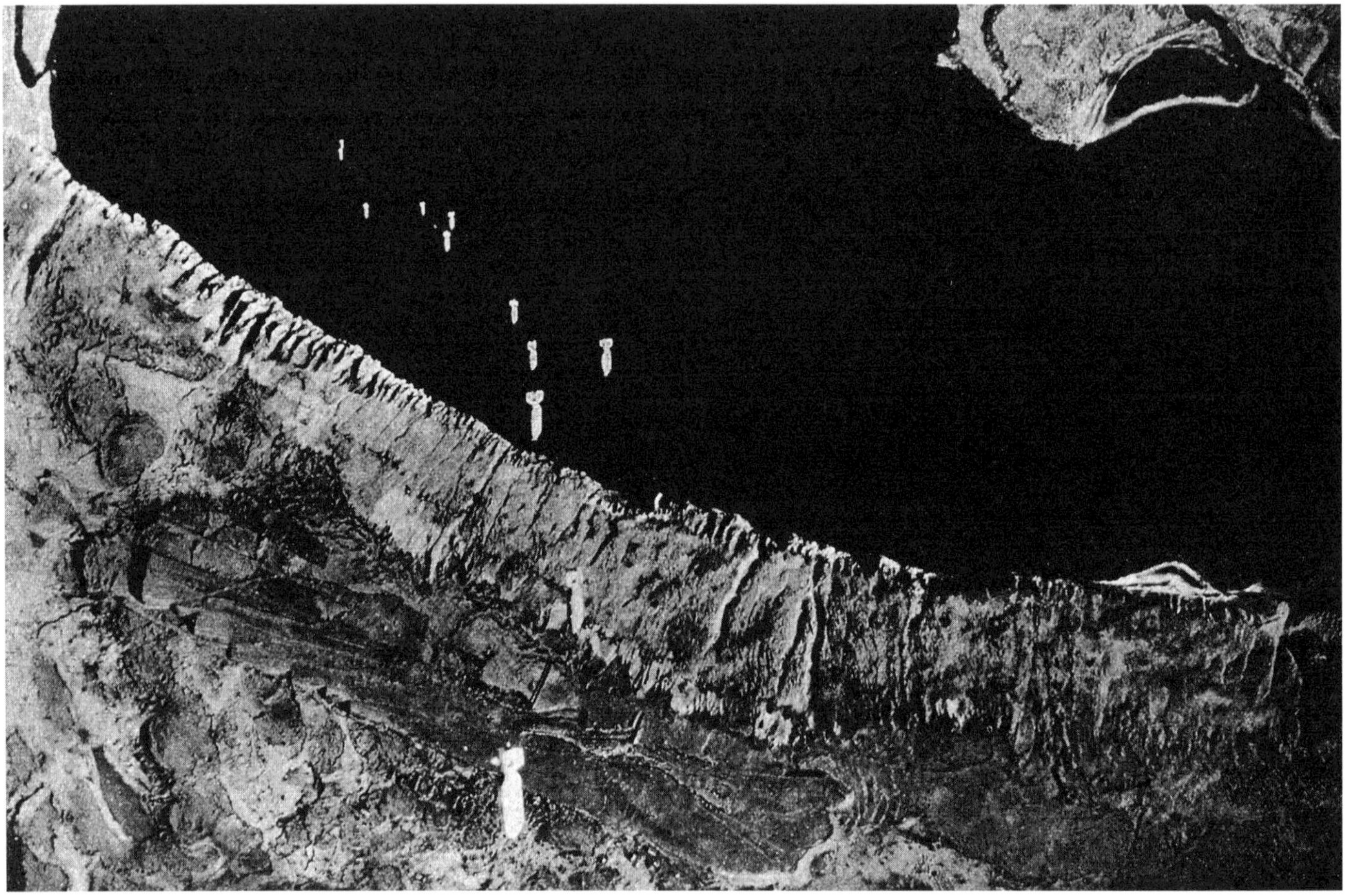

炸阿留申群岛

日本为牵制北太平洋美国海军，于1942年6月占领接近阿拉斯加的阿留申群岛的阿图，吉斯卡，阿加图诸岛，该三岛在战略上并无关重要，美军仅时以飞机往炸。1943年夏始相继收复，图为轰炸日本北部之基地。

Bombing the Aleutians

In June 1942, the Japanese occupied Attu, Kiska and Agattu of the Aleutians near Alaska to menace America from the north. But they were never able to make much use of them. The U.S. air forces bombed the islands from time to time. They were recovered in summer 1943.

アリューシャン諸島を爆撃

日本は北太平洋の米海軍を牽制する為、1942年6月にアラスカのアリューシャン諸島を占領した。この諸島は戦略上にはそれほど重要ではないので、米軍は時時飛行機を出動して爆撃に行くだけだった。1943年の夏次々と諸島を奪還して、日本本土の北部を爆撃する為の基地として使った。

北非沙漠战场

北非关系大西洋与地中海交通，轴心在1940年秋季即开始对英军作战，英属索马利为意军占据，英军增援击退之。希特勒调非洲师团来攻，侵入埃及，重要城市相继沦陷。1942年冬季由英军蒙哥马利将军指挥第八军，沿海发动反攻，肃清埃及及利比亚之轴心军。11月7日盟军复在北非登陆，分三路夹攻轴心军。将其逼至突尼西亚，德军忙于应付欧洲东线战事，北非只好放弃了。

The Battle-Field in the North African Deserts

The importance of North Africa in the communication lines between the Atlantic the Mediterranean led the Axis powers to launch an attack on the British forces in the area in the autumn of 1940.

The Italians occupied British Somaliland, but British reinforcements succeeded in indicting losses on the Italian invaders.

Hitler ordered the German African divisions to this theatre and Egypt was invaded, many cities in this country falling into Axis hands.

In the winter of 1942 the British 8th Division, commanded by General Montgomery, opened a counter-attack and annihilated the Axis forces in Egypt and Libya.

More Allied troops were landed on North Africa in November of that year and the Axis forces, hemmed in on there fronts, were forced to retreat into Tunisia.

By this time, the Germans had their hands full in Europe, and North Africa had to be abandoned.

北アフリカの砂漠戦場

北アフリカは、大西洋と地中海との交通に関係していた。枢軸国は、既に1940年秋からイギリス軍と戦ってきた。イギリス領のソマリランドはイタリアに占領されたが、イギリスは援軍を増員させ、それを撃退した。ヒトラーは「ドイツアフリカ師団」を派遣し、エジプトを進入した。多くの重要都市が相次いで陥落してしまった。1942年冬、モンゴメリ将軍が第八軍を指揮し、海に沿って反撃を開始した。その結果エジプト及びリビアにいる枢軸国の軍隊を全滅させた。11月7日、連合軍は北アフリカに上陸し、三つに分かれ枢軸国軍をチュニジアまで追い込む挟み撃ちの作戦を取った。ドイツ軍はその時、ヨーロッパ東戦線に気を取られ、やむを得ず北アフリカを断念しなければならなってしまった。

北非沙漠战场

The Battle-Field in the North African Deserts

德军沙漠攻势

非洲战争，是争取控制以中东苏伊士运河为中心之水道和陆路的战争，继续3年之久。1940年6月起英意作战6月，意军在利比亚和埃塞俄比亚失败，希特勒调非洲兵团沙漠之狐隆美尔指挥增援，1941年占班加西，巴第亚，深入埃及，英军一时几招架不住。上为驰骋非洲沙漠之德军在攻势中。

The "Desert Fox" Advance

The supremacy over the North African desert is of great importance. Hitler's Afrika Korps, under Rommel, the "Desert Fox", made its first appearance there in 1940. For once, it penetrated deep into Egypt.

ドイツ軍の砂漠攻勢

アフリカ戦争は中近東のスエズ運河を中心とする水路と陸上の交通をコトロールするための戦いであり、3年間も続いた。1940年6月から英国とイタリア両者のリビアとエチオピアにおける交戦では、イタリア軍が失敗した。ヒトラーは急いで「砂漠の狐」と呼ばれるアフリカ軍団を増援軍団として派遣した。ドイツは1941年スペインなどを占領してからエジプトの中心地に攻め込んで行った。英軍は一時支えなくなりそうになった。図は砂漠を駆け回るドイツ軍の攻撃ぶりである。

非洲英军反攻

北非利比亚沙漠，于1942年5月发生大规模坦克战，双方使用坦克在千辆左右，英军仍处劣势地位，10月间由蒙哥马利将军指挥之英第八军，沿海发动反攻，肃清埃及轴心军，重入利比亚，轴心军损失60,000人。德苏战争吃紧，德军调欧，盟军实力增强，故轴心形势愈趋不利。上为在利比亚作战之英坦克在沙漠上驰骋。

British Counter-attack at Lybia

One of the tank duels of the North African desert. In May 1942, the British army under General Montgomery counter–attacked along the coast and cleared Egypt of Axis soldiers.

英国軍のアフリカでの反撃

北アフリカのリビアでは1942年5月に大規模なタンク混戦が起きた。双方は千台のタンクを使って英国軍が少々劣勢であった。10月にモンゴメリー将軍は英第八軍を指揮し海沿いで反撃を始めた。先ず、エジプトにばんきょしている枢軸国軍を敗れ、そしてリビアに入った。枢軸国軍側は60,000兵士は死傷した。この時、ドイツとソ連の戦いも激しくなったからドイツは増援のためにヨーロッパにある軍隊を召還した。連合軍の実力はますます強くなったの反面、枢軸国軍は徐々に衰弱していった。図はリビアの砂漠で駆け回っている英軍タンクの姿である。

盟军登陆北非

盟军为开辟大西洋到地中海陆地交通线，策应苏联对德作战，1942年11月7日用船舰850艘，在艾森豪威尔将军指挥下登陆于阿尔及尔（上图）及法属摩洛哥。盟军分三路进攻，将轴心军趋至突尼斯，轴心军数度反攻，均被击退。

Allied Troops Landing at Aigier

Under General Dwight D. Eisenhower, Allied troops landed in North Africa in late 1942, and later drove the Axis to the sea at Tunisia. This success re-opened the Mediterranean and greatly strengthened the hardpressed Russians.

連合軍の北アフリカ上陸

連合軍は大西洋から地中海までの陸上輸送線を開通して、ソ連の対ドイツ戦争に応援するために、1942年11月7日に850隻の船艦を使って、アイゼンハワー将軍の指揮の下で、3路に分かれ進撃していた。枢軸軍をチュニジアまで追い詰めた。枢軸軍は数回反撃したが、皆撃退された。

北非德军解体

两年11个月又25天的北非战争，于崩角失陷时宣告结束。自北非之战开始以来，轴心军被俘虏者40万人，被击溃之德军11个师，意军26个师。希特勒原命令非洲师团战至最后一弹，但非洲已无容身之处，只有逃向欧洲大陆了。

The End of the Superior Race

The North African campaign ended after the Axis surrendered at Cape Bon. In two years 11 months and 25 days, the Allied forces annihilated 11 German and 26 Italian Divisions, capturing 400,000 men.

北アフリカのドイツ軍の解体

北アフリカ戦争が2年11ヶ月25日間続いた結果、ドイツ軍は失敗に終わった。北アフリカ戦争始まって枢軸軍は40万人も捕らわれた。ドイツ軍の11個の師団、イタリア軍の26個の師団が撃滅された。元々ヒトラーは最後まで戦っていこうとアフリカ軍団に命令したがアフリカで失敗してしまったため、軍隊はヨーロッパ大陸まで撤退するしかなかった。

打落德机

1943年4月英美在非洲爱尔桂塔尔会师，齐向突尼斯与比塞大进逼，5月6日发动总攻，占领两大港口，轴心退至崩角，作背水之战。上为被英空军击落之德国麦塞基米特一一〇式机。仅突尼斯一役中，德机损失在2,300架以上。

Another Messerschmitt-110 Downed

In April 1943, the attacking Allied forces from the east and west of Africa met at El Gueter, whence they converged on Tunis and Bizerta. The Germans lost 2,300 planes in Tunisia alone.

ドイツの飛行機が撃落

1943年4月英軍と米軍はアフリカで会合しチュニジアに進攻した。5月6日総攻撃をはじめてすぐ二つの港を占領した。枢軸軍は最後の戦いをしていた。図は英軍に撃落されたドイツの飛行機である。チュニジア戦役だけでドイツは2,300機以上の飛行機を失った。

“无条件投降”

“无条件投降”一词，创于罗斯福丘吉尔于1943年1月举行的北非卡萨布兰卡会议中，意思是盟国与轴心谈判的唯一条件，只有无条件投降。此会举行于盟军在北非登陆两月之后，先解决德意再来对付日本之原则由此会确定，进攻西西里和南意大利后再在法国南部登陆的作战计划，即成熟于此次会议中。上系罗邱会后招待记者。

“Unconditional Surrender”

“Unconditional Surrender” is the only form of surrender acceptable to the Allies. This is decided at the Casablanca Conference of January 1943. The Big-two are disclosing it to the press.

無条件降伏

「無条件降伏」と言う言葉は1943年1月の北アフリカのカサブランカ会議にチャーチルが初めて使った言葉である。その意味は、枢軸国軍は連合軍と談判する唯一の選択肢が無条件降伏である。図はチャーチルが会議後の記者会見する場面である。

德意崩溃

德黑兰会议决定了摧毁德意轴心的战略，盟军先于1943年7月踏上西西里，再登陆意南，1944年6月4日解放了罗马，两日之后，在艾森豪威尔指挥下的百万以上盟军在诺曼底滩头登陆，德军虽拼命抵抗，以兵员有限，不能阻止盟军进攻。旋盟军又在法国南部登陆，解放了巴黎。盟军由法比边境进入德境；是年冬希特勒仍图反攻作最后的挣扎，而昙花一现，又被击回。雅加达三巨头会议之后，盟军从东西夹攻柏林，会师于易北河上，柏林终为盟军占领；希特勒据宣称是死了。

The Collapse of Germany and Italy

The Teheran Conference decided the strategy for the destruction of the Axis powers. In July 1943 the Allies landed at Sicily and next found themselves on South Italian soil, Rome was liberated on June 4, 1944.

Two days later, on June 6, the Allied Forces more than 1,000,000 strong commanded by General Eisenhower made their landing on the Normandy coast. The stubborn resistance offered by the Germans at that point proved of no avail and the Allies progressed rapidly.

Further landings were effected in southern France. Paris was liberated. The Allies soon found themselves in German territory, marching via the Franco-Belgian frontiers.

Hitler staged a last desperate attempt at a counter-offensive, but was immediately repulsed.

After the holding of the Yalta Conference the Allies began a concerted attack on Berlin from both the East and the West joined forces on the Elbe, and Berlin fell into Allied hands with the death of Hitler announced by the German authorities.

ドイツとイタリアの崩壊

テヘラン会議では枢軸強国を破壊するための戦略を決めた。連合軍はまず1943年7月にシチリアに足を踏み入れた、続いてイタリア南部に上陸した。1944年6月4日にローマを解放した。二日後アイゼンハワー司令官の指揮の下、百万以上の連合軍がノルマンディー海岸に上陸した。ドイツ軍は必死に抵抗したが、兵力が弱く相手にならなく、連合軍の侵攻を阻止できなかった。更に連合軍はフランス南部にも上陸し、パリを解放した。これにより、連合軍はフランスとベルギの辺境からドイツに入った。この年の冬に、ヒトラーはまだ最後の抵抗を試したが、すぐに撃敗された。ヤルタ会談後、連合軍は東西からベルリンを挟み撃ち、エルベ川で合流した。ベルリンはついに連合軍に占領され、ヒトラー死亡の噂も流れた。

德意崩溃

The Collapse of Germany and Italy

德黑兰会议

开罗会议后，罗邱赴伊朗京城德黑兰与斯大林会晤。1941年以来，苏联担负了大部分在欧作战的任务，殷望第二战场开辟，英美则认为非有充分准备，不应轻动；三国意见颇见分歧。德黑兰会议消除了误解，决定从法国打击德军的时间和地点。图为罗斯福在会议中参观丘吉尔携来英王送斯大林对斯大林格勒人民致敬之宝剑。

At Teheran

President Roosevelt is inspecting a sword presented by Great Britain's King George to the people of Stalingrad in honour of their gallant stand against the Nazi invaders. The Teheran Conference resolved the differences among the three powers and decided the time and location for a second front in Europe.

テヘラン会議

チャーチルはカイロ会談後、スターリンに会いに急いでイランの首府テヘランに行った。1941年以来、ソ連はヨーロッパの大部の地域での戦闘任務を担い、第2戦場の切り開くことを望んでいたが、英米は充分な準備ができてないと考えた。三国の意見は分かれた。テヘラン会議ではその誤解が解け、フランスからドイツ軍に打撃を与えることが決定された。写真は、会議中にルーズベルトが英国ジョージ王からスターリンに贈った剣を見ている場面である。英国王はこの剣でスターリングラードの人民への敬意を表している。

火箭炮摧毁坦克

巴佐卡火箭炮的威力打在坦克上，发出喷泉似的火花，在坦克铁甲上打出一个3吋大小的洞。火箭炮对击毁坦克，破除强固之防御巢穴，摧毁墙壁桥梁，效果显著，为准备开辟第二战场武器之一。

Rocket Gun Wrecks Tank

A shower of molten metal is spread by an armour-piercing projectile shot at a tank from a "Bazooka" rocket. This weapon has distinguished itself as a powerful tank-killer, smasher of concrete pillboxes and destroyer of ponderous walls and bridges.

ロケット砲に粉砕される戦車

戦車がロケット弾に打たれ、噴水のように火花が出た。戦車には大きさ3インチの穴が貫通された。ロケット弾は戦車を打ち壊すこと、強固な防御線を突破すること、壁や橋を撃ち壊すことに著しい効果がある。第２戦場を開ける為に準備した武器の１つである。

火树开花

为准备开辟第二战场，盟国新武器在加紧制造中，大西洋岸美国120糎高射炮，在夜晚炮兵训练营同时实弹演习，火光照明天际。此炮能射出50磅火力至12哩空中。

Trees of Fire

Sheets of flame brighten the night sky as U.S. 120mm anti-aircraft guns fire simultaneously during practice. The new guns can fire 50-pound projectiles approximately 12 miles into the air.

炎の木は花が咲く

第2戦場を切り開く為に、連合軍は新しい武器の製造に急いだ。大西洋における米国の120ミリの対空銃は夜に砲兵訓練基地にて実弾演習を行っている。光は夜空に輝いた。この大砲は12マイルの空中まで50ポンドの火力を発射できる。

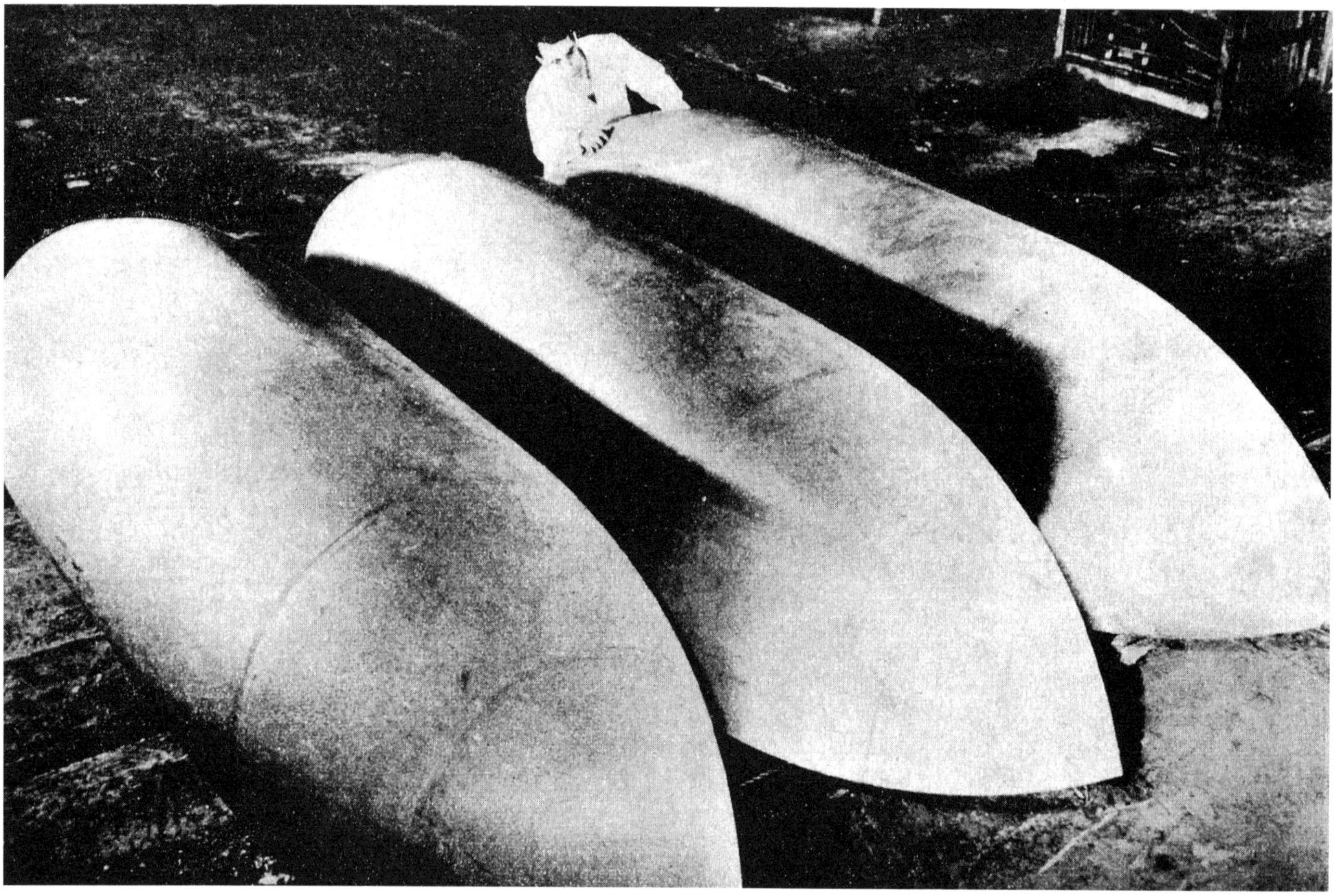

十吨重的火山炸弹

英国航空生产部专家发明十吨重之火山炸弹一种，专为英国兰开斯特式机轰炸巨大的特种目标而用，此项新武器长25英呎10英吋，直径3英呎10吋。此弹系在美军火工厂制造，正由一工人加以检查。

10-ton Volcano Bomb

The experts of the British Ministry of Aircraft Production devised these 10-ton Volcano bombs to be used by RAF Lancaster planes in attacks on specific enemy targets of great size. The new projectile is 25 ft. 10 in. long, and 3 ft. 10 in. in diameter.

10トンの大型爆弾

英国航空生産部の専門家は、巨大の目標を攻撃する英軍のランカスタ式爆撃機の為に重さ10トンの爆弾を造った。この新しい武器の長さは25フィート10インチ、直径は3フィート10インチである。米国の工場で造られた。図は一人の労働者はそれを検査している光景である。

制空权的转变

1941年年底以前欧洲的制空权掌握在德国手中，1942年到1943年盟军仅能靠空军封锁德国，到1943年底，盟国始展开对德空中攻势，制空权亦落入盟军手中。图为美飞行堡垒袭击德国占领之下法国亚眠。

Turning of the Air Power

Before the end of 1941, the air power in Europe is belong to Germany. From 1942 to 1943, the allied can only use their limited air force, to blockade its enemy. However, at the end of 1943, the air power has turned over to the Allies hands. Above, Flying Fortresses bombing Amiens–Glissy, France, occupied by German.

制空権の奪還

1941年末まで、ヨーロッパの制空権はドイツ軍に掌握されていた。1943年末に、連合軍はドイツ軍への空中攻撃を始め、制空権を奪還した。図は米軍の大型爆撃機が占領されたフランスのアミアンを爆撃している光景である。

毁灭德国飞机厂

从1942年春到1944年夏的2年时间内，英美为准备攻破西墙，不断地实行战略轰炸，破坏其工业生产，军火制造，空军力量。上为美国第十五航空队之飞行堡垒炸维也纳德国米氏战斗机工厂，开始起到1944年初，英美投于德国之炸弹达33万吨。

Blast German Aircraft Factory

Extensive strategic bombing was carried out by U.S. and British airforces from spring 1942 to summer 1944 to annihilate the German war potential. Picture shows Messerschmitt fighter plant at engulfed in fire.

ドイツ飛行機工場を打ち壊す

英米の空軍は1942年春から1944年夏まで二年間に亘りドイツの工業生産地や軍備製造地と空軍の施設を絶え間なく爆撃していた。図は米軍第十五航空隊の大型爆撃機がウィーンにあるドイツ飛行機製造工場を爆撃している場面である。攻撃開始してから1944年の初めまで英米は計33万トンの爆弾をドイツに落とした。

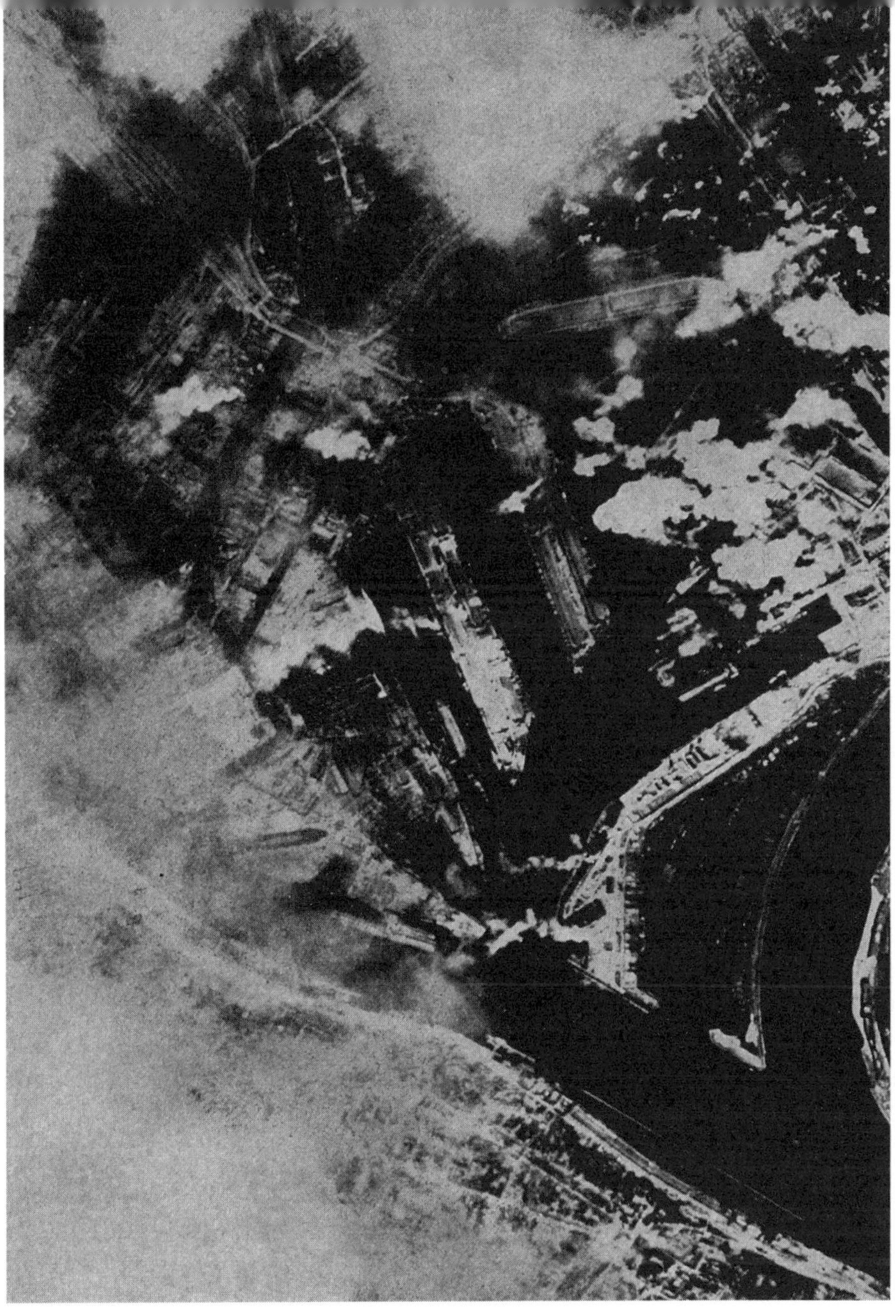

英美空中攻势

英美对德空中攻势开始于1943年夏季，英国兰开斯特式和威灵顿式重轰炸机夜晚数百成千地飞到德国作战区域轰炸，白天美国空中堡垒又去作目标轰炸，使德国工业军事经济体系和民气陷于解体和软化。上为德国基尔海军基地被炸之情况。

Attack from Air

In summer 1943, Germany was subjected to systematic bombing by British Lancasters and Wellingtons by night, and by American Fortresses by day. It greatly weakened the Germans industrially, militarily, economically and morally. The picture shows the bombing of Kiel naval base.

英米の空中攻勢

1943年夏から英米は空中からの攻撃を始めた。英国の数百から数千機のランカスター式とウェリントン式爆撃機は昼晩問わず次から次へドイツの軍事区域を爆撃し、続いて昼に米軍の大型爆撃機は爆撃を行い、ドイツの工業や軍事システム及び民用システムを破壊した。図はドイツの海軍基地が爆撃された模様である。

登陆西西里

盟军肃清非洲后，经两个月的休息与准备，进攻到西西里的踏脚石——西西里岛。盟军用了3,266艘船，装载着16万人，1,000尊大炮，600辆坦克，于1943年7月10日实行登陆。上为盟军庞大舰队之一部，在非洲待命出发之壮观。

March to Sicily

The allied forces used 3,266 vessels to transport 160,000 men, 1,000 guns and 600 tanks for the landing operation in Sicily on July 10, 1943. Part of them are shown here off the African coast.

シチリア上陸

アフリカの敵軍を殲滅した後、連合軍は二ヶ月間休憩と準備してから、シチリア島への攻撃を始めた。連合軍は3,266隻の戦艦に16万人の兵士、1,000の大砲、600台の戦車を乗せた。1943年7月10日に上陸を実行した。図は連合軍の膨大な艦隊の一部がアフリカに於いて待機している壮観である。

西西里天空的火网

西西里登陆之夜，德意轰炸机，降下照明弹，企图发现盟军登陆地点，盟军舰队乃一致发出强烈的高射炮火网，使其目标迷惑，藉以阻止其轰炸。西西里经38天的激战，落于盟军手中，盟军死伤25,000人，轴心军损失30,000人。

Maenad's Hair over a Sicilian Night

In the first night after the allied landing in Sicily, German and Italian bombers were met with dazzling anti-aircraft barrage in their effort to locate the newly landed force. Sicily was liberated after 38 days of extensive warfare.

シチリアの空に火の網

連合軍はシチリア島に上陸した夜、ドイツ軍は上陸場所を見つける為、爆撃機から照明弾を投下した。連合軍は一斉に対空砲を発射したことでドイツを惑わせ、爆撃を避けられた。シチリアは38日間の激戦を経て連合軍の手に渡った。連合軍は2万5千人、枢軸軍は3万人の死傷者を出した。

撒丁岛上的弹雨

像密雨一般，美国飞行堡垒上的炸弹落在萨丁岛的意国机场上。1943 年 9 月，意大利在地中海的三个重要岛屿——撒丁，西西里，班泰雷利亚岛尽落入盟军手中，进军德军控制下之意大利本土之战，旋即进行。

Bombs Pour Down on Italian Air Base

A closely packed mass of bombs from a Flying Fortress drops toward on Italian air base near Calgliari, Sardinia. By September 1943, Sardinia, Sicily and Pantelleria in Mediterranean islands were in allied hands and the successful invasion of the German-held Italian mainland was under way.

サルジニア島の弾雨

米軍の大型飛行機からの爆弾は豪雨のようにイタリアのサルジニア島の飛行場に投下された。1943年9月イタリアは地中海にある三つの島サルジニア、シチリア、パンテレリアは全て連合軍に占領された。ドイツ軍に支配されたイタリア本土への進攻も直ちに始めた。

在意大利作战

盟军英加部队于1943年9月3日清晨，从西西里跨国海峡首次踏上意大利的本土尼齐俄卡拉贝利亚城，同时巴多格里奥将军与盟军缔结秘密和平条约（定于9月8日生效），9月9日英美部队，冒险登陆那不勒斯以南之萨伦诺（上图），纳粹死命反攻抵御，企图击退盟军，8日以后盟军形势始行好转。

Action in Italy

Action on the Italian mainland started with the occupation of Reggio Calabria by allied forces in early September 1943. then a further attack was made at Salerno (picture) to the south of Naples. The Nazis held up the advance of Allies for eight days in bloody war.

イタリアでの戦い

1943年9月3日の早朝、連合軍はシチリア海峡を渡り、初めてイタリアの本土に着いた。図は9月9日英米部隊が強引にナポリ南のサレルノに上陸する光景である。ナチスは連合軍の進攻を阻止しようと必死に抵抗した。

意大利投降

墨索里尼因战事逆转，失去信任。意国爱麦虞限任命巴多格里奥组织政府，8月中旬（1944年）向盟国要求光荣的和平，9月4日秘密签定投降协议，将可以交出之军事力量全部交出，在德国控制下之本土，仍继续对盟国作战。图为持白旗投降之意大利军队。

Italy Surrender

Italy signed a surrender agreement with allies on September 4, 1944. to put effect the agreement, Italian soldiers waving white flags of surrender march into a small town to place themselves under the jurisdiction of the allies.

イタリアの降参

戦事の逆転によりムッソリーニは失脚した。改めて成立された政府は8月中旬頃（1944年）連合軍に停戦を求めた。9月4日に降参協定は密かに調印した。軍事用品と装備を全部相手に渡った。その時ドイツに支配された本土に於いては連合軍との戦いはまだ続いていた。図は白旗を持ち上げて降参するイタリア軍隊である。

转夜为昼

在进攻罗马的路途上，盟国第五军向米格纳诺德军阵地猛攻，155糎巨炮的火光照红了黑夜的战场。把凯撒和但丁的土地都震裂了。

Illumined Italian Night

Amid mud and rain the allies pushed slowly toward Rome. The Italian Night was lit up near Mignano by 155 mm guns which rocked the land of Caesar and Dante.

照らされたイタリアの夜

ローマへ進攻する途中、連合軍第五軍はドイツ陣地を猛烈に攻撃し、戦場の夜空は155ミリの巨砲から発射された砲弾に赤く染められた。

登陆罗马之南

盟军为绕过格斯塔夫防线，迅速占领罗马，于1944年1月23日在罗马以南36哩的勒图诺和安济奥登陆，希特勒调戈林机械化师团来攻，安济奥滩头阵地盟军苦守达4月之久。

Landing in South of Rome

To avoid attacking the Gustav Line and to hasten the liberation of Rome, the Allied High Command decided to land at Nettnno and Anzio, south of Rome. Hitler sent the Goering Korps thither in an effort to drive the attackers back into the sea, but the Allies held the beachhead for four months.

ローマ南部上陸

ローマを速やかに占領する為、連合軍はグスタフ防御線を迂回して、1944年1月23日、ローマ南部から36マイル離れたところに上陸した。ヒトラーは慌ててゲーリングの機械師団を用いて反撃した。連合軍は4ヶ月間かけ、ゲーリングと攻防戦を繰り広げた。

罗马解放

意大利法西斯的都城罗马，终于在1944年6月4日被盟军美国第五军克拉克部队攻入，德军在罗马没有抵抗，即向北引退。罗马是轴心第一个陷落的都城，意大利人民受了22年的法西斯统治，这天以最大的热忱欢迎盟军。

Liberation of Rome

Rome was liberated on June 4, 1944 by the U.S. fifth Army under general Clark. The Nazis withdrew northward without putting up any resistance. Thus the first Axis capital that had lasted twenty-two years ended on this way.

ローマ解放

1944年6月4日、米第五軍団はイタリアファシズムの首都ローマに入り、ドイツ軍は抵抗せず北部に退いた。ローマは枢軸国の初めて陥落した都市である。イタリア人民は22年間に亘ってファシズムに支配され、虐げられてきたが、この解放された日に、ローマの市民は連合軍を熱く迎えた。

偷袭挪威

盟军远征挪威罗佛吞岛，登陆破坏其油库。图为完成任务后盟军安全驶返原舰。

Attack Norway

Expedition to the Lofoten Island, Norway, when Allied troops were landed to slow up the oil tanks. Having completed their work of destruction, the troops are seen returning to their ship.

ノルウェー奇襲

連合軍は遠くノルウェーのロフォーテン諸島を奇襲して、石油タンクを破壊した。図は襲撃の目的を果たしてから連合軍の兵士達は戦艦に戻る場面である。

登陆诺曼底

第二次世界大战的一个最高峰，联合国人民期待已久的日子——进攻欧洲大陆，经过两年的准备终于在1944年6月6日来到。盟国4,000艘船只，载着百万大军，由800艘军舰，1,000架飞机护航，齐向法国北部诺曼底从事有史以来空前的军事大进攻。上为在英吉利海峡向法国海岸推进之登陆船，船上升起阻塞气球，防止敌机俯冲轰炸。

Off the Normandy Coast on D-Day

The opening of the long-awaited Second Front on June 6, 1944 marks the climax of World War Ⅱ. Barrage balloons hover over Allied ships steaming across the English Channel for landing along the French coast.

ノルマンデイー上陸

世界各国の人々は首長く期待していたヨーロッパ大陸への総攻撃の日を迎えた。これは第二次世界大戦のクライマックスである。二年間の準備を経て1944年6月6日に連合軍百万の兵士を乗せた4,000隻の戦艦が800隻の軍艦と1,000機の戦闘機の掩護の下で、フランス北部のノルマンデイーに空前の大進攻を始めた。図はイギリス海峡からフランス海岸に向けて進んでいる場面である。敵の爆撃機を防ぐ為、数え切れないほどの風船が上げられている。

巨炮开路

在登陆的前夜，1,000架盟国重轰炸机在狂炸法国海岸时，美国主力舰又在怒吼了，从夜半起盟机送过10,000吨炸弹岛仅仅60哩长的海岸线，640艘军舰又向着要登陆的滩头阵地发射了2,000吨炮弹，为登陆部队打开一条上岸的道路。

Clear the Way from Landing

On the night before D-Day, 10,000 tons of bombs and 2,000 tons of shells were dumped by 1,000 Allied planes and 640 naval ships on the narrow strip of land to pave the way for the landing forces.

道を開く巨砲

上陸の前夜、連合軍の1,000機の大型爆撃機はフランス海岸を爆撃すると同時に、米戦艦からの攻撃も始まった。夜半から僅か60マイルの海岸線に10,000トンの爆弾が落とされ、道を開く為に、更に640隻の戦艦は予定された上陸地点の浜辺に2,000トンの爆弾を落とした。

蜂拥登陆

在火幕张开时，成千的登陆艇向海滩蜂拥前进，不顾纳粹设置之阻碍与强烈的炮火，在卡恩岛芒特堡5个滩头登陆。巡洋舰奥古斯达号正在海面掩护登陆。

Swarming toward Beach

When the actual landing took place, thousands of landing craft shoot toward the beach under strong Nazi fire. Five beachheads, however, were established between Caen and Montaburg on the first day. The U.S.S. cruiser Augusta in above picture is protecting the landing.

上陸に殺到

爆撃の最中、沢山の上陸艇はナチスの激しい砲火にも顧みず、浜辺に殺到した。連合軍の巡洋艦は海上で上陸を掩護している。

瑟堡滩头一瞥

盟军于法国海港瑟堡建立滩头阵地后，装备与供应品源源在滩头登陆。德军由名将隆美尔指挥防守海岸，因后备军不足，不能有效制止盟军的展开。

Beachhead at Cherbourg

Cherbourg was the first sizable seaport that fell to the Allied attack. It had been defended by more than ten Nazi divisions, under Rommel, but it unsucceeded before superior attacking forces.

シェルブール港の光景

連合軍はフランスのシェルブール港に陣地を作った後、軍用装備が次々と送られてきた。独軍はロンメル将軍の指揮の下で抵抗したが装備不足で連合軍を阻止することできなかった。

伞兵飞往敌后

进攻的开始是美国空运军两师和英国伞兵于6月6日（1944年）夜2时在哈佛港与瑟堡间德军后方着陆，在4小时之内用运输机和滑翔机降落了3个师，这是历史上最大一次的空运工作。上为首先飞越英吉利海峡之美国空运部队在运输机中。

Paratroopers before Landing

In the small hours on D-Day, more than three divisions of American and British Paratroopers landed behind the German lines, between Le Havre and Cherbourg.

敵後方のパラシュート

1944年6月6日夜2時、米軍は二つの師団の兵士と英国のパラシュートは、ハーバート港とシェルブールの間の独軍の後方に着陸した。4時間内、運送機とグライダーを使って3つの師団の兵士を運んできた。これは史上最大な空運であった。図はイギリス海峡を飛び越えている米軍運送機に乗っている米軍の兵士達である。

瑟堡之战

诺曼底滩头阵地之美国炮兵用反坦克炮射击藏匿之德军，藉以打入内地德军阵线。兵士3人匿于墙下，旁卧殉难伙伴2人。盟军向西推进越过瑟堡半岛，进到西海岸，6月23日（1944年）向北进攻，抵战略性港埠之瑟堡。

Battle of Cherbourg

U.S. gunners, battering their way into German lines in the interior of Normandy, fire their anti-tank gun point blank at a nest of enemy soldiers. Thrusting westward across the base of the Cherbourg Peninsula in North Normandy, Allied forces fought their way to the west coast of the promontory. Swinging north they reached Cherbourg on June 23, 1944.

シェルブールの戦い

ノルマンデイーの灘の陣地にいる米軍の砲兵は隠れている独軍を射撃している。三名の兵士は壁の下に隠れ、側に死亡した二人の兵士が横倒れている。連合軍はシェルブール半島を越えて西海岸まで進んだ。1944年6月23日引き続き北部へ進め戦略要地のシェルブールに着いた。

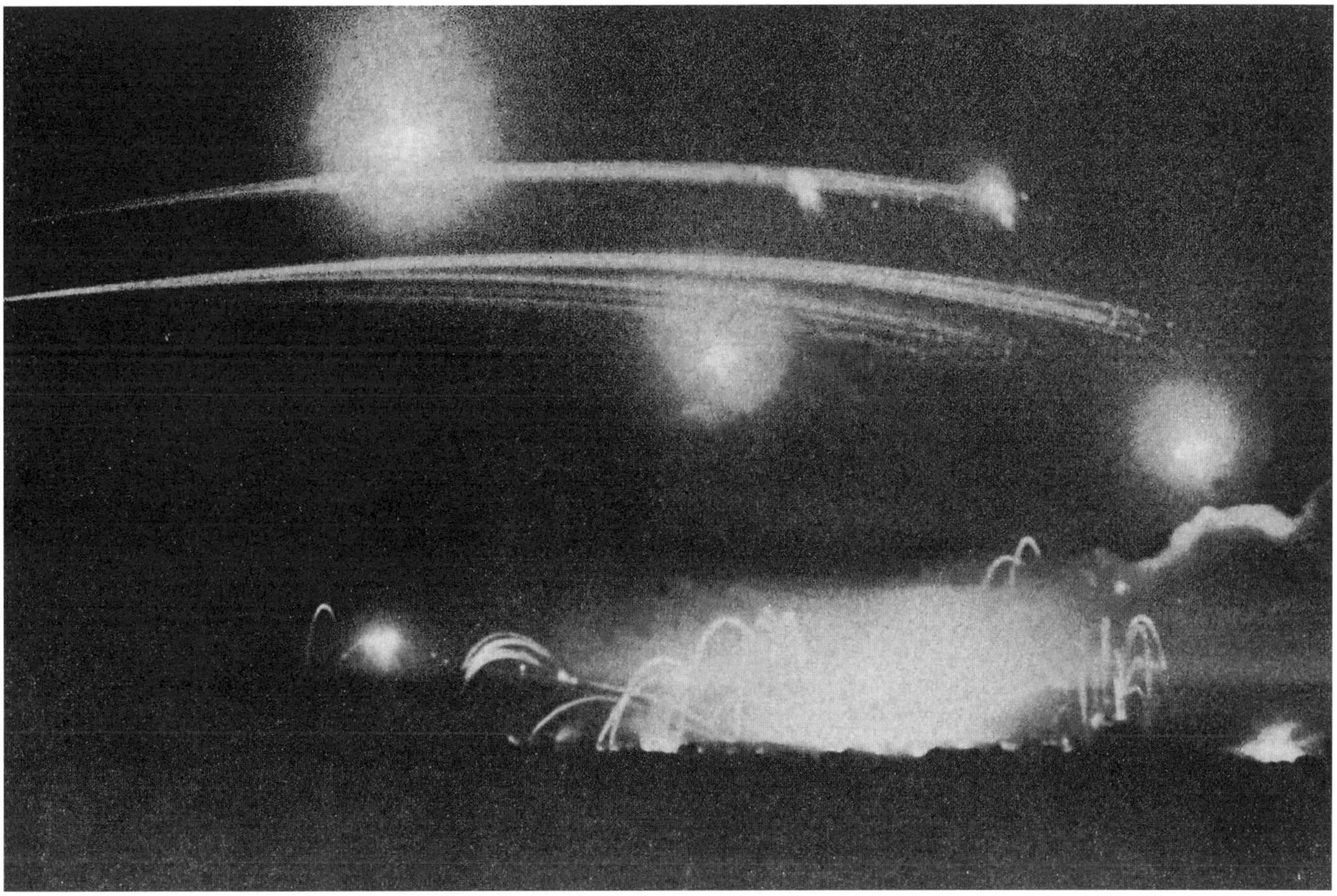

克恩夜战

克恩是德军在瑟堡半岛交通与防卫的中心，德军隆美尔将军率兵十一师在此抵抗，克恩城虽于7月9日（1944年）为盟军占领，然德军仍步步疯狂血战，藉以阻止盟军洪水似的进攻，图为8月7日夜间克恩以南夜炮战之动人场面。

Battle of Caen

The city of Caen was the central pivot of German resistance on the Cherbourg Peninsula. Rommel directed eleven German divisions against the Allies, but was unable to halt them. Picture shows gun duel at night in August 1944.

カーンの夜戦

カーンはシェルブール半島の交通と防衛の中心地である。独軍のロンメル将軍は11の 師団を率いてここで抵抗したが、7月9日に連合軍に占領された。しかし、ドイツの兵士は砲弾を浴びて狂気じみに抵抗した。図は8月7日夜カーンでの戦う場面である。

空军增援攻势

美B-24解放式机落弹炸法国之杜而的德国工事。白烟为向目标投弹之烟幕记号。1944年7月25日盟国为支持在诺曼底新的攻势，出动飞机3,000架，半数为重轰炸机。

Air Forces Support New Drive

B-24 Liberators release their deadly explosives during a raid on German installations at Tours, France. The white streamers are smoke markers dropped to mark the targets. On July 25, 1944, 3,000 planes took to the air in support of the new drive in Normandy.

空軍の応援

米軍B-24解放式爆撃機はフランスにある独軍の陣地に攻撃している。白煙は爆弾の投下後の痕跡である。1944年7月25日、連合軍は3,000機の大型爆撃機を出動しノルマンデイーへの攻撃に応援していた。

飞弹在天空中

这是一张难得的照片，飞弹以每小时350到400哩的速度向英伦进袭中，尾部露着白烟，在空中摄下来。左上角是一没有爆炸的飞弹。此项火箭飞机由每小时200哩的原动力弹床发射而出，长25英呎又4吋，翼宽16英呎，后部为推进器。燃料用完后飞弹就整个落下来。德国在盟军登陆诺曼底后，图以此秘密武器来延缓战争。

A Flying Bomb Across the Sky

This is a very valuable picture of a flying bomb which travels toward London in a speed of 350—400 miles per hour. It has length of 25 ft. 4 in. with a wing scan of 16 ft. It falls when its fuel is exhausted. Insertion shows an unexploded one.

空の飛弾

これは珍しい写真である。飛弾は時速350から400マイルのスピートでイギリスへ飛んでおり、後ろから白い煙が噴出している。連合軍がノルマンデイーの上陸は成功した後、ドイツ軍はこの「飛弾」という秘密武器を使って戦争を延びさせようとした。

黑夜打飞弹

英国防御飞弹，第一线用战斗机迎击，第二线在沿海边建立高射炮火网，集中轰击，高射炮队半数均妇女，上为夜晚高射炮射击之奇观。

Stop the Flying Bombs

A more effective way of discounting the damage of V－Ⅰ's and V－Ⅱ's was the use of extensive barrages of anti–aircraft fire. This is one o them. It illumines the night sky in spectacular batteries of which half were manned by women.

夜空に飛弾が飛ぶ

英国が飛弾に対する作戦は、第一線では戦闘機を使って迎え撃ち、第二線では海辺から対空砲を使って一斉に発砲する。対空砲隊の砲手は半数ぐらい女性である。図は対空砲が飛弾に向いて射撃している光景である。

云海与气球

1944年夏为抵御V－1和V－2飞弹，英国空前地升起2,000只阻塞汽球，以保卫伦敦和英国南部。阻塞汽球的效力并不大，因为V－2飞得六七十哩高，高射炮及阻塞汽球均够不到。8,000个飞弹中只有300个给阻塞下来。德国所发2,300飞弹，使英人死伤25,000人，毁屋20,000余幢。

Sea of Clouds Balloons

Hitler began to use pilotless V－Ⅰ and V－Ⅱ flying bombs in the summer of 1944. These secret German weapons caused both heavy damage and bewilderment. Thousands of balloons were floated high above the clouds to stop them but the result was not very satisfying.

雲海と風船

1944年夏末頃、独軍のV-1とV-2飛弾を抵御する為に、英国は2,000個の風船を上げロンドンとイギリスの南部を守る。しかし、V-2は60か70キロも高く飛んでいるから対空砲と風船はそこまで届けないので、8,000個の飛弾に対して、3,000個しか阻止できなかった。独軍が発射した23,000枚の飛弾は、イギリス25,000人を死傷させた。また20,000棟の家屋は壊された。

法国南部登陆

德军在法国北部遭受盟军猛攻时，联合国部队于8月15日（1944年）在法南马塞与尼斯宽广阵地登陆而受到另一打击。降落伞队由C–47运输机载运在新的滩头降落区降落，陆地部队由800艘船只运兵源源登陆。

Landing in Southern France

While the Germans were reeling under heavy Allied attacks in Normandy, they were dealt another blow when the Allies landed between Nice and Marseilles on Aug. 15, 1944. This paratroopers were just from C–47's.

フランス南部の上陸

独軍はフランスの北部で連合軍に激しく攻撃され、さらに連合軍は1944年8月15日にフランス南部のマルセイユとニースにも上陸して、両方から独軍を挟み打つ。パラシュートは次々と空から降りてきて、陸軍も800隻の戦艦に運ばれてきた。

巴黎巷战

法国爱国青年为迫使德军投降，于巴黎街心与法军及法奸巷战，法国第二十装甲师坦克予以协助。坦克在发炮，炮口尚留有白烟。法国内地军及成千之爱国者，使用各色武器，卒使巴黎获得解放。

Street Fighting in Paris

Assisted by a tank, French patriot fought a bitter war of revenge against the Germans and traitors in Paris. Armed with various weapons, the French Army of the Interior and thousands of others forced the Germans to surrender before the Allied arrived.

パリの市街戦

独軍を降参させる為、フランスの愛国者武装はパリの中心地で売国奴傀儡軍と戦った。フランスの第二装甲師団のタンクはそれに応援している。発砲後のタンクは白煙が漂っている。フランス各地の愛国者武装はいろいろな武器を使ってパリの解放に携わった。

法国内地军捕获德军官

法国内地军在巴黎捕获德国高级军官，在警戒中行经市区大剧院前，当盟军逼近巴黎时，巴黎城内内地军50,000人与非武装平民揭竿而起，4天酣战中解放了巴黎。

German Officer Captured by F.F.I

A German officer was captured by the French Forces of the Interior and was escorted through the streets in front of the opera. 50,000 FFI and civilians of Paris liberated the capital in four days of bitter fighting.

フランス内地軍がドイツ将士を捕まる

図はフランス内地軍隊はパリでドイツの将校を捕まって市内の大劇場を通過している場面である。連合軍はパリに攻めてきた際、パリ市内の50,000人の軍人と市民は連合軍に呼応して四日間の激しい戦いを経てパリを解放した。

巴黎解放

8月25日（1944年）盟国失陷的一大都市巴黎，首先获得解放。法兰西人民狂热地欢迎入城盟军。8月末，法国全部获得自由。

Paris Liberated

Paris was liberated by the French underground forces on Aug. 25, 1944. No stranger could stand unmoved by the milling, overjoyed French crowds on the streets. The entire French nation was freed by the end of the month.

パリの解放

1944年8月25日、パリは解放された。フランス人は熱烈に連合軍を迎えてきた。8月末頃フランスは全部解放された。

卢森堡炮战

由法国边境向比利时卢森堡推进之盟军，于4日中推进200哩，上系盟军推进至卢森堡某处，以155糎炮轰击纳粹强固据点，强烈火光下黑夜变为白昼。

Gun Duel in Luxembourg

Allied forces, pushing from the French border toward Belgium and Luxembourg, advanced 200 miles in four days. The 155mm guns were turning night into day.

ルクセンブルクの砲戦

フランスの国境からベルギーとルクセンブルクに推進している連合軍は、四日間で200マイル程進めた。図は連合軍がルクセンブルクのある町に着いた光景である。155ミリの大砲はナチスの強固な拠点を爆撃し、夜は昼に化した。

盟军越过齐格飞防线

围攻柏林之战，在西线以越进齐格飞防线为主体，美军于1944年9月首先进入齐格飞防线上之大城亚琛。北面盟军用伞兵占安亨与尼美根，绕过齐格飞防线。

Leave the Siegfried Line Behind

The Siegfried Line was the security of Germany. Allied forces penetrated it on Sept 1944, by entering Aachen. Paratroops captured Arnhem and Nijmegen by flying over it.

連合軍は西防御線を乗り越す

ベルリンに攻め込みたいなら、西部の防御線を突破しなければならない。米軍は1944年9月25日先ずアーヘンに突入した。パラシュートは北部から攻撃してきて、ドイツの西の防御線を挟み撃つ態勢ができた。

英军击沉德船

英空军战斗机于1944年9月17日希立哥兰拜特攻击德国武装船两艘，一艘被炸沉没，另一艘被炸起火，无法控制。上为英机之火箭炮正向船上发射。

British Beaufighters Blow up German Ships

Beaufighters of the RAF on Sept. 9, 1944, attacked two heavily armed German ships in Helgoland Bight. One had sunk while the other was left blazing and out of control.

英軍はドイツの軍艦を撃沈した

英軍は1944年9月17日にドイツの軍艦2隻を攻撃し、1隻は沈没、もう1隻は命中され抑えきれない火が燃え騰がった。図はイギリスの爆撃機がドイツの軍艦に発射している場面である。

德军殊死战

德国境内盟军长程巨炮于雪夜中向敌人阵地炮击。1944年12月中旬德军向德比卢边境阿登来斯作孤注一掷之反攻，德军集中15个师向盟军突击，来势甚猛，盟军空运部队在巴斯吞被围，终以德军进分凸出，预备兵有限，很快的退至科伦平原。

Hitler's Last Desperate Attempt

In snowy December 1944, the Reich mustered fifteen divisions for the last attempt to save its skin. These Allied "Long Toms" were doing their best to repel the attacking enemies.

独軍は必死に戦い

ドイツ領土に突入した連合軍は、ロング巨砲で雪の夜に敵の陣地に爆撃した。1944年12月中旬に、独軍はドイツ、ベルギー、ルクセンブルク国境のラインラント地区で必死に抵抗した。独軍は15個の師団を集めて連合軍にとびかかてきた。連合軍の空運部隊はドイツ軍に包囲され、結局は予備部隊がついてこないからケルン平原に引き上げた。

巴尔干解放

1944年秋天苏军进抵波兰，巴而干纳粹卫星国家发生动摇，罗马尼亚首先对德作战，保加利亚继之对纳粹宣战、南斯拉夫游击队最后与苏军会合，巴尔干乃获得解放。图为南非航空队轰炸南斯拉夫堡垒城市，地面炮火予以还击。

Liberation of the Balkans

The German satellites in the Balkans began to break away in Autumn 1944. At first, Romania, and then Bulgaria declared war on Germany. Yugoslavian guerillas joined force with the Russians to fight the German garrisons. Picture shows a Yugoslavian castle city exchanging fire with an Allied bomber.

バルカンの解放

1944年の秋、ソ連軍はポーランドに突入した。ナチスに支配されたバルカン地域の国々は先ず、ルーマニアがドイツに宣戦し、つづいてブルガリアも宣戦した。最後にユーゴスラビアの遊撃隊はソ連軍と会合し、バルカン地域の国々はついに解放の日を迎えた。図は南アフリカ航空隊はユーゴスラビアの中心都市を爆撃した際、地面の対空砲は反撃している光景である。

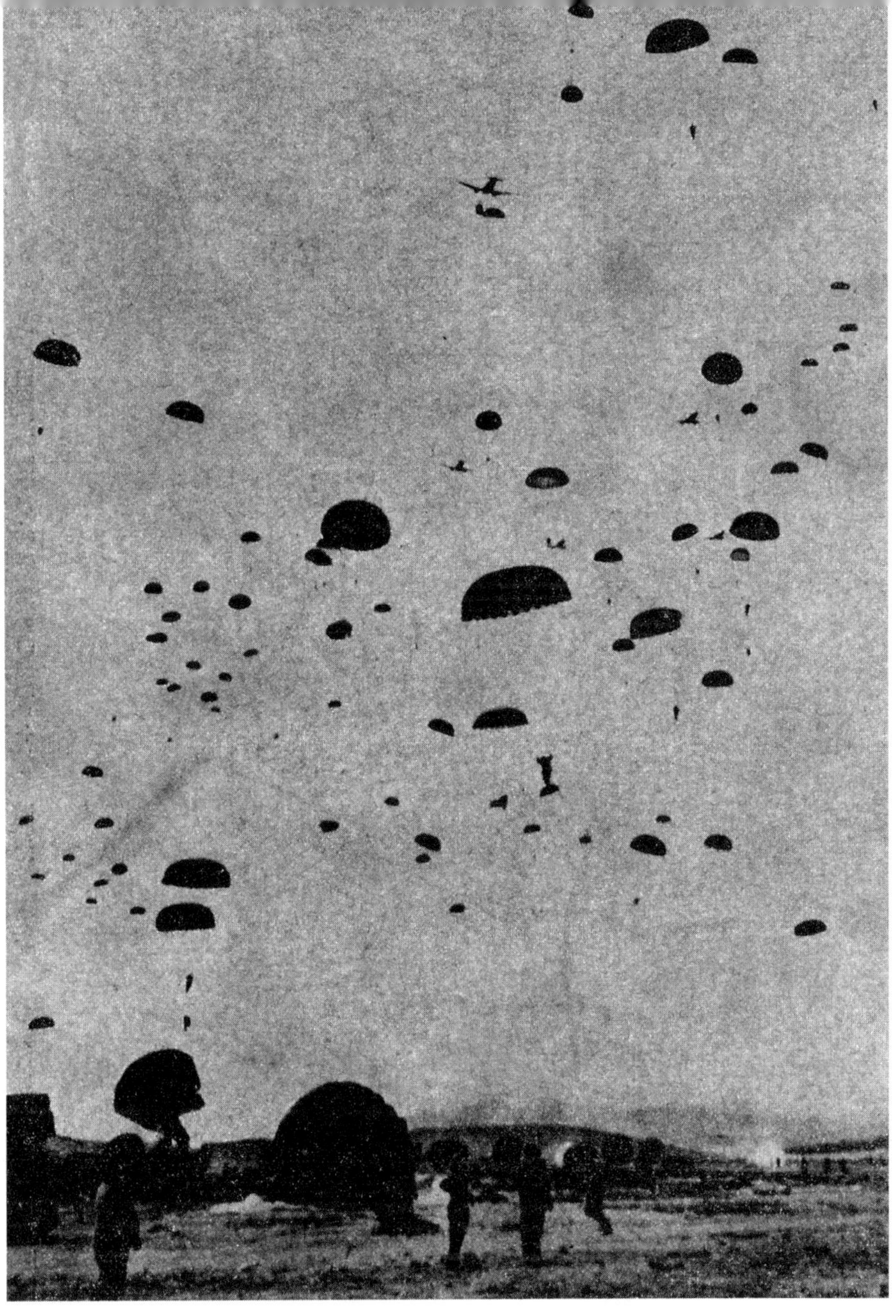

天兵解放雅典

美机载英国伞兵于希腊首都雅典附近降落，快乐的希腊人民在地面欢迎他们的解放者。希腊爱国分子得到这批军队及海上登陆部队之助，1944年10月14日雅典获得自由，结束了3年多敌人的压迫。

Paratroopers Liberate Athen

U.S. planes drop British paratroopers near Athens while jubilant Greek civilian wait on the ground to greet their liberators. Aided by these troops and others who land by sea, Greek patriots liberated Athens on Oct. 14, 1944, ending more than three years of enemy oppression.

パラシュートはアテネを解放

米軍の飛行機は英国のパラシュートを乗せギリシアの首都アテネに降りて来た。喜んでいるギリシアの人人は解放者を歓迎する。1944年10月14日にて、3年間の屈辱な日々はアテネの解放によってやっと終わった。

向德军反攻

阿登山区盟军于1945年1月初展开反攻，22日德凸出的阵线崩溃，急退至齐格飞防线。图为英军中型炮开始攻击，作为反攻之前奏。

Counter-attack in the Oden Valley

The Allies counter–attack in the Oden Valley in early 1945. The Germans collapsed and hastily retreated before the end of the month toward the Siegfried Line. Medium–sized British guns were used to herald the attack.

ドイツ軍に反攻

連合軍は1945年1月に反攻を始めた。図はドイツ軍が英軍の大砲の攻撃を受け、慌てて逃げている光景である。

法德边境坦克战

配合盟军反攻，法国边境阿尔萨斯省城斯特拉斯堡盟军坦克车于隆冬对德展开攻击，1月21日（1945年）一役中击毁德国坦克8辆。

Tank Battle at France-German Border

Allied tank units attacked from Strasburg form a part of the general Allied push against the Germans. On January 21, 1945 alone, eight enemy tanks were destroyed.

独仏国境で戦車の混戦

連合軍に呼応する為、1945年1月21日フランス国境のストラスブールにて、連合軍の戦車は真冬にドイツ軍の戦車と混戦していた。

德城战影

盟军与德国飞机于圣诞节（1944年）发生一场“狗斗战”，于废垣断瓦的阿登荷文上空掠过，留下道道的雾痕。该城于11月21日为盟军占领。

War Scene in Germany

Vapor trails from Allied and German planes engaged in a Christmas Day (1944) dog fight are streaked across the German sky above ruins in Aldenhoven. The city was captured on Nov. 21, 1944 by the Allied forces.

ドイツの町での戦い

1944年のクリスマス、連合軍の空軍はドイツの空軍と激しく空戦した。図は戦闘機が町の上空をかすめて飛んでおり、煙は霧のように空に残した画面である。

攻入科伦

著名的德国科伦大教堂内，一片瓦砾。科伦为德国大都市之一，1945年3月6日为美国第一军占领，1周后莱因河以西已无德军。12日盟军渡过莱因河。

Cologne Cathedral

The awe inspiring wall of the famous Cologne Cathedra look down silently on a floor of debris as the Allies entered on March 6, 1945. The west bank of the Rhine was cleared of German soldiers in a week.

ケルンに攻め込む

図は名高いドイツのケルン大教堂の地面の瓦礫場である。ケルンはドイツの大都市での一つで1945年3月6日米軍の第一軍団に占領された。一週間後ライン川の西側に駐在したドイツ軍は全部消えた、12日に連合軍はその川を渡した。

进入波恩

美国第三十师步兵乘巡逻车于预备攻击中进入火烧之德国波恩城。美军于1945年4月14日渡过前往柏林之最后一道河流易北河后，4月18日即占领波恩。

Roll into Born

With rifles alert, 30th Division Infantrymen entered the burning town of Born atop a reconnaissance car, after crossing the river Elbe on April 14, 1945. The river was the last barrier before Berlin.

ボンに入る

図は米国第30師団の兵士はパトカーに乗ってドイツのボンに進入している光景である。1945年4月14日米軍はエルベ川を渡り4月18日にボンを占領した。

纳粹焚毙俘虏

此人系由纳粹活活烧死，死前曾力图逃出此种可怕之刑罚。彼与苏法波犹政治犯至少有150人，被骗入德国加得勤镇附近一马房内，强迫坐于浇有汽油之稻草上，着火后被这关于屋内焚尸。

Nazi Burn Prisoner to Death

This man was burned to death by Nazi S.S. troopers. He is shown as he died struggling to escape a horrible torture. He is one of at least 150 Russian, French, Polish and Jewish political prisoners who were herded into a huge barn near Gardelegen, Germany, and forced to sit down on gasoline-soaked straw.

ナチスは捕虜を焼き払う

この人は生きてままナチスに焼死された。死の前に逃走しようとしたが逃げ切れなかったようとみえる。ソ連、フランス、ボーランド、イスラエル等国の捕虜150人はドイツ軍に厩に入れて、ガソリンの撒いたわらに座らせ焼き殺された。

受难者的戒指

德国威玛附近布成瓦德集中营发现之数千结婚戒指之一部份，此项戒指乃自奴役或死亡之俘虏手上取下。美国第三军于1945年4月13日占领布城，解放苏波法意捷俘虏21,000人，过去在该集中营已有70,000人死于饥饿或虐待。

Rings from Victims

On entering the Buchenwald concentration camp near Weima, American soldiers of the Third Army discovered trays full of wedding-rings. They were the relic of innocent people, taken prisoner by the Nazis, who died later of starvation or terror.

被害者の指輪

ドイツの捕虜キャンプに、数千枚の結婚記念指輪を見つけた。これは捕まれた人々や死亡した人たちから奪い取ったものである。米軍の第三軍団は1945年4月13日にこの町を占領してから、ソ連、ポーランド、フランス、イタリア、チェコスロバキア等の国の21,000名の捕虜を救出したが、この捕虜キャンプには既に70,000人が虐殺されてしまった。

雅尔塔会议

罗斯福，邱吉尔，斯大林三巨头为计划最后如何击败德国，奠定和平之基础，1945年2月4日至11日又会晤于黑海边克里米亚的雅而塔，图中圆桌左前方为斯大林及其高级军官，右前方为罗斯福与其私人参谋长李海及陆军参谋长马歇尔，左下角衔大雪茄者为邱吉尔。此会为使苏联参加对日战争，曾允以中国东北权益之一部让与苏联，为一大憾事。

The Yalta Conference

President Roosevelt (right) Marshal Stalin (upper left) and Prime Minister Churchill met once more at Yalta on the Black Sea coast, February 4 to 11, 1945, to discuss the final attack on Germany and the peace after the war.

ヤルタ会議

如何にドイツを抑えて、平和の基盤を築き上げることを討議の為、ルーズベルト、チャーチル、スターリン三人は再びヤルタで1945年2月4日から11日まで会議をした。図の左前方はスターリン及びその他の将校、右前方はルーズベルトと陸軍参謀長官、左下にシガを吸ているのはチャーチルである。ソ連が対日戦争に参加してもらえる為に、中国東北部の利益をソ連に譲る事がこの会議で決められたことは非常に残念なことである。

东线德军陷入泥淖

当轴心军在非洲被肃清，第二战场的呼声响彻云霄时，德军在苏联正陷于不能自拔的泥淖中。乌克兰，克里米亚，列宁格勒，加里宁及大部份白俄罗斯均被苏收复。

Reich Bogged Down

With Africa cleared of the Nazis, and the opening of the second front imminent, the Germans were deeply bogged down in the mud of the steppes of Russia. The tide of the war is turning.

ドイツ軍はソ連での立ち往生

枢軸国の軍隊がアフリカから追い出された時に、ドイツ軍もソ連で立ち往生となっている。ウクライナ、コロミーヤ、レニングラード、及びベロルシアの大部分地域は皆ソ連に奪還された。

苏军反攻

苏军自斯城之战胜利后，自1942年12月起由南到北1,500哩前线同时举行大反攻，德军死伤遍野（上图），至1943年底德军所占三分之二领土已被苏军夺回。

Soviet Counter-Attack

Close upon the heels of the Stalingrad victory, the Russians counter–attacked along a front that ran fifteen hundred miles. The Germans retreated hurriedly to the west, leaving their dead strewn everywhere.

ソ連軍の反攻

ソ連軍はスターリングーラド戦役の勝利を収めた後、1942年12月から南部から北部へ1,500マイルの長い戦線から一斉に反攻を始めた。図は野原のあちこちに横倒れているドイツ軍の死体である。1943年末頃まで、ドイツ軍に占領された領土の三分の二はもうソ連軍に収復された。

喀尔巴阡山中炮战

盟军在诺曼底登陆后，苏军对德亦展开大规模反攻，喀而巴阡山的苏军巨炮在雪山中怒吼。苏联用政治攻势辅导军事攻势，屈服了罗马尼亚，保加利亚，1944年底解放匈牙利，加重了南方对柏林的威胁。

In the Carpathians

After the opening of the second front, the Russian counter-attacked along the eastern front. Picture shows Russian guns roaring in the Snowy Carpathians.

カルバート山の砲戦

連合軍はノルマンディーに上陸後まもなく、ソ連軍もドイツに大規模な反攻を始めた。カルバート山脈にソ連軍の巨砲は雪の山にこだましている。ソ連は政治と軍事両方の手段を使ってルーマニア、ブルガリアを降伏した。そして、1944年末、ハンガリーを解放した。これからベルリンへの圧力を強めた。

塞巴斯托波尔港解放

1944年被解放之塞巴斯托波尔，是苏联海舰队的根据地。1942年德军以10万大兵猛攻8次，牺牲三师之众，塞港乃为德军占据。图为严寒中苏舰巨炮结冰情形。

Liberation of Sebastobol

Sebastobol, Soviet naval base on the Black Sea, fell to the attacking Nazis after heroic resistance in 1942. Now Soviet guns were resting after its liberation in 1944.

セバストボル港の解放

1944年解放されたセバストボルはソ連海軍の基地である。1942年ドイツ軍は10万の兵力で8回も攻撃を繰り返した結果、この港は占領した。図はソ連の戦艦の巨砲に氷がかかっている光景である。

反攻在波兰

苏军的总反攻（1944年6月）开始，冲过苏联边界，越过桑洛克河（上图），解放了华沙。苏军180个师的兵力，不过7个月的时间至1945年初即掠过波兰全境，进入德国本土。

Poland Liberated

The Red Army opened their general offensive in June 1944. In the duration of seven months, it dashed from the Soviet border to Germany proper. Poland was liberated Early 1945.

ボーランドでの反攻

1944年6月ソ連軍が全面的に反攻を始め、まもなくワルシャワを解放した。ソ連軍は180個の師団の兵力を持ち七ヶ月間もかからない内にボーランドの全土を横断してドイツの本土に突入した。

美苏会师

在德国东西两线作战之盟军苏联与美国部队，终于在4月25日（1945年）作历史性之会师于易北河上之突尔高。美苏官兵各携国旗于会师后并肩在易北河边行进。

Reds and American's Happy Meeting

Battering respectively from the east and the west, the Russians and the Americans met in this historical joining of forces at Torgau along Elbe River.

米軍とソ連軍の合流

1945年4月25日それぞれドイツの東部と西部から進攻してきたソ連軍と米軍はエルベ川で会合した。図はアメリカとソ連の軍人が合流した後肩を並べてエルベ川の畔に行進しているぶりである。

柏林巷战

苏军首先攻入纳粹巢穴柏林；柏林曾经12日之巷战，日夜大火，德军作无望之防御战，卒于5月2日完全为苏军占领。柏林之战，据估计死伤34.3万人，德军投降者70,000人。上为4月30日夜晚苏军于火焰中与德军巷战。

Street Fighting in Berlin

The Russians entered Berlin first. For twelve days, street fighting raged on in flames and smoke. The Nazis put up a stiff yet hopeless resistance which ended on May 2, 1945. The battle of Berlin cost the Germans 343,000 casualties, besides seventy thousand who surrendered.

ベルリンの市街戦

ソ連軍は米軍より早くベルリンに突入した。ベルリンには12日間に亘って市街戦を行ったので、昼も夜もで戦火が燃えていた。ドイツ軍は必死に抵抗したが結局5月2日ソ連軍に占領された。ベルリン市街戦は死傷者343,000人にも出した、ドイツ軍は7万人が降参した。図は4月30日夜、ソ連軍とドイツ軍は市街戦を繰り広げている光景である。

莫斯科德国俘虏大游行

德国俘虏57,000人行走于莫斯科街上；此为苏军反攻后在白俄罗斯捕获俘虏之一部。

German Captives Marched in Moscow

Fifty-seven thousand captured Germans were marched on Moscow streets. They formed part of the Reich soldiers that fell into Russian hands in White Russia.

モスクワのドイツ捕虜

図は57,000名のドイツ捕虜はモスクワの町を行進している場面である。

柏林残景

炮声与建筑爆炸声平息之后，欧洲第一大城市之柏林已变为一片瓦砾场。上为布兰登堡门一瞥。5月1日（1945年）希特勒继承人杜尼兹海军上将宣布希特勒业已死亡。

The Fall of the Proud Reich

The death of Adolf Hitler was announced on May 1, 1945, by his Successor Admiral Karl Doenitz. A few days later, the European part of World War II came to an end. The Brandenburg Gate in central Berlin now stands in ruins.

ベルリンの残景

大砲の音と建物を爆発する音が静かになったら、ヨーロッパ第一の大都会ベルリンはほぼ廃墟となってしまった。図はブランデンブルグ門の概観である。1945年5月1日ヒトラーの後継者デーニッツ上将はヒトラーの死亡を宣告した。

帝国之凯旋
Imperial Victory
帝国の凱旋

德国投降

德国战斗意志丧失，希特勒传于5月1日（1945年）在柏林作战阵亡，遂由继任元首杜尼兹命令所有德军投降。5月7日初步签字式于巴黎附近之里姆斯小学校举行。德国由参谋长约德尔代表，盟方有英美苏法四国代表，仅5分钟签字完成。8日在柏林签订正式投降书。

German Surrender!

Announced by Admiral Doenitz, successor of Hitler who said killed in Berlin, Germany surrendered unconditionly to the Allies. The surrender document was firstly signed in Reims, Germany, on May 7, 1945, and three days later formerly signed in Berlin.

ドイツの降伏

ドイツは戦闘の意志を失って、ヒトラーは1945年5月1日にベルリンでの市街戦で戦死したという噂も流れ、そして後継の元首デーニッツは独軍に投降するようと命令した。5月7日に投降書の仮調印式はパリの近くにある小学校で行い、僅か五分間で終了した。8日にパリで正式な調印式を行った。

伦敦胜利夜

庆祝德国投降，伦敦于胜利日举行庆祝，晚间泰晤士河畔燃放烟火，蔚为壮观。

London Victory Night

To celebrate the German surrender, Londoners ran wild on Victory Day and Victory Night. Photo shows a wondrous fireworks display held on the Thames.

ロンドン勝利の夜

ドイツの降伏を祝うために、ロンドンは勝利の日に慶祝大会を行い、夜にテムズ川の畔で花火を上げ、とても壮観であった。

自由的狂欢

德国投降，全世界均陷入疯狂的欢笑中。世界各地钟声齐鸣，礼炮声震耳，人民拥挤于街头，欢呼歌唱舞蹈，图为苏联首都莫斯科于1945年5月9日胜利日下午10时庆祝对德胜利，燃放烟火鸣炮，向红军致敬。

Joy of Liberty

German's surrender made the whole world immerged in an excited and frantic joy. Bells ringing, guns sounded, people dancing and singing on the street etc. Above, at 10 p.m. on Victory Day, May 9, 1945, Moscow marking complete victory over Germany and salutes glorious troops of the Red Army.

自由のカーニバル

ドイツの降伏により、全世界がカーニバルのように狂喜に陥れた。世界各地では一斉に鐘を鳴らし、礼砲の音が耳に震動する。図は1945年5月9日勝利の日に、ソ連の首都モスクワで勝利の慶祝を行う場面である。爆竹や花火を上げて紅軍に敬意を表する。

莫斯科庆祝胜利

纳粹崩溃，联合国一致庆祝，6月24日（1945年）莫斯科红场前举行胜利大游行，夺自德国之旗帜排列成行，倒置于地，左起第一人所执者为希特勒个人飞鹰与卐字标帜。

Victory Celeberated in Moscow

Moscow held solemn celebrations of victory on June 24, 1945. Parades and processions were held in the Red Square. These captured Nazi banners were exhibited head downward. On extreme left is the personal ensign of Adolf Hitler with the Flying Eagle and the Swastika.

モスクワ勝利の祝典

ナチスの崩壊、国連の国国は一斉慶祝する。1945年6月24日モスクワ赤グランドで勝利大行進を行った。ドイツ軍から押収した軍旗を逆さまに地面に並んでいる。左から一人目の手に持たれているのはヒトラーの個人の飛鷹と卐字がついている軍旗である。

波茨坦会议

英美苏三国领袖阿特里（大选后继丘吉尔），杜鲁门，斯大林为解决德国投降后的若干问题及加速结束对日战争，7月17日（1945年）至26日集会于柏林附近之波茨坦；最后对日发出文告，限令无条件投降。上为会场情况，着白衣立者为斯大林，斯左第5人为杜鲁门，斯右第5人为阿特里。

Botsdum Conference

Since German surrender, British Prime Minister Atlee, President Truman of America and Marshal Stalin of Russia met in Potsdum, Germany, on July 17, 1945. With the name of China, British, America and U.S.S.R., a warning was issued to Japan for surrender. Russia would join war against Japan also decided in this conference.

ポツダム会議

1945年7月17日、英米ソ三国の首脳はポツダムで会議をした。会議は日本に対する無条件降参しろという通告を出した。図はポツダム会議の会場である。白い服のはスターリンで、スターリンの左五人目はトルーマンで、スターリンの右五人目はアテリーである。

中国为联合国胜利而战

中国始终是抵抗日本的一个有力的支柱，太平洋战争之前中国已经整整打了4年，太平洋战争后，中国与英美荷各盟友并肩作战，中国以其人力、物力协助盟军在中国及印缅战场打击敌人，同样的，中国亦自盟国获得物资的援助，中国与英美盟友在战时的合作，形成二次大战史中光辉的一页。

China's Contribution to Allied Victory

Throughout the war, China remained a pillar of strength against Japanese aggression. The war in China was already four years old when hostilities broke out in the Pacific. From that time China became a full-pledged partner of the United States, Britain, the Netherlands and other Allied powers, fighting the common war shoulder to shoulder.

China's manpower and resources were fully placed at the disposal of her Allies in the fighting against the enemy in both the China and Burma theatres, While China in turn had access to the material assistance given by the Allies.

The unprecedented cooperation among China, the United States and Britain in the fight against the common enemy constituted one of the most glorious pages in the history of World War Ⅱ.

中国は連合国勝利のために戦った

中国は終始日本を抵抗する重要な支柱だった。太平洋戦争まで、中国はすでに四年間も戦争をしてきた。太平洋戦争後、中国はアメリカ、イギリス、オランダなどの連合国と肩を並べて戦った。ビルマの戦場では、敵陣を打撃するのに、中国は人力、物資をもって連合軍に協力をした。同様に中国もまた連合国から物資の援助受けた。共通の敵に対する戦いにおける中国、アメリカ、イギリスの空前の協力は第二次世界大戦の歴史における栄光の一ページのであった。

中国为联合国胜利而战

China's Contribution to Allied Victory

开罗会议

在德国投降以前，中英美领袖蒋中正，丘吉尔，罗斯福于1943年11月22日会议于开罗。此为三国领袖第一次的会晤。会中盟国决定进行长期战争，自日本占领地逐出日本武力，使之无条件投降；战后须剥夺日本所占一切岛屿，满洲，台湾，澎湖群岛归还中国，相当时期后使朝鲜独立。

Cairo Conference

Generalissimo Chiang Kai-shek, Prime Minister Churchill and President Roosevelt for the first time in the war met at Cairo On November 22, 1943, to decide how Japan should sue for peace. China international position was greatly enhanced after this meeting. It was decided at this conference to return Formosa and Manchuria to China when Japan is defeated.

カイロ会議

ドイツ投降した前、中英米三が国の首脳蒋介石、チャーチル、ルーズベルトは1943年11月22日にカイロで会議をした。これは三が国の首脳の初めての会談であった。会議は長期戦争で日本を占領地から追い出して、無条件降参をさせ、戦後には日本に占領された島々を剥奪し、満州、台湾、ポンフー諸島などを中国に返し、そして朝鮮を独立させる内容であった。

水上游击队——雁翎队

河北省白洋淀一带的渔民、猎户等，自发组织起抗日的水上游击队，凭借千顷苇塘，神出鬼没，英勇善战，坚持抗敌七八年，为白洋淀抗日根据地的重建和发展以及支持冀中军民的抗日战争作出了很大贡献。

Water Guerilla —— Yanling-guerilla

The fisherfolks and hunters, settling throughout Baiyangdian in Hebei Province, organized a band of anti-Japanese water guerilla of themselves. They haunted in the reed marshes, fought bravely, and persisted about 8 years, contributing greatly to the development of Baiyangdian Anti-Japanese Base Area and the War of Resistance Against Japan in Central Hebei Area.

水上遊撃隊雁羽隊

河北省白洋淀一帯の漁民、猟師達は自主的に抗日の水上遊撃隊を組織した。生い茂った葦の湖で神出鬼没し、7,8年もの間勇敢に敵と戦った。白洋淀を抗日根拠地としての再建と発展及び冀中軍民の抗日戦争へのサポートに多大な貢献をした。

雁翎队组图
Two Pictures of Yanling-Guerilla
鴈羽隊に関する図

雁翎队的船头会议。
Meeting on board
鴈羽隊は船で会議をする

水上游击队捕获敌官兵5人。
Five enemies captured
水上遊撃隊に捕まれた敵の軍人五名

抗日游击队

在中国抗日战争中，人民游击队一直是重要的抗日武装力量。他们在东北、华北、江南和华南等广大地区不断采用各种积极、灵活的斗争方式打击敌人，很大程度上牵制分散了敌伪的精力，有力地配合了正规军的对敌作战。

Anti-Japanese Guerillas

Anti–Japanese Guerillas were important armed forces during the whole China's War of Resistance Against Japan. They struck the enemy in many active, flexible ways in Northern China and south of Yangtze River. They played an important part in scattering the enemy's strength as well as cooperating with the regular army effectively.

抗日遊撃隊

中国人民の抗日戦争中、遊撃隊は重要な抗日武装の一つである。彼らは東北や黄河中下流地域と長江中下流地域及び華南地区の広い範囲で積極且つ融通のある方法で敵に打撃を与え、敵と傀儡軍を牽制して、よく正規軍の作戦に応援していた。

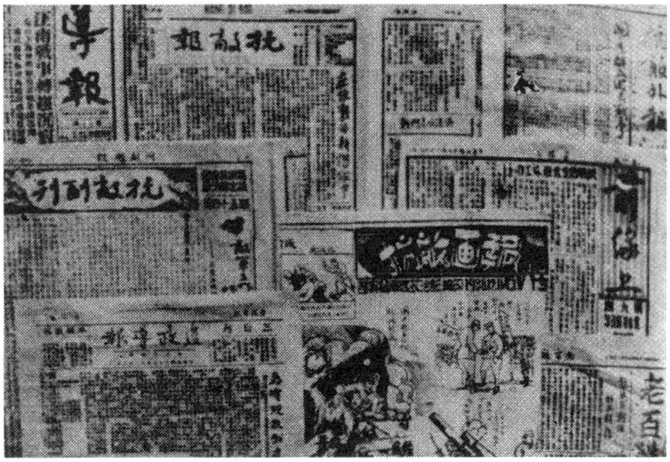

抗日游击队组图
Four Pictures of Anti-Japanese Guerillas
抗日遊撃隊に関する図

山西游击区的民兵
Possemen in Shanxi guerilla zones
山西省遊撃区の地方武装

游击队突袭敌堡
Taking the enemy's fort by surprise
遊撃隊は敵のトーチカに奇襲する

游击队员及战利品
Guerillas and their capture
遊撃隊とその戦利品

华北游击区之油印报
Newspapers distributed in North China guerilla zones
華北遊撃区の新聞紙

抗日的钟声

1942年，抗日战争正处最艰难时期，但每个中国人都坚信抗战必定胜利。河北省平山县下藩松村的普通小脚妇女戎冠秀就是其中的一位。有敌情时、游击队集合时、村民下地生产时，都根据戎冠秀敲响的钟声而行动。她身上所表现出的伟大母性的光辉，使她成为了享誉全国的支前模范。这幅当年才19岁的摄影记者江波拍摄的照片，后来成了传世名作。

Anti-Japanese Bells

In 1942, War of Resistance Against Japan came into the hardest time. Rong Guanxiu, was an ordinary housewoman lived at Pansong village, Pingshan county of Hebei Province. She usually warned the people of the enemy' s advance by ringing the bells. For her maternal spirit, she became a nationally known model in supporting the front. This photo, taken by a young photographer was regarded as a masterpiece later.

抗日の鐘

1942年は抗日戦争の一番辛くて困難な時期だった。しかし全ての中国人は抗戦の勝利を確信していた。河北省平山県下藩松村の普通の纏足女性戎冠秀はその一人であった。敵を感知した時も、遊撃隊員を集合する時も、村民が畑仕事する時も、彼女が鳴らす鐘の音を合図に行動した。彼女から滲み出る偉大な母性の輝きが、彼女を全国に名を轟かす前線支援のモデルにならせ、人々からは「人民軍の母」と親しまれる。この当時19歳の撮影記者江波が撮影した写真は後世まで伝わる名作になった。

游击队的妈妈

卢沟桥事变爆发第二天，一个东北乡下老太太从北平偷偷带回了 8 枝毛瑟枪和 2 枝勃朗宁枪。这些枪成为一支游击队的原始实力和武库，不到一年，它就有了上万条枪。老太太的长子赵侗后来当了这支军队的司令。这位赵老太太后来以“游击队的妈妈”而闻名中外。

Guerilla's Mama

On the following day after the Marco Polo Bridge Incident, an old lady from the countryside of the Northeast brought home 8 Mausers and 2 Browning pistols, and they became the initial arsenal of a Guerilla. Then, the arsenal added up to thousands of guns in less than a year. Zhao Dong, the eldest son of the old lady, became the commander of this guerilla. After that, the old lady went by the name of “Guerilla' s Mama”.

遊撃隊の母

盧溝橋事変勃発の二日目、一人の東北の老婆が北平から密やかにモーゼル銃8丁と白朗寧銃2丁を持ち帰った。これらの銃は遊撃隊の初期の武装となり、一年経たない内に、万を越すほどの銃が増えた。老婆の長男趙侗は後にその部隊の司令となり、その老婆は「遊撃隊の母」として国内外に名声が上がった。

长沙巷战

长沙在抗战中4次遭受敌人的猛攻，国军得地利之助，加以士气旺盛，人民合作，在前3次进攻中均使敌人遭受重大失败而溃退。上为长沙城中，我军与敌巷战。

Street Fight at Changsha

Changsha, the capital of Hunan, was the target of four successive enemy attacks. They were frustrated three times by the heroic defenders of the mountainous town. Above shows city defenders engaging the Japanese in street fighting.

長沙の市街戦

長沙は抗日の戦争中四回も敵の猛攻をうけた。中国軍は有利な地勢を利用して、闘志旺盛、前三回の日本軍の侵攻を打ち破れた。図は長沙市内で我が軍は敵と激しい市街戦をしている現場である。

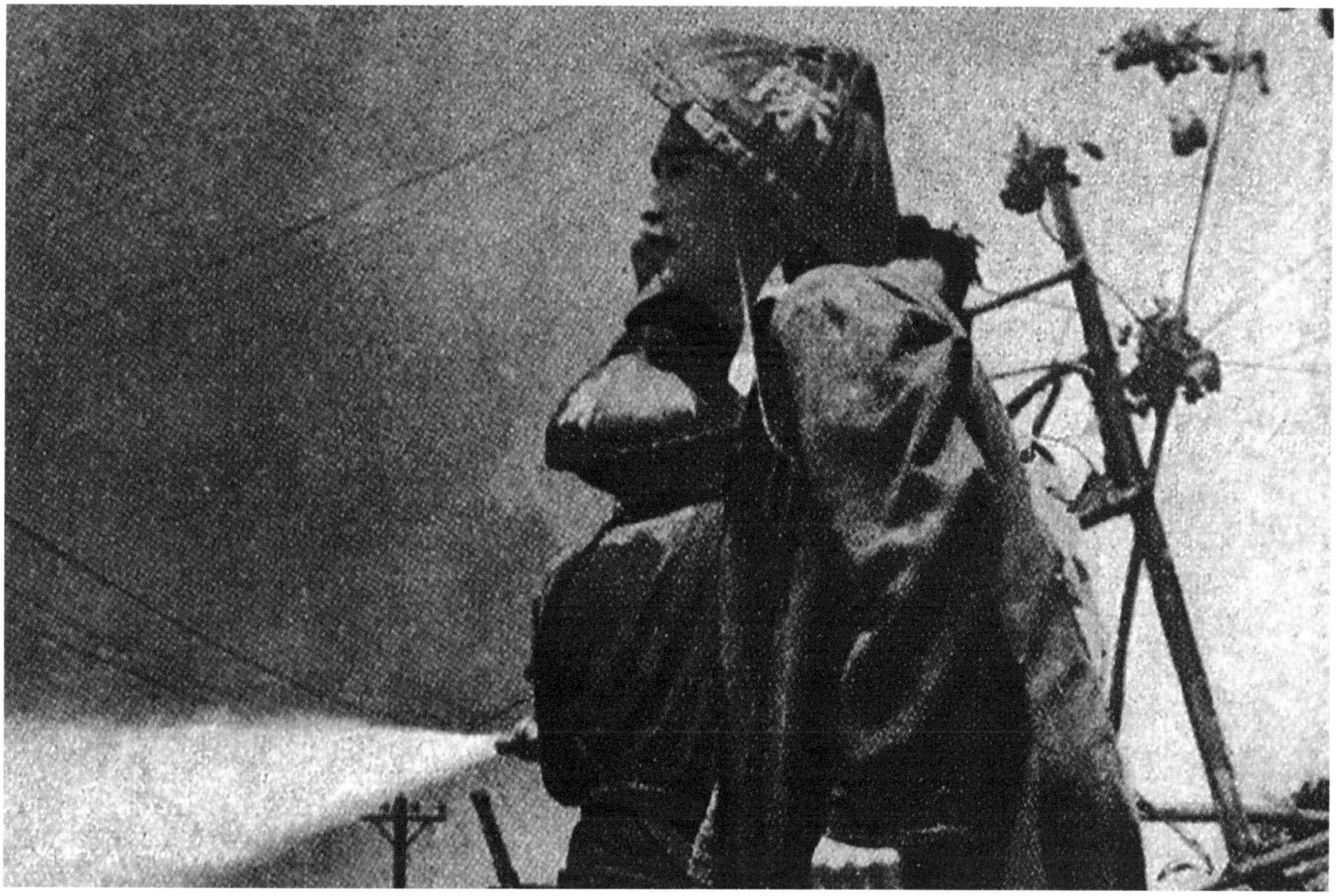

重庆在空袭下
Chungking Under Air Raids
空襲下の重慶

重庆一大悲剧

敌机狂炸下之重庆，于1941年6月6日发生大隧道窒息惨案，数逾万人之避难平民死于大隧道中。彼等因日夜连续空袭，大隧道中空气不足，管理者缺乏经验，致避难者发生骚动，相互倾轧闷毙。

Tragedy at Chunking

More than ten thousand civilians smothered to death in an underground tunnel during the heavy raids in Chungking in June 6, 1941. It was one of the tragedies due to poor administrative work.

重慶の大悲劇

1941年6月6日、日本軍の空爆を受けた重慶にて、防空隧道のなかに避難していた難民一万人以上も窒息で死亡してしまった。これは極悪非道な日本軍がやったもう一件のむごたらしくて見るに忍びない大惨劇であった。

鄂西之战

在鄂西山林中行进之我军，遭遇敌机袭击。鄂西为四川之门户，1941年3月敌抽兵进攻我军阵地，前后6日，敌死伤数千人。

Battle of West Hupeh

Chinese vanguards marching in mountainous western Hupeh were strafed by Japanese bombers. In March 1941, the enemy attacked this direction in an attempt to menace Chungking, but was frustrated with a loss of several thousand lives.

湖北西部の戦い

湖北西部の山林に進行している我が軍は敵の戦闘機の襲撃を遭遇した。湖北西部は四川省に入る門戸だから、1941年3月敵軍が六日かけて我が軍を猛攻した。結局敵側が数千人の死傷者も出た。

常德会战

常德守军在炮火中前进。敌人集结大军10万人（1943年11月）进攻湘西门户常德，我守军在敌机轰炸，大炮猛射下历15日，屹然不动，双方反复冲杀30余次，常德一度失守，卒被克复。此役我阵亡师长3人，敌伤亡近40,000人。

Battle of Changteh

Changteh defenders advanced under enemy fire. The Japanese amassed 100,000 men in the assault of Changteh, the gate to western Hunan. The defenders bathed themselves in blood and cost the Japanese more than 40,000 casualties.

常徳会戦

1943年11月、湖南省西部の門戸である常徳は、日本軍10万人からの進攻を受け、猛烈な空爆や大砲の爆撃に忍び耐え、激しい攻防戦であった。この戦役で我が軍は師団長3人が戦没したが、敵の死傷者も4万人近くある。

飞翔在喜马拉雅山上

中国被封锁后的唯一国际交通线是用运输机飞过喜马拉雅山。一架C—46运输机正在驼峰上飞行。所有飞机均飞至18,000英呎山峰，其中失事之飞机亦甚多。

Over the Hump

When the Japanese blockȧde was at its height, China was linked with the outside world only by the skyway over the Himalayas, known as the "Hump". It was a dangerous flight and many such C—46' s were lost on the snow—capped peaks.

ヒマラヤ山脈の上空を飛翔する

中国は日本に封鎖された後、唯一な国際交通線路は運輸飛行機でヒマラヤ山脈を飛び越えることである。図はC—46運輸機はヒマラヤ山の峰を飛び越えている場面である。墜落した飛行機も数多であった。

昆仑关大捷

我军夺回昆仑关，热烈欢呼。日军为切断我国西南国际路线，由广西钦州防城攻占南宁及军略要地昆仑关（1939年）。我军于12月18日开始反攻，于31日确实占领昆仑关，敌军一旅团全军覆没。

Victory of Kunlungkwan

In the later phase of the war, the Japanese attempt to cut the Chinese line of communication from the southwest. They started from the coast and penetrated deep into Kwangsi. The Chinese counter-attacked on Dec. 18, 1939 and recaptured the important mountain pass, Kunlungkwan, by the end of the month.

崑崙関大勝

図は我が軍は崑崙関を奪回した後熱烈に歓呼している場面である。日本軍は我が南西の国際交通線路を切断するために、1937年広西省の南寧と軍事要地の崑崙関を占領した。我が軍は12月18日から反撃し始め、31日崑崙関を奪回した。その戦役で敵の一つの旅団が全員戦死した。

国军远征缅甸

日军为彻底打击西南亚英军，切断我国际路线，于1942年春进犯缅甸；国军应英国之请，入缅协助英军作战（上图）；敌我数度激战。后以敌军自缅甸东部侧攻腊戍，遂与英军退入印度。

Chinese Expedition Army in Burma

When the Japanese penetrated into Burma, the Chinese national forces answered the call of the British High Command to reinforce the meagre British garrisons. But the Japanese took Lashio by surprise and forced the Allied forces to retreat into India.

我が軍はビルマへ遠征する

日本軍は南西アジアにいるイギリス軍を打撃し、中国の国際線路を切断するために、1942年の春ビルマに侵入した。我が軍はイギリス軍の要請に応じビルマに入って英軍と協力しあって戦いをした。

反攻缅甸

中国军队在1个月包围巨战后进入八莫。国军于1943年10月在印训练完毕，开始对缅甸反攻，在史迪威将军领导下开始艰难的丛林战争，费时1年又2个月，国军在滇缅边境会师。

Counter-attack at Burma

The general offensive in Burma opened with the entering of Bhamo. Newly-trained Chinese troops, under the leadership of General Stilwell fought for more than fourteen months in the tropical jungles to join force with the attacking force from west Yunnan at the Sino-Burma border.

ビルマへ反撃する

1943年10月中国軍隊はインドでの訓練を終え、ビルマへの反撃を開始した。スティルウェル将軍の指揮の下で一年又二か月をかけて、苦難に満ちているジャングル戦争を行った。

日军在缅甸损失重大

中国军队持枪路过日军尸体，进入一新克复之缅甸城市。日军在中国反攻战中，死33,082人，伤42,760人。日本封锁中国大陆之梦，宣告破灭。

Japanese Losses in Burma

Chinese army re-enter a Burmese city. Japanese losses in Burma amounted to 33,082 dead and 42,760 wounded. The Japanese blockade of the Chinese mainland was broken.

日本軍ビルマでの損失

図は銃を持っている中国の軍人が日本軍の死体の横を通っている。日本軍はビルマで中国から猛烈な反撃に食われ、33,082人が死亡、42,760人が負傷した。日本の中国大陸を封鎖する夢は完全に破滅してしまった。

赤手成大业

四川50万纯朴的中国农民的一部分，拖着碾石机，在压平新建的成都机场，天空翱翔着一架军用飞机；这是中国人民参加联合国作战最好的写照。在中国最前线和后方，无数的大小基地，都是由农工胼手胝足来建造的。成都B—29空中堡垒的大基地，可以直飞日本轰炸。

Gigantic Construction by Bare Hands

Hundreds of thousands of Chinese peasants offered their share in the holy war of resistance. They built airstrips with their bare hands for B—29's to bomb Japan from Chengtu.

素手で大事業になる

図は四川省の純朴な農民たちが石をひき砕く轆轤を引っ張って、成都の新しい軍用飛行場を建設している光景である。空に一機の軍用飛行機が飛んでいる。成都はB—29軍用機の基地であり、そこから直接日本へ飛んで空爆することができる。

由成都基地飞炸台湾

由新建之成都基地起飞之B-29超级堡垒已飞临台湾上空（下部黑色处），前机弹门大开准备投弹，时在1944年10月盟军登陆菲律宾之前。

Bomb Formasa from Chengtu

From newly built base at Chengtu, capital of Szechuan, these Super fortresses are flying Formosa. The Smash was preliminary to Allied landings in the Philippines in October 1944.

成都の基地から台湾へ空爆する

新しくできた成都空港から離陸したB—29軍用機は既に台湾の上空まで飛んで来た。前機の爆弾の門はもう開けられ、ダイナマイトを落とす準備ができている。時は1944年10月連合軍のフィリピンを上陸する前であった。

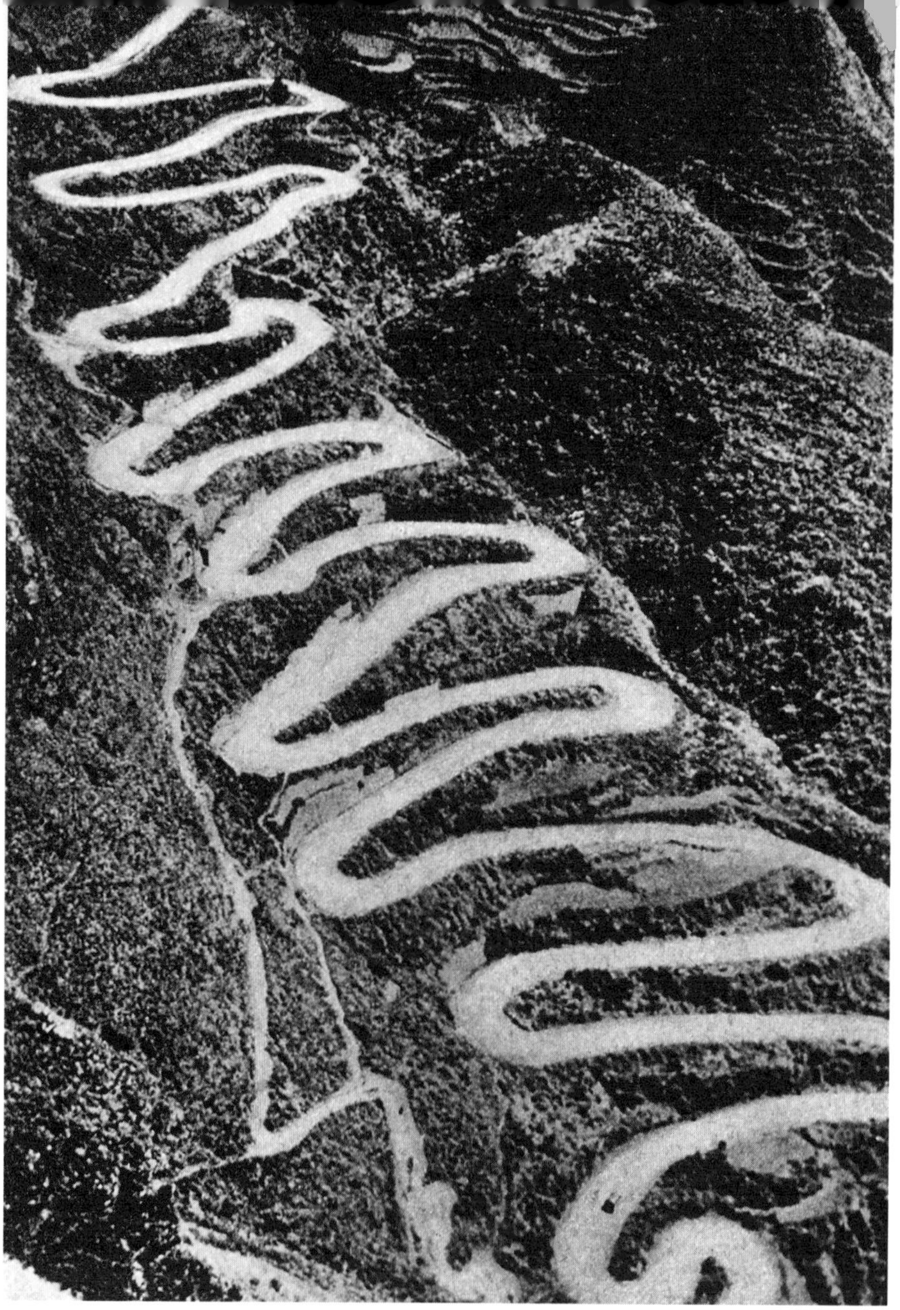

史迪威公路

史迪威路的完成，是一首壮丽的史诗，该路起自印度阿萨密的雷多，经过中缅边界而到昆明，全长1,044哩，是由中美军队一边作战，一边修路完成的。盟军在畹町会师（1945年1月20日），全路亦即畅通，打破了日军对华3年的封锁。图为该路在中国境内之二十四拐高度斜坡。

Stiwell Road

The construction of the Stilwell Road which ran 1,044 miles, from Ledo in India' s Assam to Kunming, was an epic of human courage and sacrifice. It was built under heavy Japanese attack and was completed on Jan. 20, 1945, when the two forces met from the east and the west at Wanting.

スティルウェル道路

スティルウェル道路の建設は雄壮で美しい史詩とも言える。道路はインドのリドから始まり、中国とビルマの国境を経て昆明に至り、全長は1,044マイル。図はこの道路の中国国境内にある一番険しい部分「二十四カーブ」と呼ばれている。

中印油管

由印度加尔各答经阿萨密至缅北再至昆明之中印油管，于1944年底完成。该油管口径6英吋，绵延千哩。从此飞机用油可不靠飞机在“驼峰”运送。图为由缅甸至中国第一次的运输队在油管旁加油。战后此油管即行废弃。

Liveline of Oil

An oil pipe line was laid before the end of 1944, from Calcutta to Kunming, via Assam and northern Burma, which ran more than a thousand miles. The pipe had a diameter, of six inches which would enable the easy flow of oil for aviation uses. It was abandoned after the end of war.

中国—インドのオイルパイプ

インドのカルカッタからビルマの北部を経て昆明に至る中国—インドのオイルパイプは、1944年の年末に完成したものである。パイプの直径は6インチで、長さは千マイル以上にものぼる。図はビルマから初めて中国に入った運輸トラックはオイルパイプからガソリンを入れている。

盟军向仰光进攻

英国十四军的印度山炮团，在中国军队打通滇缅路后，向仰光挺进，于夜间发射37糎炮，阻止敌人的反扑。

Back to Rangoon

The Indian Artillery units of the British 14th Army are fighting hard on their way back to Rangoon. These 37 mm mountain pieces were widely used at night to stop enemy counter-offensives.

連合軍はヤンゴンを進攻する

イギリスの第14軍団のインド山砲団は、中国軍隊が中国ビルマ道路を打開した後にヤンゴンへ進んでいる途中、敵の反撃を阻止するために37ミリの大砲で発砲している。

血战太平洋

1942年秋天起，盟军在西南太平洋开始对日反攻，从所罗门群岛起，先是逐岛推进，继而是越岛进攻，日军工事异常强固，仅在吉尔贝特岛塔拉瓦一战，美军即损失3,000人，其他塞班，关岛，雷伊泰，硫磺岛。盟军均付过极重大的血的代价，战争愈近日本本土，战斗愈形激烈，日本像疯子一样的抵抗。1945年4月盟军在大硫球登陆，日军以神风攻击队作自杀攻击，盟国舰队与塞班大硫球起飞之空中堡垒轰炸机猛炸东京，横滨各大城市，使成一片火海，5月仅在东京，两日间投弹10,000吨，可见一斑。盟军已完全掌握日本海空权。

Bloody Fighting in the Pacific

In the autumn of 1942 the Allies had commenced their counter-offensive in the Southeastern Pacific. Starting from the Solomon Islands the advancing Allies took practically everything that lay in the path of their progress meantime accelerating their speed of progress.

The Japanese defences, it was to be admitted were exceptionally strong. In the fighting at the Gilbert Islands, for instance, the Allies lost 3,000 men. In other places, like Saipan, Guam, Leyte, Iwo Jima, great sacrifices in life were also offered by the Allied forces before the enemy was brought to book.

As the war approached the Japanese mainland the fighting increased in fierceness. The Japanese became maddened in the face of approaching collapse and offered unbelievably stubborn resistance. When the Allies in April 1945 reached the Okinawa Islands, the Japanese even resorted to a final desperate attempt to save themselves with the use of "suicidal" attack squads from Tokyo aimed at the destruction of Allied naval units.

Allied planes based at Saipan. Okinawa, and on carriers intensified their bombings of Tokyo, Yokohoma, and other Japanese cities and seas of fire were virtually caused to rise in the attacked areas. In two days in May 1945, for instance, 10,000 tons of explosives were dropped on Tokyo alone. The Allies had complete mastery in the sky and on the sea.

太平洋の血戦

1942年秋から、連合軍は南西大西洋から日本への反撃を始めた。ソロモン諸島から始まって、まずは一つ一つの島に推進し、そして「島跳戦」という作戦で進攻した。日本軍の防衛工事は非常に強く、ギルバート諸島の戦いだけで、アメリカ軍は、三千人の損失も出した。他にはサイパン、グアム、レイテ、硫黄島でも連合軍が大きな損失を負った。戦争が日本の本土に近づくに連れ、激しさを増した。日本は狂ったように抵抗を続けた。1945年4月、連合軍は沖縄諸島に上陸した。日本は「神風特攻隊」を使って自滅的な攻撃を始めた。連合軍の艦隊とサイパン、沖縄諸島からの空中爆撃機は東京、横浜各大都市を火の海に化したほど激しく爆撃攻撃を与えた。五月に東京だけに対して僅か二日間で一万トンのもの爆薬を落とした。連合軍は完全に日本の海と空を掌握した。

血战太平洋

Bloody Fighting in the Pacific

给东京的礼物

2,000磅重一个的炸弹，在布肯维尔一军火库前排成列阵，等待轰炸机来临，向前行进。这些炸弹将一一投向日本目标。

Gift for Tokyo

These two-thousand-pounders were lined up on Bougainville island awaiting to be loaded on the bombers which would loose them on Japan.

東京への「おみやげ」

重さ2千ポンドの爆弾は火薬倉庫の前に列に並んで、空爆機に載せるのを待っている。これらの爆弾は一つ一つ日本に投下するつもりのものである。

夜战所罗门群岛

1942年秋天盟军从西南太平洋向日军反攻，先自所罗门群岛开始，攻占瓜达康纳尔与杜拉吉，丛林战争持续经年；1943年11月再攻所岛最后据点的布肯维尔岛。上为美巡洋舰主炮轰击日军布卡机场。

Solomon Island Lit-up at Night

In the autumn of 1942, the Allied forces started their counter-attack from the Solomon Islands. Guadalcanal, Tulage, and Bougainville fell one after the other, but only after fierce fighting. Above, main batteries of an American cruiser open fire upon Buka airfield, Bougainville.

ソロモン諸島の夜戦

1942年の秋、連合軍は南西太平洋から日本軍に反撃を始めた。ソロモン諸島からすごしつつ前進して、苦しいジャングル戦争も長く続いた。図は1943年11月にソロモン諸島の最後の拠点を進攻して、巡洋艦から日本の空港に大砲で攻撃している光景である。

伞兵降落新几内亚

西南太平洋盟军在1943年6月30日开始反攻新几内亚，伞兵在烟幕掩护下，降落于马甘山谷，与雷区盟军会合进攻。此为盟军在太平洋广泛应用伞兵之第一次。

Paratroop Attack in New Guinea

Paratroops were used for the first time in the south-western Pacific when Allied forces counter-attacked near Markham Valley and Lae in New Guinea.

パラシュートはニューギニアに降りる

1942年6月30日、南西太平洋の連合軍はニューギニアへの反撃を始めた。パラシュートは煙幕の掩護でマカン谷に降りて、地面の連合軍と合流して敵を攻撃する。これは連合軍が太平洋戦区において始めてパラシュートをつかった作戦であった。

空中增援

盟军占据拜亚克岛（罗姆佛）后，交通线为日军切断，乃由空中输送降落伞队增援。

Reinforced from the Air

The Allies' line of supply was cut by strong Japanese forces after the Allies had successfully landed at Biak. Reinforce had to be rushed through the air.

空中増援

連合軍はバイアーク島を占領した後、交通供給路線は日本軍に切断された、仕様なく空中からパラシュートを運んできて増援する。

夜攻所罗门群岛

所罗门群岛的全部攻占，费时年余。1943年10月21日之夜，盟军主力舰的5英吋巨炮，在作攻击前的怒吼。

Under Cover of Night

The occupation of the Solomons took the Allies more than a year. Picture shows a battleship shelling the Japanese garrison in the night of Oct. 21, 1943.

ソロモン諸島へ夜の攻撃

ソロモン諸島を完全に占領したのは、一年以上もかかった。図は1943年10月21日の夜、連合軍の主力艦に据え付けられている5インチの巨砲は吼えている。

野猫出奔

野猫式机为美国海军战斗机，在美航空母舰列克星敦的甲板上，野猫听到敌人来袭，直向空中奔去应战。

Hellcat Run Wild

American fighter Hellcat roar off the flight deck of the"Bellghost"——the U.S.S. Lexington. They are answering the call to engage the attacking enemy in the air.

野猫の走り

「野猫」式戦闘機はアメリカ海軍の戦闘機である。アメリカの航空母艦リキシントーン号に停留している「野猫」式戦闘機は敵の来襲の際に直ちに応戦に空へ飛んでいく。

本克希尔之厄运

美航空母舰本克希尔号在大硫球附近作战，不幸为日本自杀飞机撞击，数秒钟后全舰变为一团黑烟，上图系自美舰巴丹号上所摄之本克希尔号燃烧情况。

Sinking of Bunker Hill

The American Air-craft Carrier "Bunker Hill" was unfortunately hit by a Japanese Kamikaze plane on the high seas off Okinawa. In a few seconds it was entirely engulfed in thick smoke. The picture was taken on board U.S.S. Bataan.

バンクシール号の悪運

米軍の航空母艦バンクシール号は琉球の海上で戦っているところ、日本の自殺飛行機に空から衝突され、数秒間で軍艦からすごい黒煙が巻き騰がった。図は米軍の航空母艦パータン号から撮ったバンクシール号の燃焼している場面である。

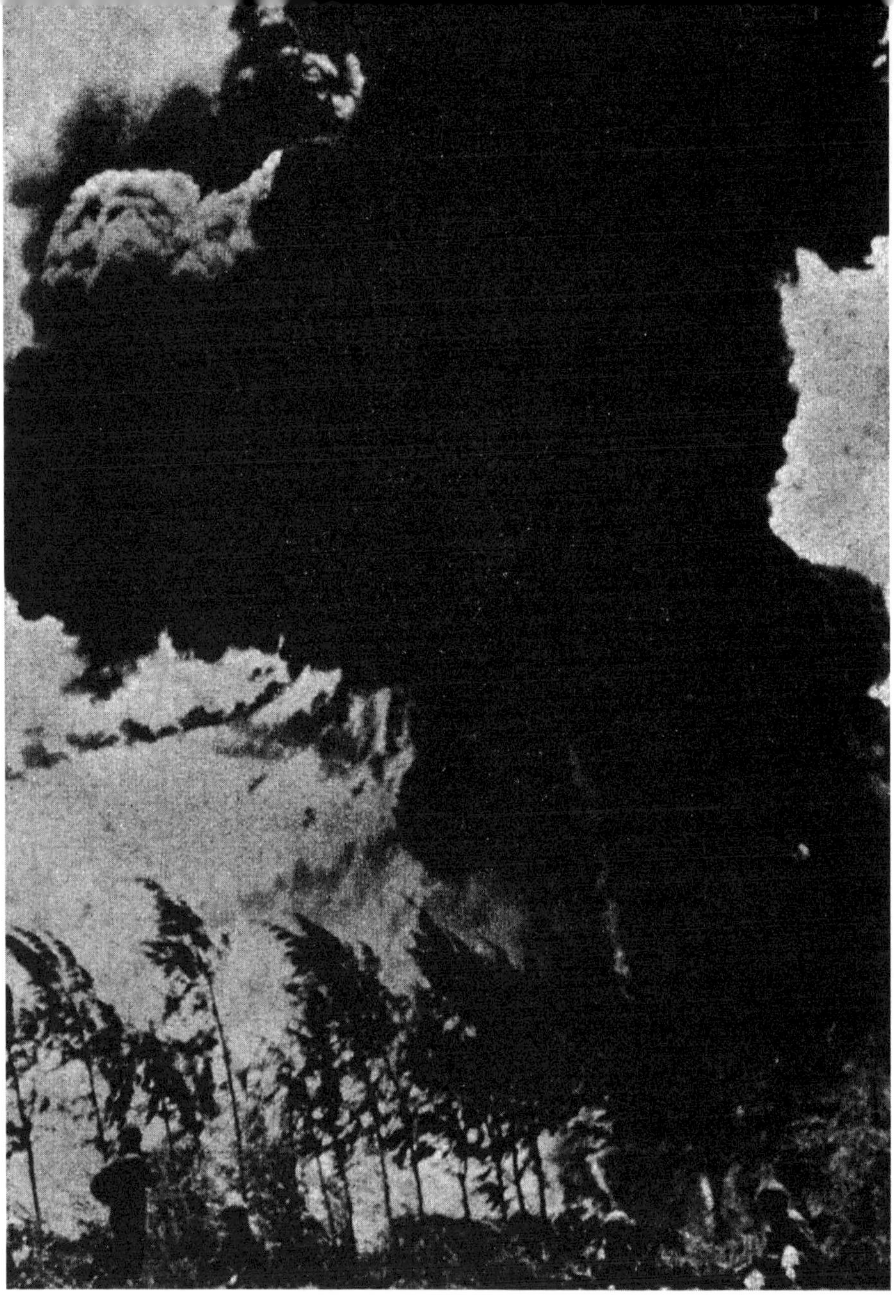

火山爆发

马利亚纳群岛之狄宁岛于盟军进攻中，一日本军火库被美国轰炸机炸中，火药像火山似地爆发着，喷出浓密的烟火。狄宁岛于1944年8月1日落于盟军之手。

Burning a Volcano

A dump of ammunitions was blasted by Allied planes on Tinin Island of the Marianas. This tiny Island was taken by American marines on Aug. 1, 1944.

火山爆発

連合軍はマリアナ諸島のディニン島において進攻中で、日本軍の一つの火薬倉庫は米軍の戦闘機から落とした爆弾に命中され、倉庫なかの火薬は火山爆発のように爆発した。

吉尔贝特群岛之战

美军于1943年11月20日进攻吉尔贝特群岛，在塔拉瓦和梅金两岛登陆，塔拉瓦有3,000日本海军陆战队防守，有坚固的炮台，美机曾轰炸炮击，但在登陆时，还是遇到日军疾雨似的炮火，初批登陆美军，仅有少数得免于死。上为美军陆战队由海岸猛攻机场。

Battle of the Gilbert Islands

The Americans timed their attack on the Gilbert Islands on Nov. 20, 1943. Before they landed, the Americans attacked the defenders from the air and the sea for several days. Now they are attacking again on land.

ギルバート諸島の戦い

1943年11月20日、アメリカ軍がギルバート諸島への進攻をはじめた。タラワとマキン両島に上陸した。初めて上陸したアメリカの兵士は日本軍からの暴風雨のような砲弾銃弾に食われ、生き残た兵士は僅かしかなかった。図はアメリカの海軍陸戦隊が海岸から空港に向かて猛攻している場面である。

塔拉瓦火网

塔拉瓦3天的苦战，美军在日军炽烈的火网下争夺一个个的据点，日军逐渐被迫至西端。日军最后曾展开一次自杀性的攻击，除一极小部分外，大部被歼灭。在塔拉瓦，梅金，阿比玛玛三岛上被歼日军达5,700人。

The Hell of Tarawa

It was like hell in those three Tarawa days. Numberless U.S. marines fell before the Japanese fire. But Hirohito also lost 5,700 men in Tarawa, Makin and Abemama.

タラワ火の網

米軍はタラワで日本軍からの猛烈な抵抗を受けながら、三日間の苦戦を経て、一つ一つの拠点をめぐって奪い合って、徐徐に日本軍を西側まで追い詰めた。タラワ、マキンとアビママ三つの島で殲滅された日本軍は5,700人にものぼった。

美军损失在塔拉瓦

塔拉瓦67小时的战争，美军损失两营约3,000人，为太平洋战争代价极高的一次。这次的代价却换得进击马绍尔和马利亚纳等群岛的基地。

American Losses at Tarawa

In the battle of Tarawa that lasted 67 hours, American losses amounted to 3,000, an all-time high. But it opened the door to the Marshall and Mariana Islands.

米軍はタラワでの損失

タラワで67時間の激しい戦闘により、米軍は3千人も戦没した。これは太平洋戦争においてアメリカ軍の極高い代償を払った戦役であった。

瓜加林之战

马绍尔群岛的瓜加林环状珊瑚岛，为日军空军基地之一，上为由航舰起飞之盟机炸瓜加林之罗伊岛上日军之建筑物，引起白烟。1944 年 2 月 1 日盟军占领该岛。

Kwajalein Atoll

Kwajalein Atoll of the Marshall Islands is a strong Japanese air-base. American bombers are doing their best to pave the way for the landing marines. Allied forces captured the island on Feb. 1, 1944.

クワジャリンの戦い

マーシャル諸島に所属するクワジャリン環状の珊瑚島は日本軍の空軍基地の一つである。図は連合軍の爆撃機がクワジャリン島にある日本軍の建物を爆撃することによって白い煙は巻き騰がる場面である。この島は1944 年 2 月 1 日に連合軍に占領された。

那摩尔日军投降

日军于那摩尔岛被美军围攻下举手投降，另一日兵正从穴中伸出他的头。那摩尔岛为瓜加林珊瑚岛之一，日军分布了8,000人，有极坚固的工事，在未登陆前美军用飞机巨炮狂炸3天，登陆之后美军用火箭炮与火焰喷射器来毁灭岛上的强固防务。

Japanese Surrender on Namur

Before they landed, the Americans had bombed and bombarded Namur of the Kwajaleins for three days. Now the Japanese defenders are walking out of their foxholes to surrender.

ナミュールの日本軍が投降

図はナミュールの日本軍が米軍に包囲され余儀なく手を挙げて投降する場面である。ナミュール島はクワジャリン珊瑚諸島の一つであり、8千人の日本軍が守備しており、米軍は上陸後ロケット砲や火炎噴射タンクで日本軍の頑丈な陣地工事を粉砕した。

陨星坠落

中太平洋马利亚纳群岛，一架日本轰炸机图攻击一艘美国航舰，被高射炮击中，拖着烟与火的尾巴，正向海中落去。

Meteor of Death

Hit by U.S. Navy anti-aircraft fire, this Japanese bomber is trailing smoke and flame to its end, near an American escort carrier in the Central Pacific off the Marianas.

りゅうせいの墜落

太平洋のマリアナ諸島で、日本軍の爆撃機が米軍の軍艦を攻撃中、対空砲に撃たれ火と煙を付いてまま海へ墜落している。

塞班滩头一瞥

马利亚纳群岛日军，为保全塞班滩头作自杀性之反攻，卒为盟军优势炮火一一击倒。上为塞班答拉班港湾附近被击毙之日军及被毁之美军坦克。

Beachhead at Saipan

Counter-attacking along a beach in a last suicidal attempt to save Saipan, these Japanese soldiers were mowed down by superior U.S. fighting forces.

サイパン島浜辺の概観

サイパン島を守るために、マリアナ諸島に駐在している日本軍は自殺的な反撃をしようとしたが、連合軍の強い砲火に食われ、狙撃されてしまった。図はサイパン島タラバン港湾辺りに射殺された日本軍兵士及び壊された米軍の戦車である。

轰击关岛
Bomb Guam
グアム爆撃

火攻日军

塞班日本守军尽藏在很深的洞穴中，虽加攻迫，亦不出洞，美军遂以喷火坦克予以正面火攻。日军在山穴中抵抗了18天，才被赶到北端一个袋形阵地。

Attack with Liquid Fire

The Saipan defenders held on desperately in their foxholes and caves for eighteen days. Flame-throwing tanks had to be used to end resistance.

日本軍に火攻め

サイパン島の日本軍守備隊は皆洞窟に隠れ、迫られても出てこないから、米軍は噴火タンクで正面から火で攻める作戦をとった。日本軍は洞窟の中に18日間も抵抗したが、結局島の北部に追い込まれた。

塞班日军全员战死

塞班首府格拉班于美军炮轰后，陆战队在火中迅速推进，进行太平洋战场第一次之巷战。塞班之战，惨烈万分，美军掩埋日军尸体19,793人。此役日本守军“全员战死”，东京震动，东条内阁因之辞职。

The Flaming Capital of Saipan

In flaming Garapan, the Capital of Saipan, U.S. marines moved fast in their first Pacific street fighting. Later, 19,793 Japanese bodies were buried; no Japanese survived. It shocked Tokyo and caused the downfall of the Tojo cabinet.

サイパン島の日本軍が全員戦死した

米軍はサイパン島の首府であるグラバンを爆撃後、陸軍は速やかに進め、太平洋戦場において始めての市街戦を行った。サイパン島の戦闘は極惨烈で、米軍は19,793名の日本軍兵士の死体を埋めた。この戦闘で日本軍が「全員戦死」という大失敗で、東京の政治界も揺り動かされ，東条内閣はこれで辞職してしまった。

塞班基地

日军于盟军登陆塞班时，由菲律宾调集海空军增援塞班，一日折机400架，船舰亦多被炸。美军据有塞班据点后，立刻修建超级空中堡垒之大基地，准备进袭东京。图为空中堡垒一架在塞班新建基地被日机炸中起火。塞班距东京1,500哩，适在空中堡垒航程之内。

Saipan Base

The Japanese military authorities tried all means to keep the Allies from using this valuable base, which is 1,500 miles from Tokyo, within the radius of B-29's. A B-29 hit by Japanese bomb in the new Saipan base.

サイパン基地

連合軍はサイパンに上陸した時に、日本軍はフィリピンから海軍を調達して応援に来たが、一日だけで、400機の戦闘機も撃落され、数多く戦艦も爆撃された。米軍はサイパンを占領した後、たちまち、スーパー空中堡塁と言われた基地を作り、東京へ進攻の準備を急いだ。図は空中堡塁に待機している米軍の飛行機は日本軍の爆弾に命中され炎上している場面である。サイパン島は東京から1,500マイル離れ、日本への攻撃できる距離である。

菲律宾海战

1944年10月日军为截击在菲律宾中部登陆之美军并破坏其供应线，出动船舰作战；第一次菲律宾海战两天，损失极轻航舰3艘，油船2艘，飞机402架；第二次菲律宾海战日舰伤沉58艘，为盟国1944年空前大胜利。上为二次大海战中美舰甘贝湾号在日舰队炮击中。

Battle of the Philippine Sea

The Japanese Imperial Navy came out in force for the last time in the two battles of the Philippines. Their appearance ended in complete failure, which helped to speed the end of the war. Picture shows U.S.S. Gambier Bay under Japanese fire.

フィリピン海戦

1944年10月、日本軍はフィリピン中部から上陸した米軍を狙撃する為に、戦艦を派遣した。第一回のフィリピン海戦は二日間に渡り、日本側は小型戦艦3隻、タンカー船2隻、飛行機402機が損した。第二回のフィリピン海戦は日本の戦艦は58隻も損傷あるいは沈没した。これは連合軍が1944年において空前の勝利だった。図は第二回の海戦中、米軍の戦艦は日本の軍艦に爆撃された場面である。

进攻土鲁克

盟国B-24解放式机群自马绍尔群岛基地起飞前往轰炸中太平洋加罗林群岛海军基地土鲁克。土鲁克珊瑚岛珊瑚广大而又深，足以停泊日本整个舰队，1944年10月中旬，已有四分之三为盟军占据。

Attacking Truk

These Liberators are shown on route from their base in the Marshall Islands to attack Truk, the Japanese base in the heart of central Pacific Caroline Islands. The Truk atoll lagoon is large and deep enough to hold the entire Japanese fleet.

トルックの進攻

図は連合軍のB-24式飛行機群はマーシャル諸島の基地から離陸、太平洋中部のトルックにある海軍基地へ向かって飛んでいる場面である。1944年10月中旬頃、島の四分の三は既に連合軍に占領された。

掩护登陆明多罗岛

盟军于1944年12月15日登陆明多罗岛，一艘美驱逐舰掩护登陆，炮手注视天空，审视头上之飞机。5吋口径巨炮两尊及高射炮均准备发射。登陆明多罗后距马尼拉仅150哩。

Escorts Landing at Mindoro

The gun crews of a U.S. Navy cruiser covering allied landings on the island of Mindoro, Dec. 15, 1944, scan the skies in an effort to identify a plane overhead. The landing placed the Allies within 150 miles of Manila.

ミンドロ島の上陸を掩護する

連合軍は1944年12月15日、ミンドロ島に上陸した。図は一隻の米軍の駆逐艦は上陸を掩護して、砲手は空を見上げて、飛んでいる敵機を監視し、直径5インチの二つの巨大な大砲と対空砲は発射の準備をしている場面である。ミンドロに上陸すればマニラまで僅か150マイルの距離になる。

盟军登陆明多罗被袭

日本轰炸机攻击在明多罗登陆之运输舰队，救急船上之炮手正仰视来袭敌机，其后之登陆艇着火。盟军不顾敌人之攻击，仍于1944年12月14日在菲律宾北部岛屿登陆。该处战事开展，得以建立若干机场，用以攻击吕宋岛之日军。

Attacked off Mindoro

Landing crews were under attack of heavy Japanese bombs. Despite this, the liberation forces landed On Dec. 14, 1944, to make several airstrips available to U.S. Planes from which to attack the Japanese on Luzon.

連合軍はミンドロ島に上陸する際に襲撃された

日本軍の爆撃機はミンドロ島に上陸しようとしている運輸船を攻撃した。急救船の砲手は攻撃に来た敵機を見上げ、その後ろの上陸艇が炎上している。連合軍は敵の攻撃も顧みず、1944年12月14日、フィリピン北部の島に上陸成功した。そこで戦闘を繰り広げられ、ルソン島の日本軍を攻撃為に、空港も建設した。

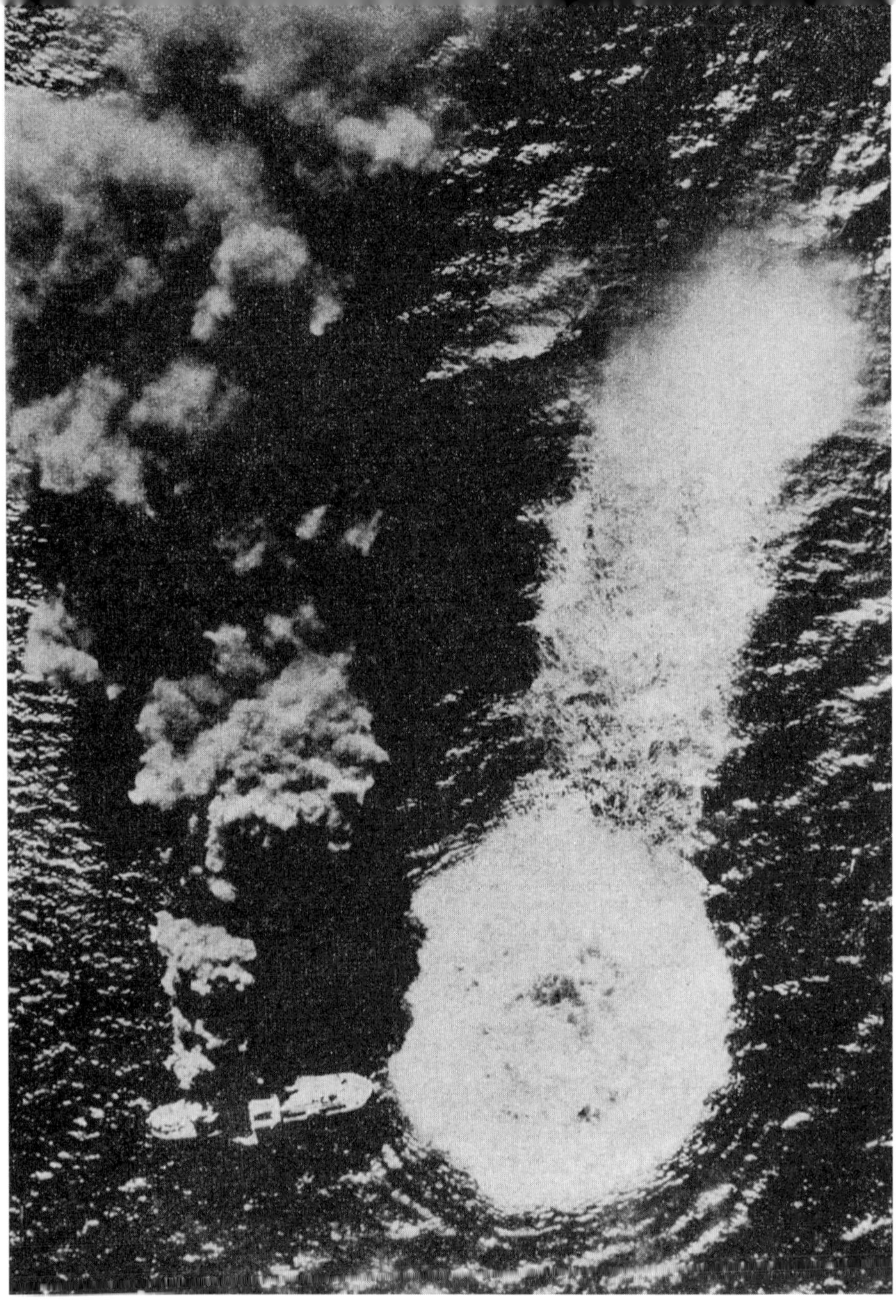

吕宋日船起火

日本商船一艘1945年在吕宋西北岸为美国航舰飞机炸中，发出一阵阵黑烟，另有一弹落于舰旁引起巨波。美第三舰队此次进击吕宋，沉敌舰12艘，毁14艘，打落及损伤敌机28架。盟军于1月9日登陆吕宋。

Japanese Ship Afire near Luzon

A Japanese merchant ship off Luzon sends up clouds of smoke after suffering a direct hit by one bomb from a U.S. plane. A huge wave was made by the explosion of another bowb.

ルソン島日本船の炎上

1945年、一隻の日本の商船はルソン島西北の岸辺で米軍の軍艦に爆撃され、黒い煙を巻き騰がっている。又、爆弾は船の傍に落ちて大きい波がはね上げられた。米軍の第三艦隊が今度ルソン島を攻撃したの戦果は、敵の軍艦12隻を撃沈し、14隻を損傷させ、28機の飛行機を撃落した。連合軍はやっと1月9日にルソン島の上陸は成功した。

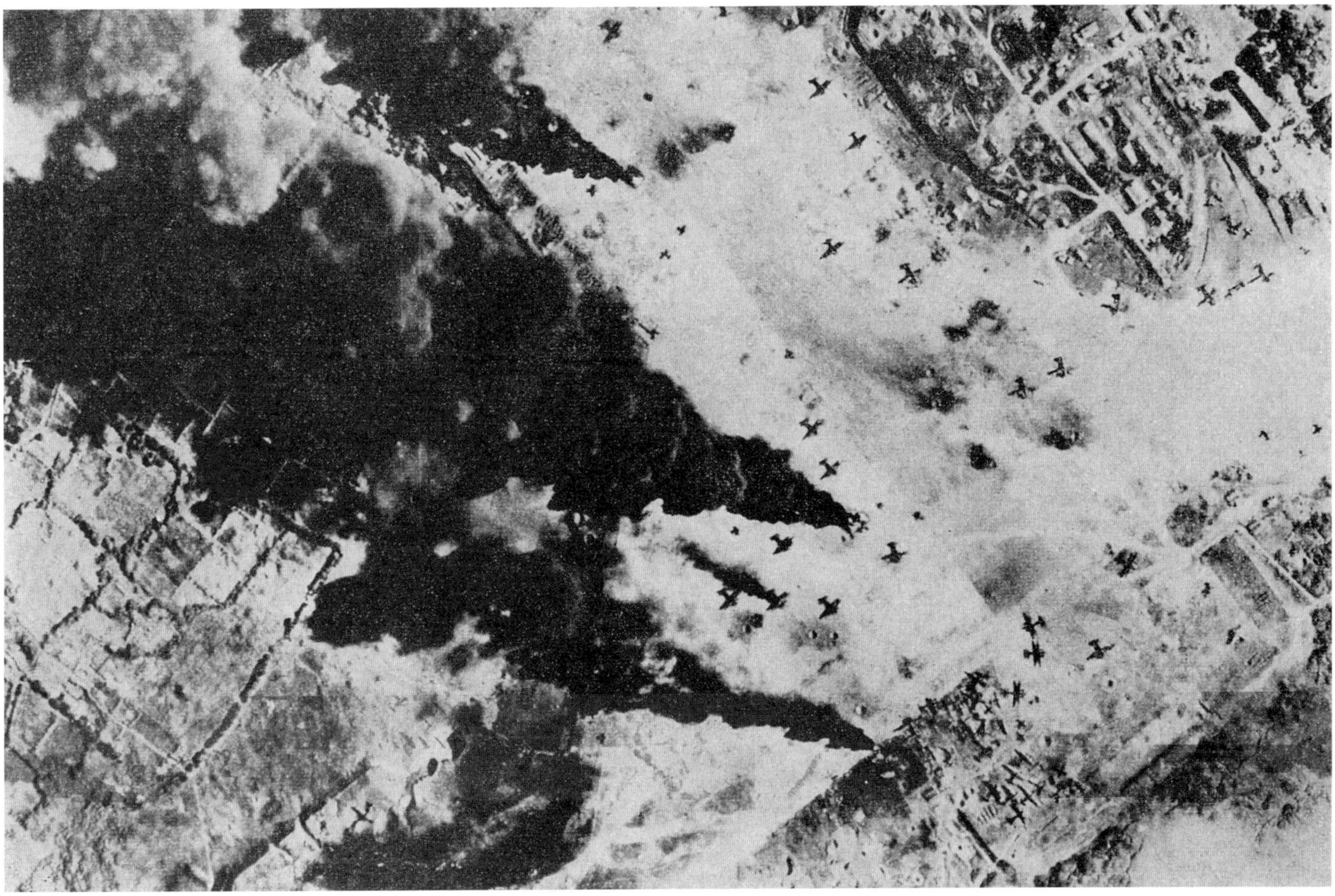

轰炸硫磺岛

火山群岛之一的硫磺岛，机场上停着无数的日本军用机，像水上的鸭子一般正等待美国第七航空队的轰炸，若干飞机已被炸中，冒出浓烟。这是登陆硫磺岛的前奏。

Bombing of Iwo Jima

Iwo Jima of the Volcano Islands was subjected to the severest bombing before marines landed there. The numerous duck-like planes show the importance attached by the Japanese to this tiny island.

硫黄島の爆撃

火山島の一つの硫黄島に待機している日本軍の飛行機は空港で米軍第七航空隊の爆撃を待っているような状態である。幾つの飛行機は既に撃中され、濃い煙が出てきた。これは硫黄島上陸の前奏である。

向硫磺岛前进

美陆战队于1945年2月18日登陆火山岛之硫磺岛，成队之水陆坦克，乘风破浪，冲向黑烟笼罩之滩头。停于岸边之巡洋舰排炮阵阵向雷钵山发射，以控制硫磺岛南部高地，该地经肉搏后于2月22日占领。

Objective, Iwo Jima

A wave of amphibian LVT's cuts through the Pacific toward the smoke-covered beach of Iwo Jirna. A cruiser (background, left) stands offshore pouring salvo after salvo into Mt. Suribachi, dominating height of this volcano island.

硫黄島へ前進

米軍の陸軍は1945年2月18日に、火山島の硫黄島に上陸した。列を編成した水陸両用のタンクは危険に恐れず勇敢に前進し、黒い煙に包まれた浜辺に進攻している。岸辺に停泊している巡洋艦から一斉に発砲し、これは硫黄島南部高地をコントロールする為の戦闘である。2月22日、激しい戦いを経てついに米軍に占領された。

硫磺岛登陆

由全部久经沙场之精兵组成的美国陆战队第四师，于1945年2月18日在东京东南750哩的硫磺岛登陆。这是盟军在太平洋最艰苦的一次登陆战，日军尽藏山中，居高临下，对准海滩登陆美军射击，陆战队及登陆艇赴汤蹈火似的向滩头仰攻，损失十分重大。

Landing at Iwo Jima

The occupation of Iwo Jima, 750 miles from Tokyo, was One of the severest tasks undertaken by the U.S. Fourth Division Marines. They landed on Feb. 18, 1945, and in the subsequent fighting suffered great losses.

硫黄島の上陸

米軍の第四師団は1945年2月18日、東京の東南750マイルを離れた硫黄島に上陸した。これは連合軍の太平洋戦争における一番苦しい上陸戦であった。日本軍は山の中に隠れて有利な地勢を利用して上陸している米軍を射撃する。米軍の陸軍及び上陸艇は水火も辞さず浜辺に向かって攻撃したので多大な損失が出た。

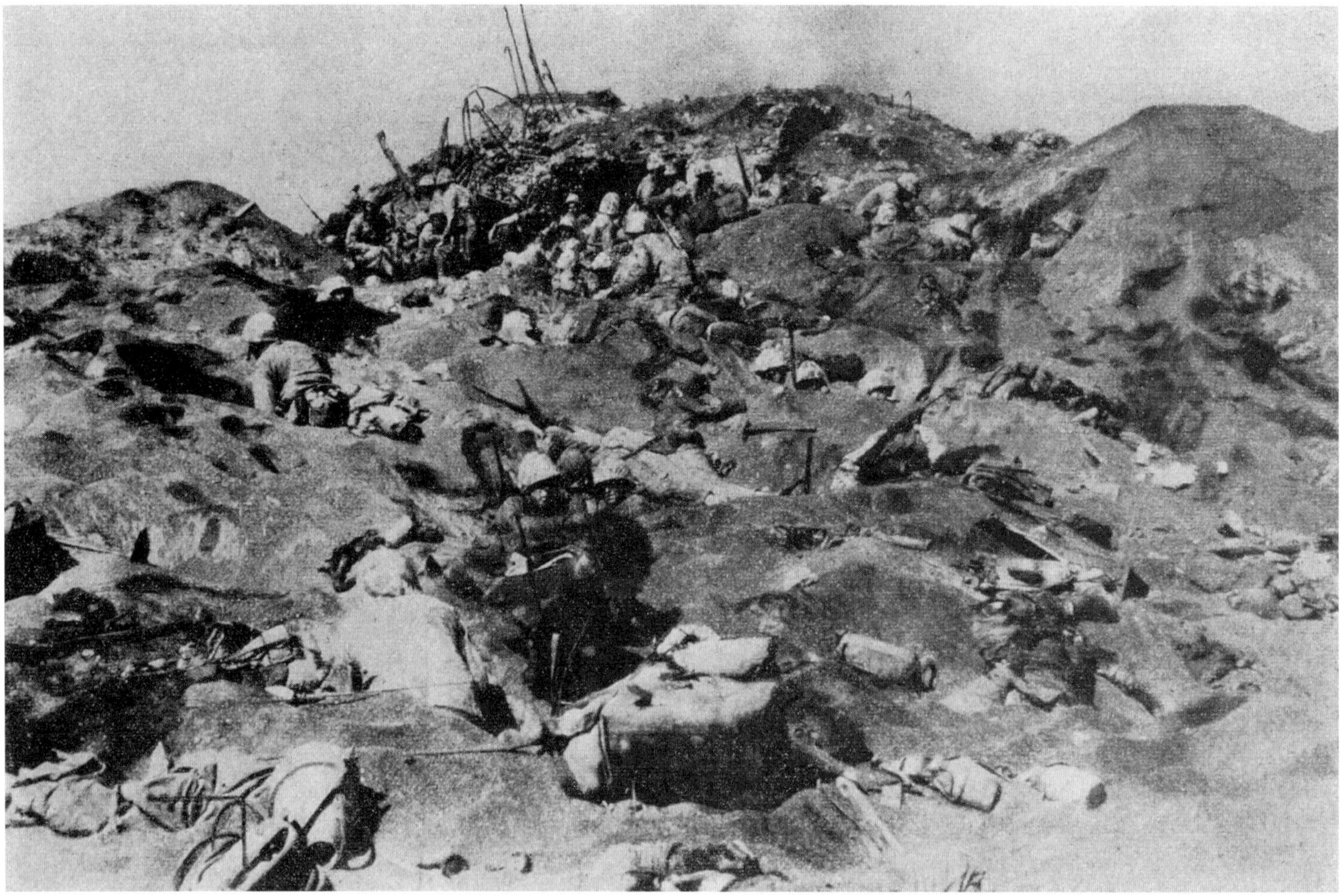

血染火山岛

苦战6天之后，陆战队付出了重大代价始逐步进展到中部之机场。上图为陆战队平息了日本巢穴之后，在仅足容身的穴中获取片刻的休息。一寸土地一寸血，硫磺岛的火山沙土上几乎被染红了。

Volcano Island Soaked with Blood

Every inch of Iwo Jima was contested with profuse flowing of blood. After silencing Japanese pillboxes, these marines are resting briefly in their foxholes.

火山島は血に染められた

六日間の苦しい戦いを経て連合軍の陸軍は多大な代償を払って徐々に島の中部にある空港に近づいた。図は米軍が日本軍の拠点を占領した後、身だけ隠れる狭い洞窟の中に一服している様子である。「一寸の土地は一寸の血を払う」のように、硫黄島の土地は血に赤く染められた。

爆炸硫磺岛敌人巢穴

硫磺岛上爆炸藏匿日军之山穴，该穴与三进岩洞相连，美军匍伏于岩石之后以防波及。美军在登陆之前曾狂轰该岛72小时，但当800艘船舰登陆时仍遇强烈之抵抗。该岛南部雷钵山争夺战尤为惨烈。血斗4日，星条旗才树立在雷钵山头。

Blast Iwo Jima Blockhouse

U.S. marines crouching behind a rock to avoid the blast as a heavy explosive charge blows up a cave connected to a three-tier blockhouse on Iwo Jima. Mt. Suribachi on the southern tip of the island was taken after fully four days of bloody and gruesome war.

硫黄島にある敵の洞窟を爆発する

図は硫黄島に日本軍の隠れた洞窟が爆発された場面である。この洞窟は三つの洞窟に繋がっている。米軍は上陸する前にこの島に72時間も荒い爆撃を続いたが、800隻の船が上陸する際、強い抵抗を遭遇した。

大硫球海空战

大硫球附近海空军打成一团，日机一架在美舰炽烈的炮火中图炸美舰，自身中弹落于海中。盟军于1945年3月31日进攻该岛起，日军图以空中攻击抵抗盟军，但自4月11日起5天内在硫球群岛被毁日机即达275架。

The Battle of Okinawa

The Japanese high command used aerial assaults to stop the Allied invaders from carrying Okinawa. But in the five days after April, 1945, Japan lost 275 planes.

琉球諸島における海空戦

米軍と日本軍の海軍や空軍は海上から空まで大混戦になった。一機の日本飛行機は激しい砲火中にアメリカ軍艦に爆撃をしているが、撃たれて海に落ちた。連合軍は1945年3月31日からこの島を攻撃し始めてから日本軍はずっと激しく抵抗した。4月11日から五日間のあいだに撃落された飛行機は275機にも達した。

海空战斗即景

日机一架在大硫球海面向美战舰作自杀攻击，未中的前被高射炮击中落于海上。上图正中为美国艾塞克斯级之航空母舰。

Aerial and Sea Fighting off Okinawa

A Japanese plane has just plunged into the Pacific. It was shot down by anti-aircraft fire before it could make its planned suicidal attack against a U.S. combat ship. In the center of the photo is an Essex-class carrier.

海空戰門の光景

日本軍の飛行機は諸島の海面でアメリカ戦艦に対する自殺的な攻撃をしたが、対空砲に撃たれ海に落ちた。図はアメリカの航空母艦である。

自杀飞机

日本在太平洋用作自杀性攻击之飞机有多种，美军名之为傻弹“Buka Bomb”（如上图）之飞机一种，乃专为作自杀攻击而设计。此机前部满藏炸药，独坐自杀飞行员1人，有翼与尾。最初在雷伊泰岛使用，后在大硫球3月战争中乃大量使用。

Buka Bomb

This rocket-propelled bomb is steered by a suicide pilot. The Americans call it Buka Bomb, which was widely used first at Leyte and then during the three months of warfare at Okinawa.

自殺的な攻撃

日本は太平洋戦争中自殺的な攻撃に用いられた飛行機は幾つかの機種がある。アメリカはこれを「Buka Bomb」と呼んでいた。図はその中の一種類である。これは自殺攻撃の為に作られたもので、飛行機の翼と尾の前部には爆薬を一杯積んでおり、パイロットは一人である。

自杀飞行员

在内卫圈遭受攻击时，日本军民均准备以一死报国，其海空军既无法赶上盟国，乃组织所谓神风特攻队，连同飞行员与飞机向敌方目的物撞击，以求同归于尽。此种作战方式，固使美舰遭受相当损失，终无法阻止盟军进展。上为日本神风攻击队员（即自杀飞行员）面向皇居告别，此辈将一去不返。

Japanese Suicide Pilots

When the Allied forces penetrated the Japancse inner defense, the Japanese air-force used large numbers of suicide pilots to charge their planes at the objectives. They inflicted some damage on their enemies but could by no means reverse the tide of war. Above, suicide pilots bid farewell in the direction where the Emperor resides.

自殺パイロット

日本の中心部まで攻められた際、日本軍は必死に抵抗した。海軍は連合軍の進攻を阻止するために、いわゆる「神風特攻隊」を組織して、パイロットと飛行機は一緒に敵サイトの目標に衝突させ、敵と共に壊滅させる作戦である。こういう攻撃はアメリカの艦船に相当な損失をもたらしたが、連合軍の前進を阻止するこうはできなかった。図は「神風特攻隊」隊員は皇居に向かてお別れを言っている光景である。

自杀飞机撞中美舰

日本自杀飞机一架自高空向美航空母舰艾塞克斯号实行自杀攻击，撞及飞行舱面二号升降机前，自天空掠过，留下一道白光。

A Successful Suicidal Crash

This Kamikaze plane succeeds in crashing on the flight deck of U.S. Carrier Essex.

自殺飛行機はアメリカ空母に衝突する

自殺飛行機は空からアメリカ空母に向かって自殺式攻撃をする。図は自殺する飛行機が上空を掠めて飛んでいく瞬間である。

美航舰被自杀机撞中

美航空母舰英特利比德号在太平洋作战，为日本自杀飞机撞中，图为船员在舱面救火之紧张场面。

A "Kamikaze" Fire

A Japanese Kamikaze plane successfully attacked the U.S.S. Carrier Intrepid operating in the Pacific. The crews were desperately trying to extinguish the fire.

アメリカの空母は衝突された

アメリカ空母が太平洋で日本の自殺式飛行機に衝突され、船員は慌てて鎮火している。

日机火葬

一架日本飞机预备去炸美国航空母舰黄蜂号，被黄蜂号的炮手打中，为它举行了一次海上的火葬，时为1945年3月18日。

Cremation of a Jap Bomber

A Japanese bomber when going to bomb Allied ships in Pacific on March 18, 1945, guners of the U.S.S. Hornet score a direct hit at it and held a cremation.

日本の飛行機は火葬された

一機の日本の飛行機はアメリカ空母を攻撃しようとするところ、米軍の空母の対空砲に撃中された。まるで、海上の火葬式をしているみたい。時は1945年3月18日である。

自杀的一刹那

日本自杀飞机一架，向美航空母舰桑加芒号撞击，未能中的，落于舰旁之一刹那。

Futile Suicidal Attempt

A Japanese Kamikaze plane caught fire in mid—air in its futile attempt to crash on the U.S.S. Sangamon, and crashed alongside. It was caught by the camera just before it disappeared from sight.

自殺の瞬間

図は自殺式飛行機はアメリカ空母をぶつかりにいったが、当たらなく、空母の傍に落ちた瞬間である。

海上自杀

1945年5月23日日本双引擎自杀轰炸机一架为美航舰高射炮击中落于海上。在82天的硫球岛战争中，日机屡图以轰炸，爆击，自杀进攻攻击海边美舰，计炸沉舰只11艘，地面飞机7架，但日机被毁者达111架。

A Suicide Bomber Dashes to its Death

On May 23, 1945, off Okinawa, this twin-engined suicide bomber, short of its target, dashes into the sea. Suicidal Kamikaze warfare tried to save the situation but was of no avail.

海上の自殺

1945年5月23日、日本の二つのエンジンがついている爆撃機は米軍の戦艦の対空砲に撃中され、海に落ちた。82日間の琉球諸島での戦争中、日本軍は爆撃や自殺式攻撃で米軍の戦艦11隻を沈没させ、陸上に7機の飛行機を損失させた。日本側も111機の飛行機を損失した。

福兰克林号被炸

美航空母舰福兰克林号满载飞机与汽油，在距日本60哩以内的海面作战，忽遭日本俯冲轰炸机攻击，计落500磅炸弹2枚，舰受巨伤倾斜，发生大火，船员损失千人，后仍驶行数千哩，返抵纽约修理。

U.S.S. Franklin Hit

Operating less than 60 miles off the Japanese coast, she was suddenly attacked by a dive-bomber, which scored two direct-hits with 500 pounders. Listing badly, the carrier limped thousands of miles back to New York for repairs.

アメリカの空母フランクリン号が爆撃された￥

アメリカ空母フランクリン号は飛行機とガソリンを満載して日本から60マイルを離れた海面で作戦した時、突然来た日本の戦闘機に上空から爆撃された。500ポンドの爆弾二枚も撃中され大きな損害になり、戦艦は傾く、炎上して死傷者は千人にものぼった。空母は負傷したままで奇跡のように1,000マイルも走行してニュヨークまで辿りついた。

在东京上空

盟军进据马利亚纳群岛后，在塞班建立B-29超级堡垒基地，专用以轰炸日本本岛防御圈（塞班距东京761哩）。上为第一次于1944年11月24日在东京工业区上空投弹，1944年仅炸东京5次，投弹1,500吨，到1945年6月在东京每月投弹达5,000吨。

Rain of Bombs over Tokyo

The air-bases at Saipan (761 miles from Tokyo) enabled the Allied Super fortress to bomb Japan proper with ease. Picture shows a fleet of B-29's from Saipan for the first time flying over Tokyo on Nov. 24, 1944. 1,500 tons of bombs were released on the Japanese capital in five trips. Until June 1945, 5,000 tons of bombs were dropped every month at Tokyo.

東京の上空

日本本土の防衛圏（サイパン島は東京から761マイル）を爆撃する為に、連合軍はマリアナ諸島を占領した後、サイパン島でB-29大型の堡塁基地を設けた。図は1944年11月24日、初めて東京工業区上空から爆弾を投げる場面である。1944年一年間で東京への爆撃はただ5回で、1,500トンだけの爆弾を投下したが、1945年6月までの半年のあいだに、東京に投下したダイナマイトは毎月5,000トンにも達した。

日人画符驱鬼

盟国航舰飞机飞袭日本本州时，在福山海岸看见上面在沙滩上画的符。是项古钱，日人悬诸门首，以避凶恶邪气者，现日人想以之驱逐“美鬼”之进攻。

Japanese Prevent Attacks with Charms

U.S. carrier-based planes attacking the main Japanese island at Honlshu, saw this drawing on the beach near Okayama. It is a presentation of an ancient Japanese coin, which nowadays is frequently hung on doorways to ward off evil spirits.

日本人は守り札を描き魔除けする

連合軍の戦艦や戦闘機は日本本州を襲撃する際、福山海岸に砂浜に描いた巨大な守り札を見つけた。札は古銭のようなかたちで、日本人が普段には魔除けするために玄関に掛けるものである。現在、これで“アメリカ鬼”の進攻を阻止しようと祈っている。

南洋交通线切断

盟国B-25解放式机于1945年4月6日在南海袭击一日本驱逐护卫舰，该舰旋被炸沉。美国舰队尼米兹宣称：1945年3月18日至4月18日大硫球及有关战役击沉日船舰百艘，毁日机2,569架。同期美船损失15艘。日南洋交通线全被切断。

Communication in China Sea Cut

An Allied B-25 Liberator attacks a Japanese destroyer in the China Sea April 6, 1945. U.S. Fleet Admiral Nimitz announced that between March 18 and April 18, 1945, at least 100 enemy vessels were Sunk.

南洋交通線の切断

連合軍のB-25爆撃機は1945年4月6日に、南海に日本の護衛艦を撃沈した。アメリカ戦艦は1945年3月18日から4月18日まで琉球諸島及びその他の戦役で、日本の戦艦百隻を撃沈し、飛行機2,569機を撃落したという。日本の南洋交通線は完全に切断された。

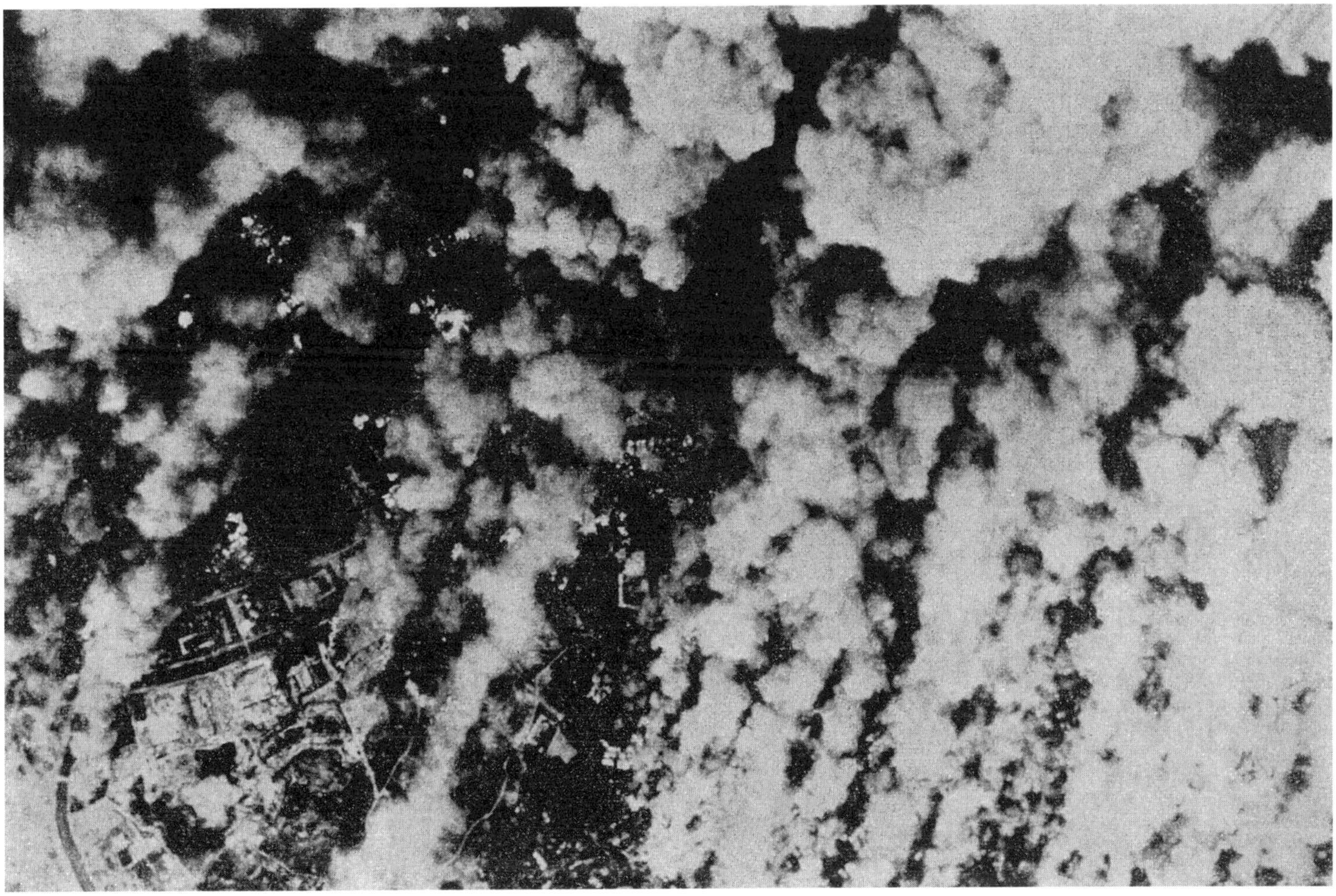

火烧横滨

美国B-29超级堡垒450架，于1945年5月29日在横滨工业区及海湾投下烧夷弹，引起大火。自马利亚纳起飞之超级堡垒，系由硫磺岛起飞之P-51野马式战斗机随行保护。硫磺岛于1945年3月15日夺自日本手中。

Flaming Yokohama

Incendiary bombs from 450 U.S. B-29 Super fortresses set tremendous fires in the industrial and port area of Yokohama on May 29, 1945. The bombers were escorted by P-51 Mustang fighters operating from Iwo Jima, captured on March 15, 1945.

横浜が燃えている

450機の米軍B-25スーパー爆撃機は1945年5月29日に、横浜工業区及び海湾に燃焼弾を投下し、大きな火災となった。マリアナ諸島から飛んできたB-25は琉球島から飛んできたP-51野馬戦闘機の援護の下で、横浜を爆撃したのである。

大阪被炸惨况

大阪为日本最大之城市，亦为最大之工商业中心，在日本投降之前，已为一连数月之B-29超级堡垒炸平，仅1945年6月1日1天，就在大阪投下烧夷弹达3,000吨。

This was Osaka

Osaka, Japanese largest city and greatest commercial and industrial center, was levelled by attack from the air. On June 1, 1945 alone, 3,000 tons of incendiary bombs were dropped.

大阪の爆撃される惨状

大阪は日本最大の都市で、最大の商工業の中心でもある。日本降参する前、米軍の空爆機の連続爆撃により既に瓦礫場になった。1945年6月1日その日だけでも、3,000トンの燃焼弾が投下された。

炸北海道

北海道东岸一城市城中建筑于1945年7月14日被炸，烟雾弥漫，车头一辆亦起火。此为盟国对本州北部及北海道南部千机轰炸的一部。

Hokkaido Attacked from Air

Flames sweep buildings on Kushiro on east coast of Hokkaido, one of the Japanese home islands, after a bombing attack by planes of the U.S. Third Fleet on July 17, 1945. The assault was part of a 1,000-plane strike against northern Honshu and southern Hokkaido islands.

北海道の爆撃

北海道東部の町にて、1945年7月14日、建物は爆撃され濃い煙が出て、汽車も炎上した。これは連合軍が本州北部及び北海道南部への荒く爆撃の一幕である。

东京工业区被炸

在美超级堡垒扫荡下之东京工业区一瞥。盟国自1945年年首起加紧对日本空袭，出动飞机超级堡垒恒在500架左右，目标为东京及各工业城市，1945年7月起美航舰飞机加入作战，使日本舰队遭受致命打击，东京工业区几成为平地。

Bombed Tokyo Industrial Quarters

A glimpse of the former industrial quarters, Tokyo. The Allied high command intensified their bombing of Japan in early 1945, often using waves of more than five hundred planes. The Japanese industries were greatly paralyzed.

東京工業区の爆撃

図はアメリカのスーパー爆撃機に空爆された東京工業区概観である。連合軍は1945年から日本への空襲を加速した。500機の大型爆撃機を次々と出動し、東京や各工業都市を爆撃した。1945年7月から米軍の母艦戦闘機も戦闘に加え、日本の戦艦に致命的な打撃を与え、東京工業区は瓦礫場となってしまった。

日本战败

日本还在顽强地抵抗时，美国的第一颗于1945年8月6日投于广岛，8日苏联又对日宣战，再加上丢在长崎的一颗原子弹，日本上下震于杀伤力的强大，同时海空军已枯竭，日本乃宣布准备投降，只要保存天皇制度；14日日本正式宣布投降。盟国派麦克阿瑟将军为进占日本之最高统帅，于9月2日在东京密苏里号上与日本代表签定降书，日本帝国主义的侵略，算告一段落，与纳粹战犯的处死，结束了二次世界大战。

The Defeat of Japan

While Japan was still stubbornly making a desperate last stand the first atomic bomb from the United States was dropped on Hiroshima on August 6, 1945. Soviet Russia than declared war on Japan on August 8, 1945, while the second atomic bomb was dropped on Nagasaki. The destructive powers of the new weapon found the Japanese at their wits' end.

Japan's military prowess was of course also fully exhausted and she announced her readiness to surrender, if the Emperor system could be preserved. Official announcement of the surrender was made on August 14.

The Allied powers appointed General Macarthur the Supreme Commander for occupation of Japan. The deed of surrender was signed on September 2 on board of the U.S.S. Missouri anchored in Tokyo Bay. Japanese imperialistic aggression was fully defeated. This, following earlier collapse of Nazi-ism, finally brought the complete conclusion of World War Ⅱ.

日本の敗戦

日本がまだ頑固に抵抗を続けていた間、アメリカは最初の原爆弾を1945年8月6日に広島に投下した。8月8日ソ連の日本に対する宣戦したことに加え、更に長崎に落とされた原爆弾、一連の強烈な圧力が日本に多大なダメージを与えた。同時に日本は、海も空も既に力が枯渇した、天皇制さえ保障されれば、投降するつもりだった。15日に、日本は正式に降伏を宣誓した。連合国は日本占領のためにマッカーサー司令官を最高司令官に任命し、9月2日、米戦艦ミズーリにおいて日本代表は降伏文書にサインされた、これにて日本帝国主義の侵略は終焉を迎えた。ナチス戦犯の処刑に合わせ、第二次世界大戦はついに終結した。

日本战败

The Defeat of Japan

盟军进入东京湾
Allied Ships in Tokyo Bay
連合軍東京湾に進入

原子弹落广岛

当日本冥顽不灵地在进行自杀抵抗时，盟国的一个惊人而可怕的秘密武器原子弹于8月6日（1945年）落于广岛，炸毁广岛城市百分之六十，死30,000人，伤17万人，两周后复死60,000人，全城大部夷为平地。

Hiroshima Atomic-bombed

The first atomic bomb ever known to mankind was loosed on Hiroshima on Aug. 6, 1945. By this one bomb, more than sixty percent of the city was destroyed, Casualties, 200,000.

広島に原子爆弾落下

日本は頑固して自殺式抵抗を行う際、米軍が驚るべく武器の原子爆弾を8月6日（1945年）に広島に投下した。広島は大いに破滅され、3万人が死亡、17万人が負傷した。二週間後、更に6万人が死亡してしまった。

原子弹落长崎

1945年8月9日在日本长崎，第二颗原子弹落下了，烟雾直冲至60,000英呎（18,000公尺）上空。此图摄自数百哩外空中，原子弹落弹处附近30华里地点房屋均荡然无存，威力可见一斑。

Atomic Cloud over Nagasaki

The mushroom-shaped cloud of boiling smoke of the second atomic bomb dropped over the Japanese seaport Nagasaki on Aug. 9, 1945 was pictured several hundred miles away from the air. Ten miles from the point where miracle missile fell, buildings were uprooted and crushed.

長崎に原子爆弾落下

1945年8月9日、アメリカは再び原子爆弾を日本の長崎に投下した。茸のような煙は6万フィート（18,000メートル）の上空まで騰がった。この写真は空中から撮ったものである。原子爆弾の落下場所の周囲15平方キロに於いて建築物は全壊された。原子爆弾の恐ろしさはこれで分かる。

原子弹炸后的长崎

第二颗原子弹炸后之长崎空中鸟瞰。此25万人口之城市，被毁三分之一，人口死亡约计25,000人，伤50,000人，房屋被毁者18,000所。此为对日本之最后一击，8月14日日本宣布无条件投降。

Nagasaki Hit by Atomic Bomb

The second atomic bomb fell on Nagasaki on Aug. 9, 1915. The city was one-third destroyed; 25,000 people estimated killed, over 50,000 injured and 18,000 buildings were flattened. On the 14th, Japan surrendered.

原爆された長崎

図は原爆された長崎の鳥瞰である。この25万人口の都市は三分の一は全滅、約25,000人死亡、50,000人負傷、18,000の家屋は破壊された。原爆が功を奏し、余儀なく日本は無条件降伏と宣言した。

苏联对日宣战

波茨坦会议中，苏联已接受盟国要求，如日本拒绝投降，苏联决定参加反抗日本侵略的战争，1945年8月9日，苏联正式履行此项约定，宣告对日立于交战状态，翌日即自中国东北边境及朝鲜突入日军阵线，飞机实行轰炸。日本遭受原子弹与苏联宣战两重新的压迫，已无法继续作战，乃决定接受投降。图为苏联第一远东战线总司令瓦西列夫斯基元帅（正中）和梅利特斯可夫司令与日本关东军代表商讨日本投降的问题。

U.S.S.R. Declare War with Japan

Stalin pledged at the Yalta Conference that U.S.S.R. would declare war on Japan six months after the defeat of Germany. The pledge was renewed in the Potsdam Conference, and on August 9, 1945, the declaration was made known to the whole world. On the next day, the Red Army of the Far Eastern district crossed the Manchurian and the Korean borders at three points and the Red Air-force carried out extensive bombing. Under the double pressure of the atomic bomb and Soviet participation, Japan has to surrender.

Above shows Soviet Marshal Vasilievsky, Commander-in-Chief of the First Far East Front of Soviet forces, and Marshal Meretskov meet representatives of the Japanese Kwan-tung Army to negotiate the capitulation. Chief Japanese delegate was Lt. General Hata, Chief of Staff of the Kwan-tung Army.

ソ連の対日宣戦

ボスダム会議中、ソ連は国連からの「対日戦争に参加してほしい」という要求に応じた。1945年8月9日、ソ連は日本に宣戦し、約束を果たした。翌日、中国東北の国境及び朝鮮から日本の戦線に突入し飛行機で爆撃を行った。日本は原子爆弾の打撃とソ連の宣戦という二重の圧力を受け降参をせざる得なくなった。図はソ連の第一極東戦線総司令官のワシレフスキ元帥(ドイツ軍)とメリトスカフ司令官は日本関東軍の代表と降参問題について交渉している場面である。

日本投降了！

1945年8月10日7时35分（东方战时时间）日本同盟社广播："日本将接受波茨坦宣言之条件，倘使天皇主权不受损害。"这一消息，立刻传遍世界每一角落，联合国人民，无论在前线，在后方，在地面，在空中，一致热烈欢呼！上为缅甸前线澳洲兵手舞足蹈之一幕。

Japan Surrendered

At seven thirty, in the morning of Aug.10, 1945, Domei broadcasted from Tokyo that Japan willing to sue for peace according to the terms laid down in the Potsdam Declaration. The picture shows Aussie soldiers on the Burma front overjoyed at the news.

日本は降参した

1945年8月10日7時35分、日本同盟社は"天皇主権を損害させなければ、日本はボスダム宣言の条件を同意するつもり"と報道した。このニュースはすぐに世界各地に伝え渡され、世界の人々は皆歓呼していた。図はビルマ前線でオーストラリア兵士は躍り上がって喜んでいる場面である。

举世狂欢

日本将接受投降消息由同盟社传出后（8月10日），全世界均为之欢欣鼓舞。上为是日下午3时40分伦敦唐宁街情形，英人欢乐之余，尽以白纸掷于街头。

Wild with Joy

The Downing Street of London was littered with paper torn by exhila-rated Londoners after hearing from the radio that Japan had decided to surrender according to the terms laid down in the Declaration of Potsdam.

世を挙げて祝う

日本降伏のニュースは同盟社により報道された後（8月10日）、全世界は狂喜となった。図はその日の午後3時40分ごろロンドンのイギリス人は大喜びのあまりに紙を町にばら撒いている場面である。

日人恭聆天皇投降广播

全世界沉浸于欢笑中时，东方日本人民于1945年8月15日正午以极大之虔诚，痛楚，悲愤恭聆日皇裕仁所作之广播大诏。日皇谓战争已不利于我，敌复使用残虐炸弹，若继续作战，不但民族灭亡，人类文明亦必被毁。各地日军，日人均在收音机前肃立恭听，上为关岛日俘听广播之悲愤恭谨形态。

The Words of an Emperor

Behind the barbed-wire of a camp on Gaum, these Japanese prisoners of war listened to the words of Hirohito, who said, for the first time on the radio, that it was time for Japan to surrender.

日本人は天皇降参の報道を仰せ

全世界は大喜びしているが、日本人は1945年8月15日正午に極複雑な気持ちを抱いて天皇裕仁の詔書を静かに聞いていた。天皇は戦争は既に日本国に不利になって、敵は恐ろしい原子爆弾を使いはじめたので、引き続き戦っていくなら民族は絶滅されるだけでなく、人類文明もこれで壊滅になってしまうと述べた。各地の軍人と庶民は皆ラジオの前で恭しく起立しながら天皇降参の報道を聞いた。図はグアムの日本捕虜は悲しく恭しく報道を聞いている場面である。

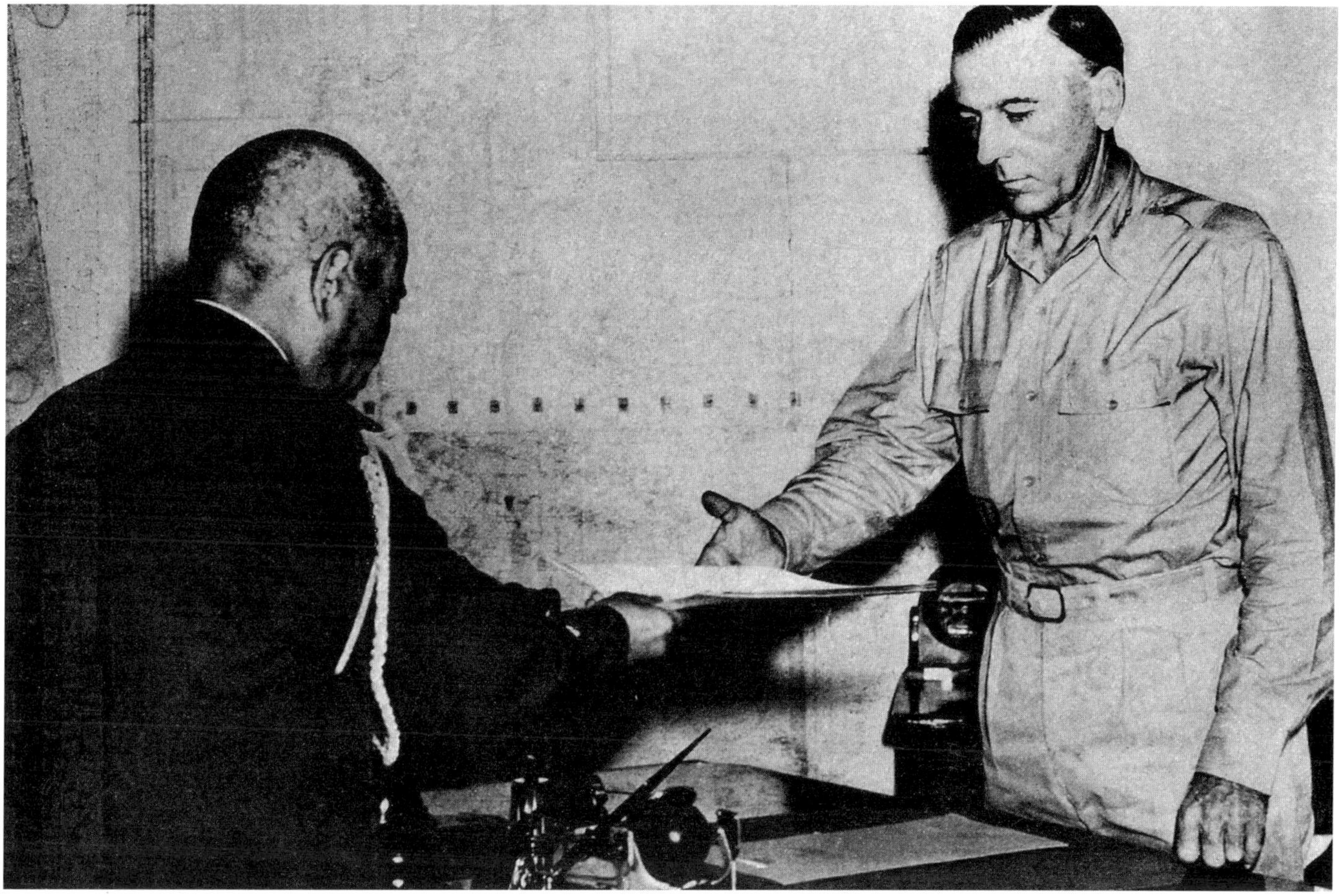

日代表到马尼拉洽降

8月15日（1945年）日本正式宣布决定投降，派副参谋总长河边虎四郎（左）赴马尼拉盟军总部向麦克阿瑟元帅接洽投降。河边正以天皇裕仁之证件交与麦帅参谋长修伯兰，正式投降仪式则于9月2日在东京湾举行。

Negotiation of Surrender

Japan made the formal surrender statement on Aug. 15, 1945. Lt. General Tarashiro Kawabe (left) was sent to negotiate surrender in General MacArthur's headquarters at Manila. Credentials are being presented to Lt. Gen. Sutherland.

日本代表はマニラでの降参

1945年8月15日、日本は正式に降伏を宣言した。副参謀総長の河辺虎四郎（左）をマニラにある連合国軍本部に派遣し、マッカーサー元帥と降参の件について交渉した。河辺は裕仁天皇の証明書をマッカーサー元帥の参謀長官に渡した。正式の降参儀式は9月2日に東京湾で行う予定である。

盟舰向日本海岸挺进

这里是一望无边的盟国舰队，在1945年8月14日日本宣布接受波茨坦宣言及美国代表中美英苏所作节略后，于8月17日集队向日本海岸挺进。

Allied Fleet Sail toward the Coast of Japan

After V-J Day, these Allied naval craft sailed in great and impressive formation toward the Japanese coast on Aug. 17, 1945.

連合軍の戦艦は日本海岸に進む

これは見渡す限りの連合軍の戦艦である。1945年8月15日、日本はボスダム宣言を受けると承諾してから、8月17日これらの戦艦は列を並んで日本海岸へ進んできた。

盟舰进驻东京湾

美国第三舰队乘风破浪，以堂堂阵势，开入东京湾，执行受降及占领工作。盟国占领军以美国为主，其它英国仅有少数军舰参加。

U.S. Fleet Entering Tokyo Bay

In stately formation, these formidable carriers of the U.S. Third Fleet are sailing into Tokyo bay to accept the Japanese surrender and to carry out occupational works.

連合軍の戦艦は東京湾に入る

日本の降参を受けることと日本を占領するために、アメリカの第三艦隊は波を破って堂々して東京湾に入った。国連占領軍は主にアメリカで、イギリスは僅かな戦艦を出した。

飞向东京

显示盟军之庞大武力，在日本签订投降书前美机1,000架举行示威飞行，上为盟机掠过英舰约克公爵号上空，飞向东京之壮观。

Armada of the Air

To impress the Japanese of the powerful might of the Allied forces, these planes, numbering a thousand, are flying toward Tokyo. In the foreground is the British battleship H.M.S. Duke of York.

東京へ飛ぶ

連合軍の強大な武力を現す為に、降参書を調印する前にアメリカの飛行機千機がデモ飛行を行った。図は飛行機の列はイギリスの戦艦ヨーク公爵号の上空をかすめて東京へ飛んで行く壮観な風景である。

密苏里号上日本签订降书

日本与盟国投降协议于1945年9月2日在东京湾美国战舰密苏里号上举行，日代表为重光外相，梅津美治郎参谋总长，盟国有中美英苏法澳加荷纽代表。签降后日本侵略战争完全结束。

The End of World War Ⅱ

On board V.S.S. Missouri on Sept. 2, 1945, Japan's Minister of Foreign Affairs, Shigemetsu, represents the Japanese Government, and Lt. Gen. Hirota, represents the Japanese Armed forces. They signed the documents of surrender and thus ended the war.

ミズーリ号での降参調印

日本と国連は1945年9月2日に東京湾に停泊しているアメリカ戦艦のミズーリ号で調印式を行う。日本側は重光外務大臣、梅津美治郎参謀総長で、国連側は中国、アメリカ、イギリス、ソ連、フランス、オーストラリア、オランダ、ニュージランドの代表が出席した。調印式の終了によって、日本の侵略戦争は完全に終止符が打れた。

皇军倦了

日本投降，在日本军人间引起极大的烦躁与悲愤，东京的军人甚至冲进皇宫示威，但是天皇陛下的命令，使他们只有接受投降之一途。日军在中国征战8年，在太平洋苦撑4年，也够疲倦了，皇军的确需休息。上为日本在越南军事负责人在西贡等待盟国管制委员会主席格莱赛少将之来临，苦苦等候5小时半之疲劳情形。

Dozing Soliders of Mikado

Perhaps the soldiers of Mikado are seeking the vanished Empire in their dreams. After years of planned aggression, they could relax and perhaps repent at last. Senior Japanese officers at Saigon waiting to surrender. Second from left, Lieutenant-General Manage, Commander of 2nd Japanese division.

皇軍は疲れた

日本の降参は日本軍人の中に大きないらだたしさと悲しみを引き起こした。東京の軍人は甚だしきに至り皇居に押し込んでその気持ちを表したかったが、天皇陛下は既に命令を発布したので彼らはそれを守らなければならない。日本軍は中国で八年間、太平洋で四年間の苦しい戦いを経て甚だ疲れた。これ以上戦うことはできなくなった。図は日本のベトナム駐在軍の責任者はサイゴンで国連管制委員会主席の来るのを待っていた。既に五時間半も待たせられたからもう待ちくだびれた。

中国战区洽降

日本在华派遣军总司令岗村宁次派参谋副长今井武夫（正中）及参谋桥岛芳雄，前川国雄二人于8月21日（1945年）由南京飞至芷江，向中国陆军总司令部洽降，由何总司令参谋长萧毅肃，美军作战部参谋长冷欣接受洽降。今井正阅一投降条款。

China Accepts Japanese Surrender

Japan's Supreme Commander in China, Lt. Gen. Okamura sent his Vice-Chief of Staff Gen. Takeo Imai to Tsekiang in Hunan on Aug. 21, 1945, to negotiate peace and the surrender of the Japanese Army of the China war-zone.

中国戦区での降参

日本の中国駐在軍総司令官の岡村寧次の命令で、1945年8月21日に、参謀長官の今井武夫及び橋島芳雄参謀、前川国雄が南京から芷江に、中国陸軍総司令部と降参の交渉に行った。何総司令、蕭毅粛参謀長、アメリカ作戦部の参謀はその交渉を受けた。

南京受降

中国战区受降典礼于9月9日（1945年）在南京举行，驻华日军最高指挥官岗村宁次偕高级指挥官代表签定降书，中国由何总司令应钦，偕受降官顾祝同，陈绍宽，张廷孟，萧毅肃受降。上为岗村在降书上签字。130万日本侵华大军放下武器，大陆政策之美梦完全破灭。

Surrender at Nanking

Japan's Supreme Commander in China Lt.Gen. Okamura put his seal on the document of surrender at Nanking on Sept. 9, 1945. China was represented by Generals Ho Ying-chin, Koo Chu-tung, and Chen Shao-kwan. 1,300,000 Japanese soldiers will lay down their arms and wait to be repatriated.

南京で投降を受け入れる

中国戦区での降参を受け入れ儀式は1945年9月9日に南京で行った。中国に駐在最高指揮官の岡村寧次は高級指揮官達を率いて降参書に調印した。中国側は何應欽総司令官をはじめ、顧祝同、陳紹、張廷孟、蕭毅肅達はその降参を受け入れた。図は岡村が降参書にサインしている光景である。これで130万の日本侵略軍は武器を卸し、その大陸政策は完全に破滅した。

英军重返香港

香港落于日人手中几将4年之久，日本投降后英太平洋舰队在哈尔柯特海军中将率领之下，重返香港。上为英军在香港登陆。

The Re-occupation of Hongkong

Hongkong was left in Japanese hands for almost four years. Now a British fleet under Rear–Admiral C.H.J. Harcourt is sailing into Hongkong again after V–J Day.

イギリス軍は香港に戻り

香港は日本に四年間支配された。日本降参後、イギリスの太平洋艦隊はハルクータ海軍中将の指揮の下で再び香港に戻ってきた。図はイギリス軍の香港に上陸する場面である。

欢笑与愤怒

日本投降，联合国人民在欢笑中包藏着对日本敌人之愤怒，上为新加坡英军登陆时华侨及马来人在一日兵前表现之情绪，请注意正中一儿童对日兵咬牙切齿之情态。

Bitterness Amid Joy

Chinese and Malayan children of Singapore overjoyed at the Japanese surrender and the arrival of British forces. The kid in the center, looking at the Japanese Soldier, reveals the bitter memory of the Japanese occupation.

喜びと怒り

日本は降参した後、人々は喜んでいるが、日本への怒りも胸一杯である。図はシンガポールのイギリス軍、華僑とマレー人達が日本兵士の前での表情である、真ん中に立つ一人の子供は恨み骨髄に達する怒りの表情に注目してください。

祖国万岁

日本投降，抗战胜利，中华民族百年来的外族压迫解除于一旦，其欢愉之情绪惟有此一代受日本磨难之中华儿女，始能领略其况味。图为新加坡华侨，于英军重返时举着“祖国万岁”的巨旗游行市上，快乐之情，溢于言表。

Vive La China!

A street scene in Singapore after V-J Day. These Chinese are welcoming the return of Allied troops. On this huge Chinese flag is written, “Long Live China!”

祖国万歳

日本は降参した、抗日戦争は勝利を挙げた。中華民族は百年来の外国の圧迫から解放された。日本から齎された苦しみを身に沁んだ中国人民は始めてその解放感を喜んで味わった。図はシンガポールの華僑は「祖国万歳」と書いている大きな旗を持ち上げ、そのよろこぶ気持ちははっきりと顔に現している。

搜查日本俘虏

南京中山门前搜查被集中之日本俘虏，日兵在华共有130万人，投降后全部被解除武装，遣送返国。

Japanese Searched before Repatriation

Before the Chung Shan Gate of Nanking, Japanese soldiers were searched before being sent to various camps awaiting repatriation. In China over 1,300,000 men were repatriated.

日本捕虜の検査

南京中山門前に集められた日本捕虜を検査している。中国駐在した日本軍は130万人もあり、降参後、全部武装を解除され日本に返送された。

鞠躬如仪

横滨一日本之俘虏营中，从前的日本看守官兵于拘留之美海军士兵离去时鞠躬送别，似甚恭敬。1945年9月3日起日本所有俘虏营由麦克阿瑟下令交由各俘虏营中被拘之最高盟军长官管理。

Bow to their Prisoners

At the gate of a PW concentration camp in Yokohama, these Japanese gendarmes bowed to their former prisoners. On Sept. 3, 1945, the administration of all PW camps was turned over to the encamped senior Allied officers.

辞儀する

日本の捕虜キャンプに拘束されたアメリカの海軍官兵は横浜の捕虜キャンプを離れた際、日本兵士が辞儀をしている。1945年9月3日からマッカーサーの命令により日本の各捕虜キャンプに拘束されている連合軍兵士の中、肩書きの一番高い長官がそのキャンプの臨時管理者に就任する。

日本小潜艇

日本投降，本州海军基地尚存有在建造阶段未及完成之5人潜水艇100余艘，正由美海军人员加以调查。此项小潜艇始终未及应用对付美国太平洋舰队。

Japanese Midget Submarines

On Y-J Day, Japan still held more than a hundred five-men submarines in various stages of construction at Kure Naval Base, Honshu, which are being inspected by a U. S. Navy party. The Japanese never had an opportunity to use them against the U.S. Pacific Fleet.

日本の小型潜水艦

日本降参後、本州の海軍基地に尚、未完成の五人乗り小型潜水艦は百隻程もある。アメリカ海軍はそれを検査している。これらの小型潜水艦は最後になっても戦争に使われてなかった。

日本大炮掷于海中

为防止日本再起，盟军总部将日本所剩军用品之一部如大炮，弹药投诸海中。执行此项工作者，为日本军人，而由盟军加以监视。

End of Empire

The Allied High Commands had decided to dump a certain amount of Japanese guns and ammunitions into the sea. The work was carried out by Japanese soldiers under close Allied inspection. Thus the dream of an empire came to an end.

日本の大砲が海に捨てられた

日本の復活を防ぐために、国連本部は日本軍の残した大砲や弾薬等を海に捨てた。この仕事は日本の兵士にしてもらった。

天皇与上司

至尊无上之日本天皇裕仁于盟军占领日本后，拜访其占领者麦克阿瑟元帅于美国大使馆(1945年9月25日)。裕仁与其外国统治者长谈35分钟，内容不祥。上图麦克阿瑟与裕仁天皇之姿态，适成一强烈的对比。

Emperor and Boss

Emperor Hirohito of Japan pays a visit to the super-ruler of Japan, General MacArthur, on Sept. 25, 1945. The interview lasted 35 minutes and its content never disclosed.

天皇と占領者

連合軍が日本を占領した後、1945年9月25日、裕仁天皇はアメリカの大使館に占領者であるマッカーサー元帥を尋ねた。裕仁は外国統治者と35分間程話したがその内容は不詳。図はマッカーサーと裕仁天皇は話す場面である。

傀儡皇帝溥仪

满洲傀儡皇帝溥仪（右）于苏军进入我国东北时在长春被捕，上系应远东国际战犯法庭之请求，由苏联军官押至东京作证。溥仪供称，彼之出任傀儡，系受日本军人之胁迫。

Puppet Emperor Pu Yi

The Puppet Emperor of "Manchukuo" Henry Pu Yi was captured by the Red Army and has since been under their custody. He appeared before the International War Crimes Court in Tokyo to testify against Japanese leaders as war criminals.

傀儡皇帝溥儀

満州の傀儡皇帝溥儀（右）はソ連軍に長春で逮捕された。図は極東国際戦犯の法廷の要請に応じて、ソ連の将校が証人としての溥儀を連行して東京へ行く。溥儀は日本の軍人の脅迫を受けたから傀儡の皇帝になったと証言した。

旧金山会议

旧金山联合国大会举行开幕式。此次会议系由克里米亚会议决定召集，中美英苏为邀请国，被邀参加者50国，会议通过联合国宪章，成立联合国机构，藉以达到永久的世界和平。

San Francisco Conference

The grand opening of the first assembly of the United Nations at San Francisco in June 1945, the time and place were agreed upon at the Crimea Conference of the Four Powers: China, Great Britain, U.S. and U.S.S.R. playing hosts. Fifty nations were represented and the United Nations Charter was passed to ensure permanent world peace.

サンフランシスコ会議

中、米、英、ソ連は五十国を要請してサンフランシスコにて国際連合成立大会を開催した。世界永久な平和の為に、会議は国連憲章を通過し、各組織を設けた。

法西斯罪魁和汉奸的下场

那些曾经不可一世、嚣张跋扈、践踏人类文明与和平的法西斯头目和汉奸们终于受到了正义的惩罚。历史和现实告诉我们：不管反人类反和平的势力多么强大、多么残忍，最终还是难逃失败的可耻下场。全世界人民都应该牢记法西斯和军国主义带给世界人民的伤与痛，决不让悲惨的历史重演！

End of the Fascists and the Traitors

The fascists and the traitors, who sabotaged the human peace, fell down at last.

History and the reality tell us, however powerful the forces of reaction had been, they are foredoomed to failure.

On the occasion of the 60th anniversary of China's War of Resistance Against Japan and Anti-Fascist World War, People all over the world, at the thought of Fascism and Militarism, should keep in mind that this page of history should not be allowed to repeat itself.

ファシストの主犯者と売国奴の結末

かつて傲慢で、のさばりはびこり、人類の文明と平和を踏みつけたファシストの頭目及び売国奴達は最終的に正義の制裁を受けることとなった。歴史と現実は我々に教えてくれた：反人類反平和勢力がいかに強大で、残忍なものでも、最終的には失敗に終わるという恥ずかしい結末から逃れられない。全世界の人民はこのファシズムと帝国主義が世界人民にもたらした傷と痛みを心に刻ませ、二度とこのような悲惨な歴史を再演させてはならない！

法西斯罪魁和汉奸的下场

End of the Fascists and the Traitors

正义的审判

二次大战终了，纳粹首要20人以从事侵略战争阴谋者与主动者的罪嫌，于1945年11月20日在国社党圣地纽伦堡正义之宫，由联合国加以审判。上图在被告栏内者左起第一排：戈林，李宾特洛甫，季德尔，罗森伯格，第二排：杜尼兹，莱德，史拉基，青年领袖绍克尔，约德尔（其它在被告栏右部者未摄入）。

Nuremburg Palace of Justice

After the termination of the war, twenty Nazi leaders were brought to court for trial as war criminals. From left to right：(front row) Herman Goering (in white), Joachim von Ribbentrop, Wilhelm Keitel, Alfred Rosenberg ；(back row) Karl Doenitz, Frich Raeder, Baldur von Shirach, Fritz Sauckel, and Alfred Jodl.

正義な審判

二次世界大戦終了後、ナチス首脳20名は侵略戦争を起こした罪で、1945年11月20日、ナチス国社党の聖地であるニュルンベルクの「正義の宮」で国連に審判された。

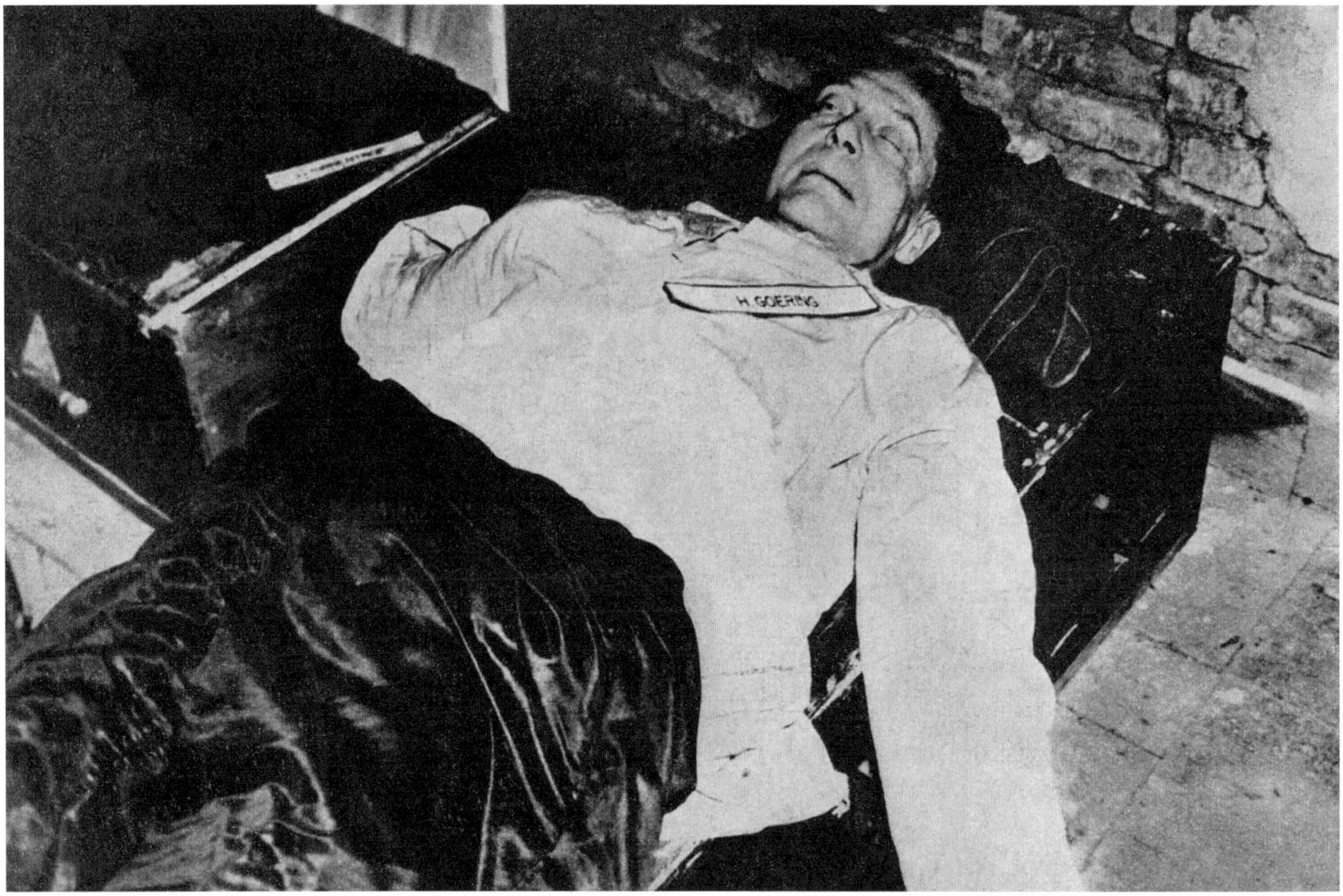

公正的判决

纳粹要犯20人经10个月的审讯，于1946年9月30日宣判，被处绞刑者戈林，季德尔等11人，终身监禁者2人，有期徒刑者4人，无罪释放者3人。死刑于10月16日执行，纳粹第二大要人戈林则于执行前服毒自杀（上图）。

Sentence of Justice

After a trail that lasted ten months, sentence were read on sept.30, 1946. Of the twenty accused Nazi leaders, eleven were to be hanged, two to serve life terms, four to serve a number of years, and three were acquitted. Goering, however, contrived to comit suicide on the eve of his execution.

公正な判決

十ヶ月続いた審判で、1945年11月30日、ナチス首脳20名に対する判決が言い渡された。ナチス首脳ナンバ2のゲーリングは死刑を執行される直前に自殺した。

赖伐尔枪决

前法国维琪政府总理赖伐尔以叛国罪被判死刑，于1945年10月15日执行前服毒未果，终为医生救活，2小时候后在巴黎监狱内执行枪决。赖伐尔要求向行刑人员发令执行及不要蒙眼睛，均被拒绝，执行时禁止摄影，此影为法国晚报记者萨特拉斯用远距离镜头之照相机在监狱外所摄。

France's Laval Shot

French's No. 1 traitor, Pierre Laval, ex–Premier of the Vichy Government, failed in a last minute attempt to escape the firing squad by taking poison in his deathcell on Oct. 15, 1945. Doctors revived him and sent him to the execution ground in a Paris prison. He asked if he could be allowed to give the order to fire and be free from having his eyes bound, but this was not granted. This picture is a sneak shot, as photographers were officially banned.

ラヴァルを銃殺する

フランスの売国奴のヴィジー政府の総理ラヴァルは反逆罪で死刑を判決された。1945年10月15日死刑を執行する直前にラヴァルは毒を呑み、自殺しようとしたが未遂に終わった。二時間後、監獄内で銃殺された。この写真はフランス夕刊の記者が遠いところから遠距離レンズで密かに撮ったものである。

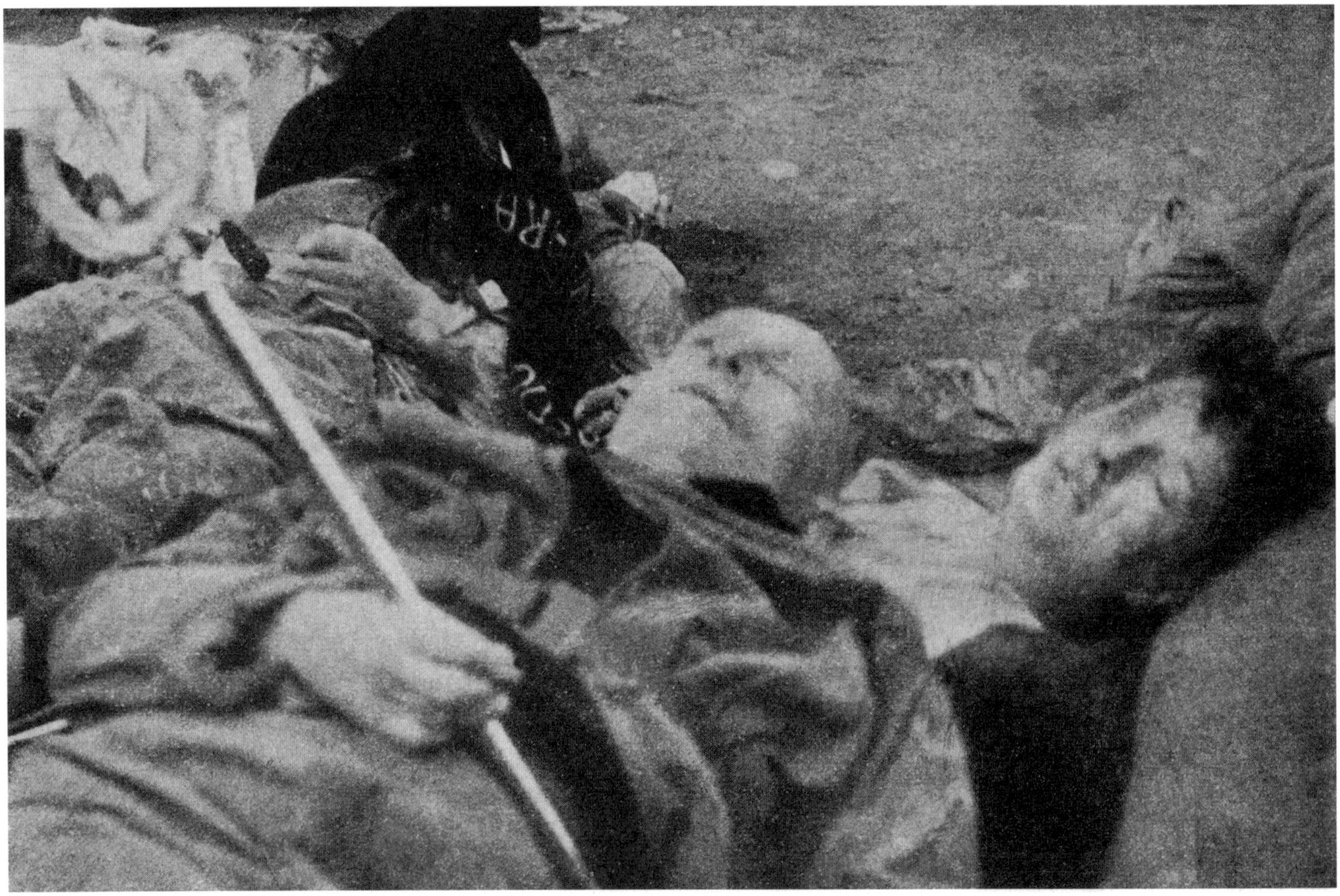

独裁者之死

意大利的大独裁者墨索里尼，1945年4月见大势已去，图逃往瑞士，被游击队在科摩湖畔捕获，与法西斯头目16人同时枪决，然后悬尸于米兰。墨氏被枪中后身体倒在情妇培达西的身上。

Death of a Dictator

Italy's Benito Mussolini now lies dead on a Milan street, after being executed by his embittered and enraged fellow countrymen. Underneath is his mistress, Clara Petacci.

独裁者の死

イタリアの大独裁者ムッソリーニは、1945年4月に大勢は既に決まったと判って、スイスへ逃走の途中で遊撃隊に捕らわれ、後にファシズムの首脳16名と共に処決され、死体はミラノに曝された。図は処決された後、ムッソリーニがの屍体愛人のペタッチの死体の上に横倒れている様子である。

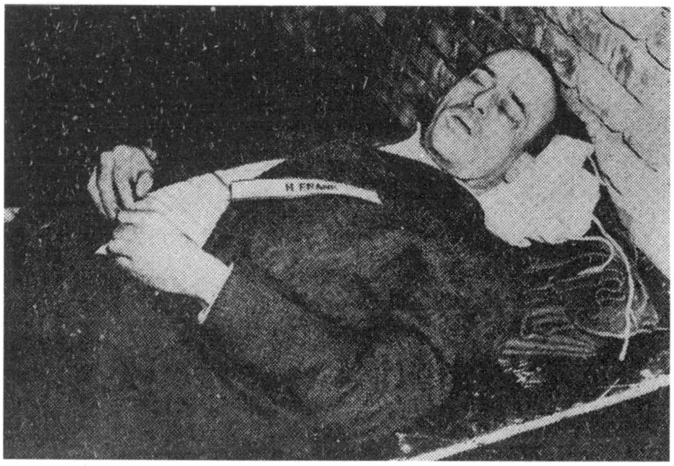

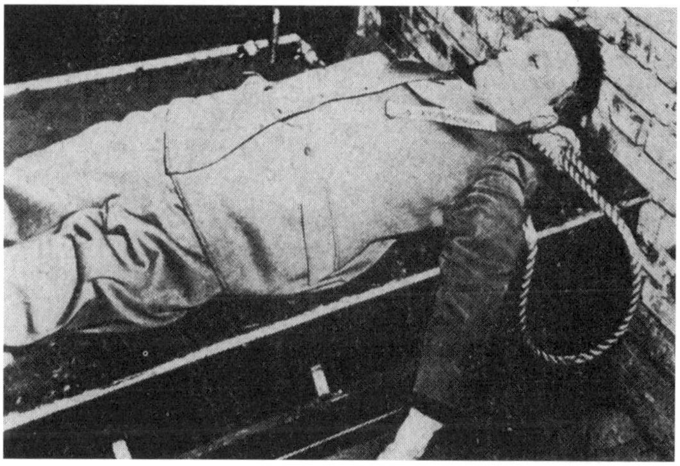

被处死的法西斯罪魁（一）
The End of the Fascists (1)
死刑されたファシズム主犯者達（一）

被绞死的德外长李宾特里甫
J.Von Ribbentrop ended up in the gallows
絞め殺されたドイツの外相J.Von Ribbentrop

被绞死的纳粹波兰总督弗兰克
The Nazi governor of Poland, Hans Frank
絞め殺されたナチスのポーランド総督Hans Frank

被绞死的前奥地利与荷兰区总督殷嘉德
The Nazi governor of Austria-Holland District, A.S.Inquart
絞め殺された前オーストリアとオランダの総督A.S.Inquart

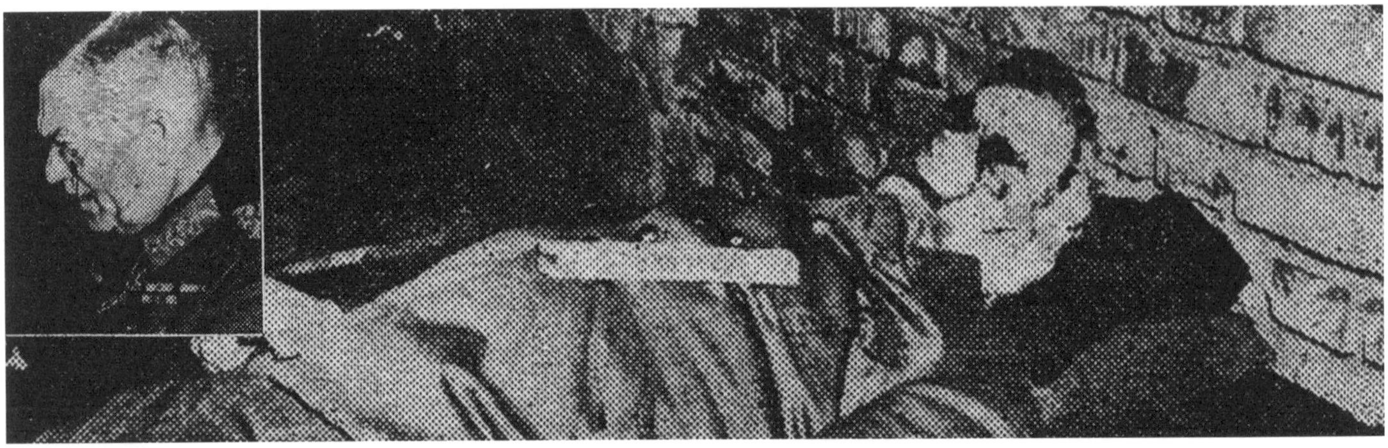

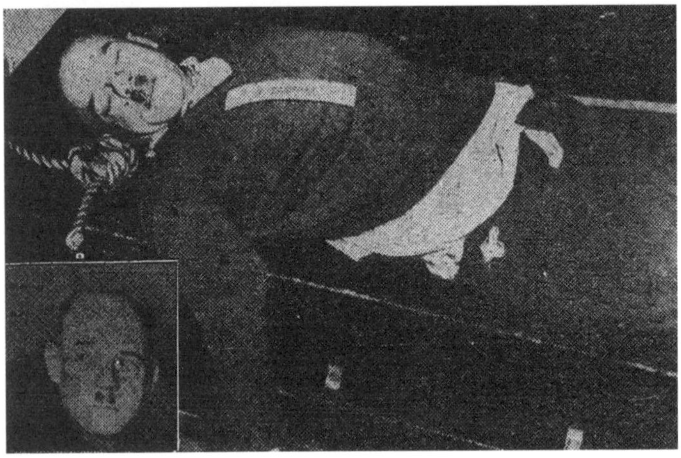

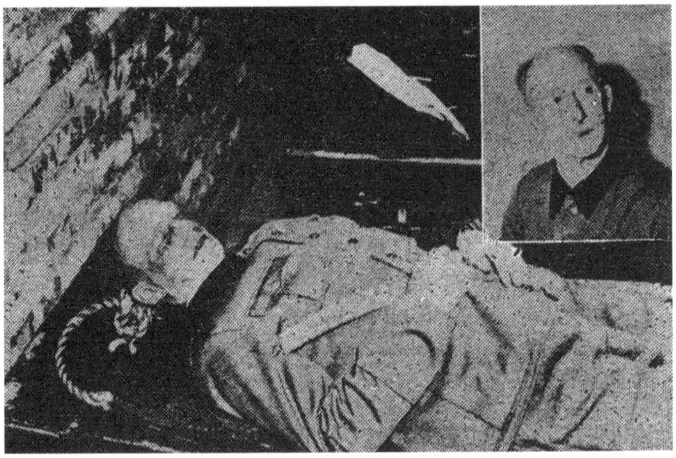

被处死的法西斯罪魁（二）
The End of the Fascists (2)
死刑されたファシズム主犯者達（二）

被绞死的东线德军总司令季德尔
Wilhelm Keitel ended up in the gallows
絞め殺されたドイツ軍の総司令官 Wilhelm Keitel

被绞死的纳粹奴隶劳工鼓吹者沙克尔
Fritz Sauckel ended up in the gallows
絞め殺された労働者を奴隷にするのを提唱したナチス Fritz Sauckel

被绞死的纳粹重要将领约德尔
Alfred Jodl ended up in the gallows
絞め殺されたナチスの重要将校Alfred Jodl

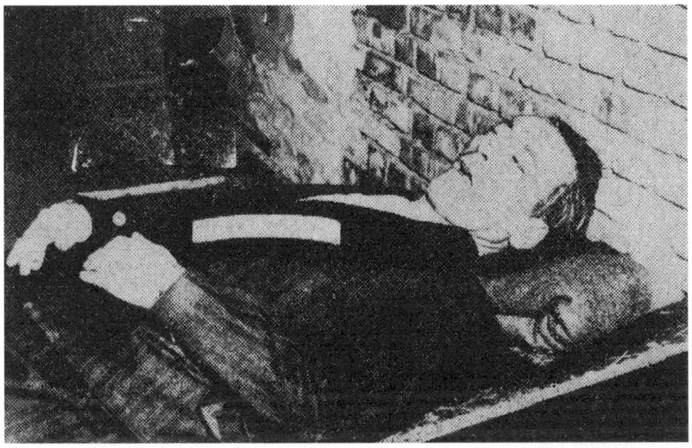

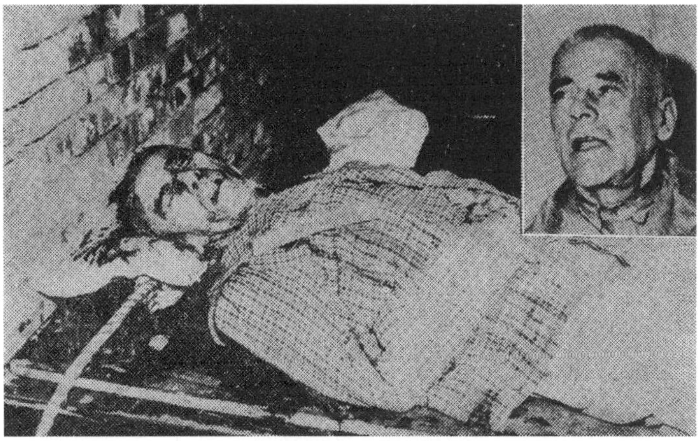

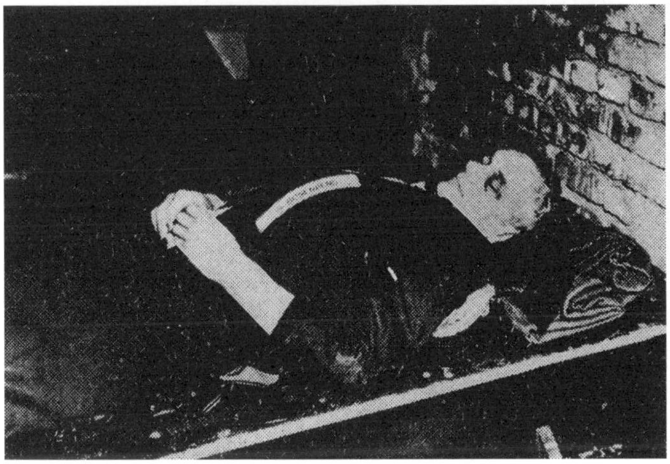

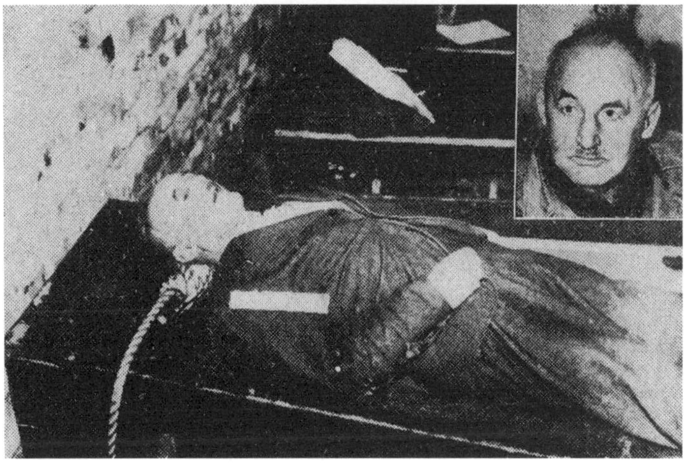

被处死的法西斯罪魁（三）
The End of the Fascists (3)
死刑されたファシズム主犯者達（三）

被绞死的德国特务头子加藤勃鲁纳
The head of Gestapo, E. Kaltenbrunner
絞め殺されたドイツスパイのボスE. Kaltenbrunner

被绞死的德内政部长非烈克
The Nazi chamber minister, lhelm Frick
絞め殺されたドイツの内務部長Wilhelm Frick

被绞死的纳粹党大哲学家罗森伯格
The Nazi philosopher, Alfred Rosenberg
絞め殺されたナチス党の哲学家Alfred Rosenberg

被绞死的迫害犹太人的刽子手史特莱辙
The slaughter of Jews, Julius Stricher
絞め殺されたユダヤ人を迫害した殺人犯Julius Stricher

日战犯受审

日本军政领袖多人被控为战争罪犯，由远东国际战犯法庭加以审判；法官进入时全体起立。前排左起：土肥原，畑俊六，广田弘毅，南次郎，东条，冈田，梅津美治郎，荒木真夫，武藤，野村，贺屋，后排左起：桥本欣五郎，小矶国昭，永野修身，大岛浩，松井石根，平沼骐一郎，东乡，松冈洋右，重光葵，佐藤，岛田，白鸟敏夫，阪垣征四郎。

Japanese Leaders on Trail

Japanese leaders on trial as war criminals (left to right) front, Doihara, Hata, Hirota, Minami, Tojo, Oka, Umezu, Araki, Muto, Noshimo, Kaga; back, Hashimoto, Koiso, Nagano, Oshima, Matsui, Hironuma, Togo, Matsuoka, Shigemetsu, Sato, Shimada, Shiratore, and Itagaki. They stand up as judges enter.

日本の戦争犯罪者が審判される

複数の日本軍人、政治家は戦争犯罪と起訴され、極東国際戦争犯法廷で審判された。図は審判中の光景である。審判官が入る時に全員起立した。前列左から：土肥原賢二，畑俊六，広田弘毅，南次郎，東条英機，岡敬純，梅津美治郎，荒木貞夫，武藤章，星野直樹，賀屋興宣，後列左から：この当時郎，小磯国昭，永野修身，大島浩，松井石根，平沼騏一郎，東郷茂徳，松岡洋右，重光葵，佐藤賢了，嶋田繁太郎，白鳥敏夫，板垣征四郎。

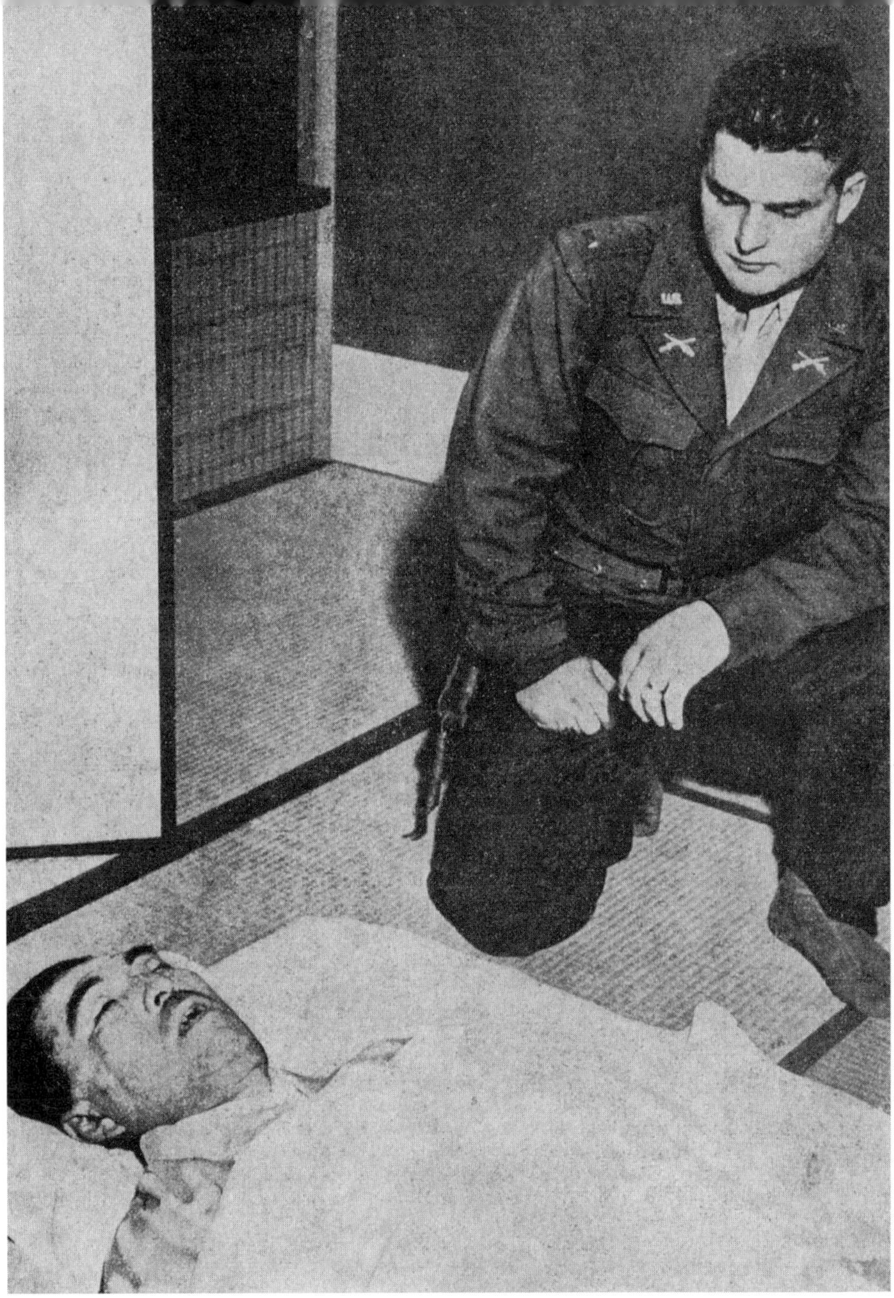

近卫服毒自杀

侵华头目之一曾3次担任首相之近卫文麿，闻将以战犯身份交付审判，于赴法庭之前夕举行招待会一次，当晚即服毒自杀而死。其后为一看守的美国兵。

Death of Konoye

Instigator of Japanese aggressive war, thrice prime minister in Japanese war cabinet, Prince Jumimara Konoye committed suicide in the eve of the day on which he was required to appear in the court of the war criminals.

近衛は毒を呑んで自殺

中国を侵略した近衛文麿は三回日本の総理に在任した。戦犯として審判を受けなければならないと判り、法廷に赴く直前に社会見をしてから、その晩毒を呑んで自殺した。

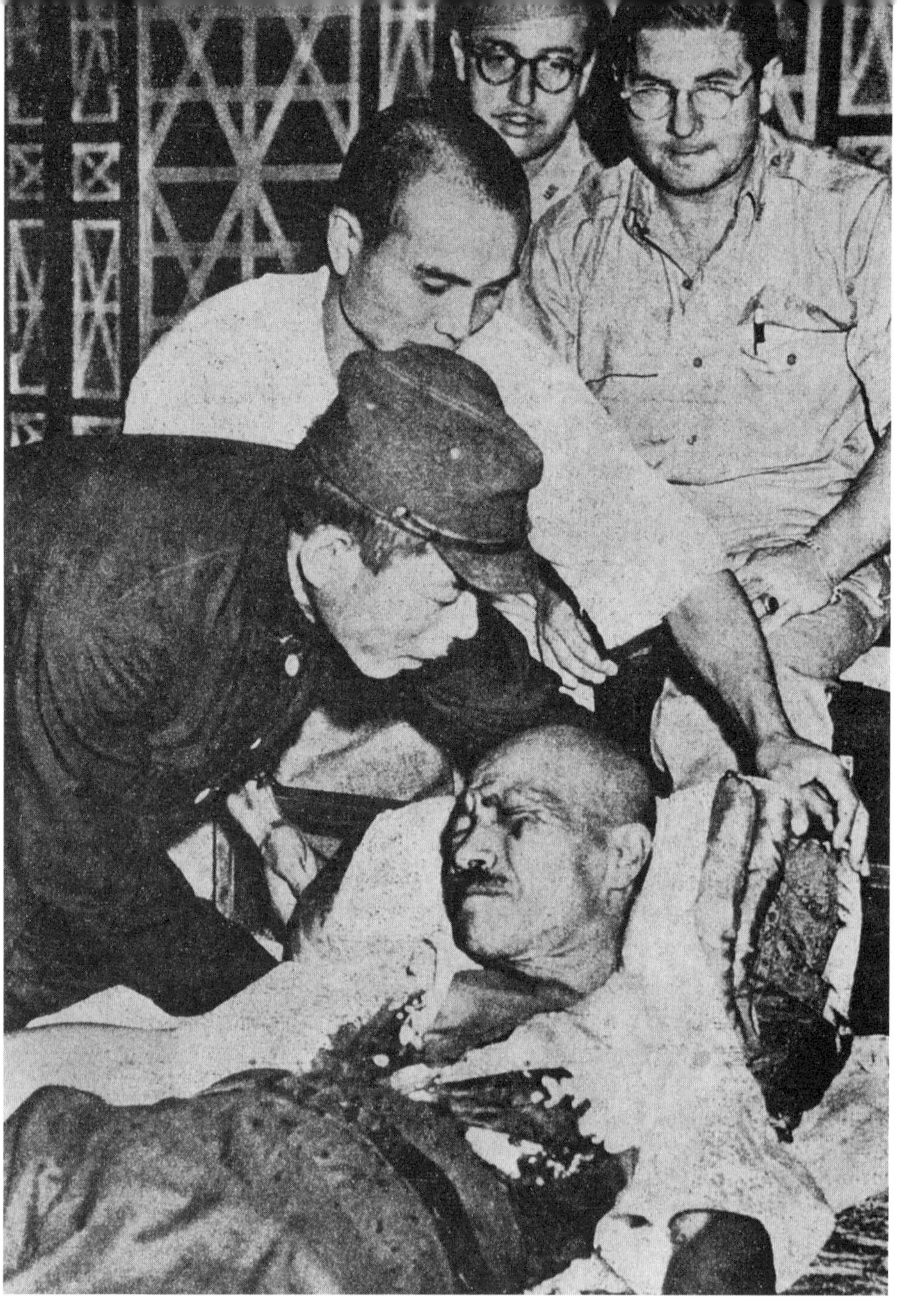

东条自杀未遂

太平洋事变时任日首相之东条英机，于被捕时以自备手枪向胸部射击，弹穿肺部，未中心脏，后为医生营救得以活命，乃由远东战犯法庭审判。图为其自杀未死之痛苦情状。

Tojo Failed in Suicidal Attempt

Tojo, the Japanese Prime Minister that planed and carried out the attack on Pearl Harbour in 1941, attempted suicide with a pistol but failed to end his life. American doctors saved his life in order that he might answer to the accusations against him in the court of justice.

東条自殺未遂

太平洋事変の際、日本総理の東条英機が捕まえられた時に、隠していた拳銃で胸に当て、自殺を図った。弾丸は肺臓を貫いたが医者に救われた。やはり、極東国際戦犯の法廷に送られた。図は自殺未遂の東条の苦しい表情である。

汪陈跪像

1938年12月，汪精卫携其妻陈璧君离开重庆，逃往越南河内，公开叛国投敌，做了中国历史上最大的汉奸。汪陈跪像于1940年10月制成，放在桂林一处公园的抗日阵亡将士纪念碑前，以示汉奸遗臭万年之意。下图是设在广东曲江的汪、陈跪像。

The Kneeling Figure of Wang Chingwei and Chen Bijun

In November 1938, Wang Chingwei, with his wife Chen Bijun, turned traitor and fled to Nanking via Hanoi to form a puppet government under the dominance of the Japanese army. The kneeling figure of Wang Chingwei and Chen Bijun, built in October 1940, was placed in the front of the Monument to the Anti-Japanese Heroes, indicating they would live in infamy forever.

汪、陳の土下座像

1938年12月、汪精衛は妻の陳璧君と一緒に重慶を離れ、ベトナムのハノイへ逃げた。公然と国を裏切り、敵陣に身を投じ、中国歴史上代表的な漢奸となった。汪、陳の土下座像は1940年10月に作られた。売国奴の悪名を後世に残すという意味で、桂林のある公園の抗日戦没将兵記念碑の前に設置された。下の図は広東曲江に設置されていた汪、陳の土下座像である。

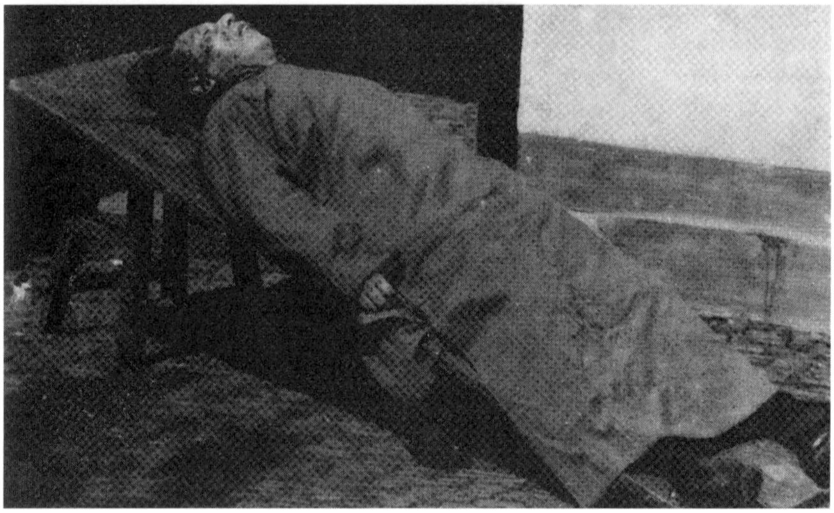

汉奸的下场 （一）

日本投降后，曾供职于汪伪国民政府的汉奸头目纷纷被捕。上图为原伪国民政府主席陈公博枪决后之尸体，下图为汪家班之另一要角褚民谊。

The End of the Traitors (1)

After Japan surrender, the Traitors, served on the puppet government, were arrested one after the other. Picture upper shows the corpse of Chen Gongbo, Chairman of the puppet government. Picture lower shows the corpse of Chu Minyi, a main assistant of Wang Jiaban.

売国奴の結末（一）

日本が降伏した後、汪の傀儡国民政府に職務についていた売国奴の頭目は次から次へと逮捕される。上の図は、傀儡国民政府の代理主席陳公博の銃殺後の死体で、下の図は、汪の傀儡国民政府の要員、漢奸の褚民誼である。

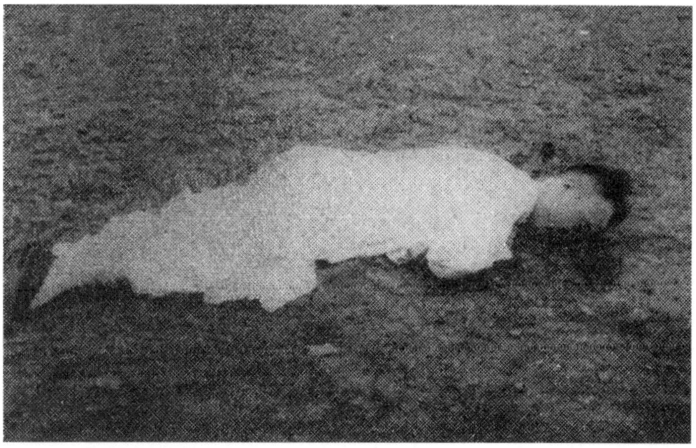

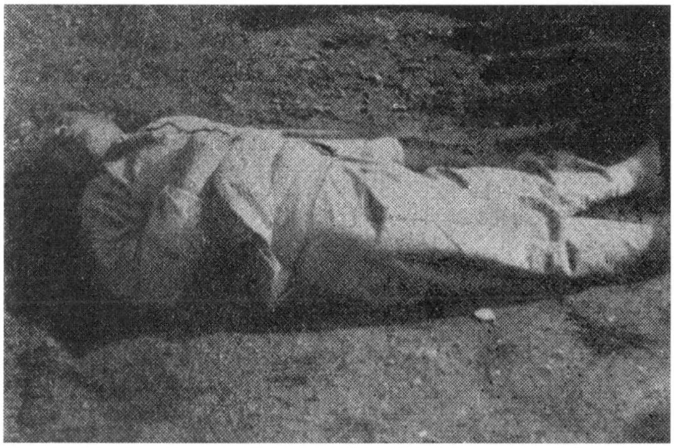

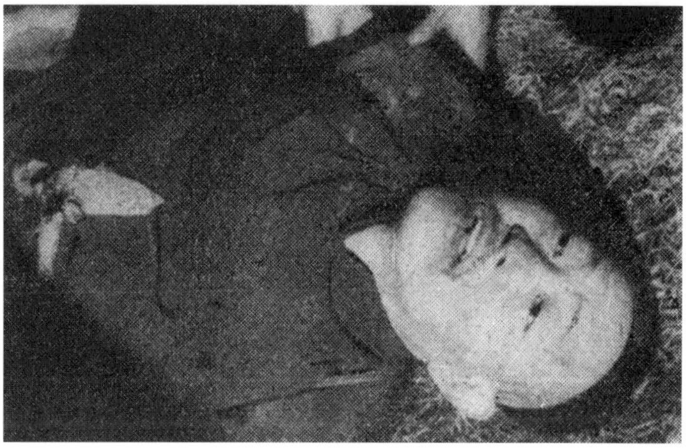

汉奸的下场（二）
The End of the Traitors (2)
売国奴の結末（二）

梁鸿志被判处死刑
Liang Hongzhi was condemned to death
死刑と判決された梁鴻志

梅思平被枪决
Mei Siping was shot dead
銃殺された梅思平

林柏生被枪决
Lin Bosheng was shot dead
銃殺された林柏生

齐燮元被枪决
Qi Xieyuan was shot dead
銃殺された斉燮元

汉奸的下场（三）

The End of the Traitors (3)

売国奴の結末（三）

周佛海被判处死刑(后改判无期)
Zhou Fohai obtained a commutation from death to life imprisonment
死刑（後無期に改めた）と判決された周佛海

殷汝根受审
Yin Rugen was on trial
審判される殷汝耕

丁默村受审
Ding Mocun was on trial
審判される丁默村

周作人与陈曾栻
Zhou Zuoren and Chen Cengshi
周作人と陳曾栻

图书在版编目（CIP）数据

二次大战照片精华／舒宗侨，魏守忠编．—北京：群言出版社，2005
ISBN 7-80080-540-9
Ⅰ.二...　Ⅱ.①舒...②魏...　Ⅲ.第二次世界大战（1939～1945）－史料－图集　Ⅳ.K152-64

中国版本图书馆CIP数据核字（2005）第092093号

总 策 划　范　芳
责任编辑　闻立鼎　陈丹丹
封面设计　曹承斌
出版发行　群言出版社
地　　址　北京东城区东厂胡同北巷1号
邮政编码　100006
联系电话　65263345　65265404
电子信箱　qunyancbs:dem@xinhuanet.com
网　　址　www.qypublish.com
印　　刷　北京雅昌彩色印刷有限公司
经　　销　全国新华书店
版　　次　2005年9月第1版　2005年9月第1次印刷
开　　本　889×1194　1/16
印　　张　19
字　　数　160千字
书　　号　ISBN 7-80080-540-9
定　　价　158.00元